D1565981

POWER ON THE RIGHT

books by william w. turner

HOOVER'S FBI: THE MEN AND THE MYTH
THE POLICE ESTABLISHMENT
INVISIBLE WITNESS: THE USE AND ABUSE OF THE
NEW TECHNOLOGY OF CRIME INVESTIGATION

POWER ON
THE RIGHT
william w. turner

Ramparts Press
berkeley, california

To Lori and her new generation.

acknowledgments

Much of the material for this book has been acquired during my roamings as a journalist and I wish to thank those on the conservative side of the fence who were generous with their time and knowledge. My gratitude is also due to Charles R. Baker, executive director of the Institute for American Democracy, Morris Rubin of *The Progressive* magazine, and others who encouraged and abetted my delving into the topic.

For this book—as for others—I am indebted to Karen Kahn for her assistance with the manuscript. And to Andrew Moss and Laurence Moore of Ramparts Press, thanks for patience extended.

CONTENTS

1
THE STATE
OF THE RIGHT

When Attorney General John N. Mitchell in an unguarded moment remarked, "This country is going so far right you are not even going to recognize it,"* he may have been engaging in only slight hyperbole. In the 1970 congressional campaigns, liberal candidates such as John Tunney of California and Adlai Stevenson III felt it imperative to outdo their Republican opponents on the law-and-order issue; Stevenson took to wearing an enameled flag pin on his lapel and harking back to his Korean War service. In traditionally liberal New York, Conservative Party standard-bearer James Buckley won a U.S. Senate seat, the first third-party candidate to sit in the upper house since Robert LaFollette Jr. of Wisconsin won as a Progressive in 1950. Buckley's victory was no freak even though the Democratic and Republican candidates split the liberal vote, as Conservative Party strength had been building since 1965. In that year Buckley's brother, William F. Buckley of the *National Review,* polled surprisingly well in the mayoral race. Four years later two "law and order" procrusteans forced John V. Lindsay to run as an independent in the general election for mayor. Brass-band patriotism, which has echoed so hollowly from the far right in years past, is now a swelling sound across the land.

The comeback began in the late stages of the Eisenhower administration when public revulsion against the excesses of the McCarthy epoch had largely faded. Major accelerants were the Supreme Court's civil rights decisions and the election of John F. Kennedy, who was not only

* The remark was overheard and reported by a journalist for *Women's Wear Daily* (September 18, 1970). A Department of Justice spokesman naturally denied that the attorney general had said quite that.

sympathetic to the civil rights movement but a Roman Catholic to boot. Still, the comeback was confined mostly to groups that were highly racist and xenophobic in character. It was not until the assassination of John Kennedy on November 22, 1963, that the political center of gravity of the nation as a whole began a perceptible shift to the right. Even the transition from John Kennedy to Lyndon Johnson marked a swing, if largely undetected and unchronicled, to the right. Journalist Thayer Waldo, then pounding the political beat for the *Fort Worth Star-Telegram,* well recalls the night in a hotel suite in 1962 when Johnson, in an expansive mood, pointed to the preoccupied Kennedy and boasted, "I'm going to make a conservative out of him." Indeed, the wealthy Texans who helped shape and advance Johnson's career, men like George and Herman Brown of the huge Brown & Root construction firm, Clint Murchison Sr., and H. L. Hunt, hardly subscribed to the liberal ethic, and neither did their protégé. But Johnson knew that Washington was not Austin, and that right-to-work laws and segregation were not politically profitable. So he was a liberal of convenience rather than conviction, at times and in ways that corresponded to his position as a power broker. His legacy to the American political scene has not been one of expanded civil liberties and workable domestic programs, but of repressive legislation* and a war that has bitterly divided the nation and left urban problems to fester.

The escalation of the war in Vietnam in 1964–65 brought on a renewed siege of "anti-communism," just as the Korean War had boosted the reactionary forces at work in Joseph McCarthy's heyday. The domestic dominoes began to tumble. When urban neglect caused polarization, and polari-

---

* Witness the euphemistically named Omnibus Crime Control Act of 1968 which harbored such opprobrious provisions as wiretap authority and limits on defendants' rights.

zation exploded into widespread violence in Los Angeles, Newark, Detroit, and other centers, latent white racism was awakened, and a harsh cry for "law and order" went up. The emergence of the New Left, with its own power base on the campuses and its call for radical social and economic change, drove the middle farther into the arms of the right. In one of the greatest ironies of our times, this process was hastened by the 1968 assassinations of Dr. Martin Luther King Jr. and Robert F. Kennedy, both passionately despised by the far right. By the time of the 1968 Democratic convention, the vaunted American sense of fair play had been so dulled by the clash of lifestyles and subcultures that an overwhelming majority of the population heartily approved of the police overkill in countering unruly demonstrators in Chicago.

As a result of these crises, the public's threshold of tolerance has been moved well to the right. What is significant about the move is that extremist groups commonly identified in the public mind as such have not shared proportionately in this newfound acceptance. For example, when the subject of right-wing extremism is raised, most people think of a John Birch Society chapter primly discussing its campaigns against the United Nations and fluoridation, or of the Ku Klux Klan exacting its terrorist toll in the South. But neither has benefited greatly from the rightward swing. A Gallup poll released on July 27, 1970, showed that the Birch Society was viewed in a "highly favorable" light by only four percent of the population, and the KKK by three percent, very small increases over five years before, while their "highly unfavorable" images stood at thirty-eight and seventy-five percent respectively. (On the left, SDS and the Black Panthers rated seven and two percent "highly favorable" respectively.) Despite being household words, neither group any longer plays a dominant role on the right.

Leadership in the right has fallen to new organizations with lower profiles and better access to power—to the

15

American Security Council, with agents and allies inside the councils of government; to God-and-flag zealots like the Reverend Carl McIntire, whose high-voltage radio voice reaches millions of Middle Americans while his political tentacles reach as far as the office of Vice President Ky of South Vietnam; to multimillionaire funders of right-wing causes like Patrick J. Frawley Jr., whose ideological complex spreads its influence from parish vestibules to the Pentagon; and even to the nation's police, whose emergent "blue power" is distinctly conservative in tone. What is characteristic of this new right is its closeness to government power and the ability this closeness gives it to hide its political extremism under the cloak of respectability.

The nature of the new right is perhaps most graphically illustrated by the Spiro Agnew phenomenon. A product of the parochial politics of Maryland and little known outside of the state, Agnew was tapped for the second highest office in the land to appease the southern Republican bloc, which was struggling to establish a foothold in the southern states. Appeasement was imperative because of the George Wallace threat. Ever the pragmatist, Richard Nixon understood that nascent Republican strength in the South was in jeopardy unless a gesture was made toward the "southern way of life."

Agnew has more than filled the bill. With his calculated outbursts against antiwar demonstrators and campus dissidents—"today's niggers," Dick Gregory calls them—the vice president has proven more atavistic than George Wallace, who at least brought some populist programs to Alabama. Surely Agnew's labeling of Albert Gore, Charles Goodell, Adlai Stevenson III, Vance Hartke, and others who have opposed the war and the ABM system as "radical liberals" was no less excessive than the Birch Society's name-calling. Yet Agnew's stock is high, while the Birch Society's is low. The difference is not one of political philosophy—if this were 1776 the Birchers would be Tories, and Agnew one of their leaders. It is simply that as an extremist of the middle Agnew operates from a base of acceptability and respectability—the Republican Party and the vice presidency—that renders unthinkable the notion that he may be an extremist.

The dangers of extremism cloaked by governmental authority are obvious. In the clamor for more police to prowl the cities, more FBI agents to watch the campuses, and more weaponry to assert global military superiority, in the waging of the Southeast Asian war and the war against the young, we are edging perilously close to the preemptive use of violence as an instrument of national policy. It is of course possible to argue that military elitism is no monopoly of the right—that John Kennedy was one of the staunchest admirers of the Green Berets, that several of the most fertile brains in the Institute for Defense Analysis, which helped develop the techniques of unconventional warfare in Southeast Asia and then adapted them for the use of police in the streets, are card-carrying members of the American Civil Liberties Union. But there is a difference—and quite a relevant one—between those who see force as a means and those who see it as an end. "Fascism," said Stanley Hoffman in *Le Mouvement Poujade*, "is above all the practice and mystic worship of violence." We are moving in the direction, and rapidly, of looking upon institutionalized violence as part of the American mystique.

It is beyond the scope of this book to discuss the Pentagon and the CIA, two major propellants of the move to the right, since they are subjects unto themselves as well as powers unto themselves, and require book-length treatment in their own right. We shall, however, examine the newfound political clout of the nation's police network, which constitutes a movement away from the traditional dispersal of power so fundamental to the prevention of a police state. We shall look at the American Security Council, dominated by retired military brass of hawkish bent and the recipient of a message of thanks from President Nixon for its role in the successful ABM fight; at the Liberty Lobby, with one foot in neo-Nazi cultism and the other in the halls of Congress; at the fundamentalist church structure and its powerful propaganda voice; at Patrick J. Frawley Jr., the Los Angeles multimillionaire angel for right-wing causes; at the pariahs of the paramilitary right led by the jailed Robert DePugh; and at other major components of the contemporary right-wing movement. I cannot claim that every piece is in place in this intricate mosaic, but I feel confident that the reader will gain a fairly accurate perspective of the current state of the right—and of its increasing familiarity with the corridors of power.

2
THE JOHN
BIRCH SOCIETY
a polemical treadmill

While IAD's annual survey of the Far Right shows the John Birch Society still speaks with the loudest voice in the movement, it does not dominate to the extent it did a year ago. Rivalries and, paradoxically, a measure of success are creating problems.
— *Institute for American Democracy's 1969 survey of extremism*

The showiest happening of the John Birch Society these days is the annual "God, Family & Country Rally" on the Fourth of July in Boston, hard by national headquarters in Belmont, Massachusetts. Over the years the list of participants in the event reads like a *Burke's Peerage* of the ultraright: Billy James Hargis of the Christian Crusade, who moderated a seminar on how to oppose sex education at the 1969 rally; Kent Courtney of New Orleans, who began promoting George Wallace for president at the 1967 affair; Otto Otepka, the fired State Department security boss who became a *cause célèbre* on the right; Colonel Curtis Dall, front man for the pressure-tactic Liberty Lobby; Lee Dodson, a former organizer for the White Citizens Councils now with the new American Lobby; and Louisiana Congressman John Rarick, a flame-tongued segregationist. The 1970 rally featured Governor Lester Maddox, who fulminated against the "communists' plan to force racial integration . . . upon public education and bring our country to its knees." But all was not solidarity: the Young Americans for Freedom boycotted the rally as "racist," contending that "racism is anti-ethical [*sic*] to individualism."

The rally illustrates the current Birch dilemma. While many of the multi-hued birds of the right occasionally come home to roost at their spiritual birthplace, most have flown off to do their own thing. The society is simply too broadly focused, too inert, and too centered around the personality of its founder to satisfy their aspirations.

Nevertheless, the John Birch Society has achieved a large measure of success. Founded in 1958 by Robert H. W. Welch Jr., retired vice president of the Welch Candy Company, the society spread swiftly across the nation, its tenets attracting in the main young businessmen pledged to "free enterprise," housewives upset by progressive trends in education and mental health, retired military officers indoctrinated with phobic anti-communism, and retired persons eager to grasp simplistic solutions to complex world problems. Welch preached that a globe-girdling conspiracy with agents in every stratum of American life was about to swallow America. "I am an alarmist," he wrote in *The Blue Book of the John Birch Society*, "and I hope to make you alarmists, too."

By 1961 the alarm had reached enough ears for the society to claim a membership of a hundred thousand and report an annual income of over $3 million in dues and donations. And it had attained a degree of respectability. The Roman Catholic bishop of Wichita, Kansas, Mark K. Carroll, remarked that the twelve guidelines behind the society's philosophy were the Ten Commandments updated, and the late Richard Cardinal Cushing of Boston praised the society's staunch stand against communism. More important, the provincial middle classes, whom Richard Nixon hails as his "silent majority" and C. Wright Mills once described as seeking "the destruction of the legislative achievements of the New and Fair Deals," provided a substantial base of acceptance. A 1962 Gallup poll found that at least ten million Americans considered Welch's "philosophy" intriguing.

The geographical distribution of Birch strength corresponds roughly to the concentrations of petty conservatism around the country. The midwestern Bible Belt is fertile soil, and the Mormon-settled states of Utah, Idaho, and Washington contain a membership out of proportion to their population. The eastern seaboard and Chicago have largely turned their backs on the society. But Texas, Florida, and Southern California are Birch country.

Southern California is the lotus land not only for the society but for ultraconservatism in general. When the Australian Dr. Fred Schwarz first set up his theological anti-communism shop in the United States, it was in Waterloo, Iowa, but the siren call of the California southland soon lured him to San Pedro and now Long Beach, where his Christian Anti-Communism Crusade has been anchored since 1958. Possibly nowhere in the nation is there a denser concentration of rightist activity than in Greater Los Angeles. Two well-known outfits are the Liberty Amendment Committee (not to be confused with the Liberty Lobby), which from national headquarters at 6413 Franklin Boulevard pushes for repeal of the graduated income tax, and the Free Enterprise Division of Coast and Southern Federal Savings and Loan Association, which supports a staff of paid propagandists struggling "to preserve a climate of economic opinion favorable to Americanism." The *First National Directory of Rightist Groups*, published in 1968 by the Alert Americans Association, lists literally dozens of smaller groups and fronts. Glendale alone boasts the United Patriotic People of the USA, Community Crusades for Americanism, the Network of Patriotic Letter Writers, Pilots for the American Republic, and the Reverend W. Stuart McBirnie, who originates a daily radio program from his United Community Church and subscribes to the motto "Free Enterprise under God." This is in addition to active branches of the National States Rights Party, the American Nazi Party, Young Americans for Freedom, the Constitution Party, and Pro-America.

No wonder that in 1964 Robert Welch announced that California was "fertile soil" for the growth of his society and opened a western headquarters in San Marino, an affluent enclave in northeastern Los Angeles. The headquarters, at

2627 Mission Boulevard, sits below a bluff dominated by the Victorian Huntington Hotel. The front of the unpretentious headquarters building houses an American Opinion Bookstore, one of some hundred eighty retail outlets for Birch-published and -approved literature around the country. The titles range from *The Blue Book* and similar tracts to W. Cleon Skousen's *The Naked Communist,* J. Edgar Hoover's *Masters of Deceit,* and *It's Very Simple,* in which Birch writer Alan Stang advances the theory that "the Communists—under the cloak of civil rights—are trying to get American citizens who happen to be black to exchange the benevolent slavery of the Old Plantation for the malevolent slavery of the New Plantation."

When I visited the headquarters in September 1965, two well-dressed matrons were browsing through the racks exchanging admiring comments about such Birch Society luminaries as Hilaire DuBerrier, billed as "a distinguished foreign correspondent and publisher of a private intelligence letter" who is an authority on communist penetration in France, Algeria, and Indochina.

In the back part of the building are the offices, carpeted in gold pile and furnished in executive-suite style. At the time, the personable John H. Rousselot was national public relations director of the society at a salary of $36,000 a year (his successor is Rex Westerfield). Gerrymandered out of a congressional seat he had held for one term, he was widely touted as the bright young heir-apparent to Welch, then a spirited seventy-six. But in 1967 Rousselot went his separate way, first as a public relations consultant, then as a congressman re-elected in 1970 in a San Gabriel Valley district—defeating Myrlie Evers, widow of slain civil rights leader Medgar Evers, who ran as a Democrat.

As I talked with Rousselot, the embers of nearby Watts were still alive. The trouble, he said, had stemmed from communist agitators who exploited black discontent. The society wasn't against civil rights, he insisted, but preferred the "constructive" approach. As an illustration, he cited a fifteen-hundred-dollar scholarship awarded to a black high school girl in Richmond, California—only one of a number of such awards nationwide. Rousselot lauded the Los Angeles police department's handling of the disturbances, which had taken several days to peak, and said the society would now step up its "Support Your Local Police" campaign.

A few weeks before, Rousselot had provoked a local furor by stating that some two thousand Los Angeles County law enforcement officers were members of his organization. The reaction of State Controller Alan Cranston, now a U.S. Senator, had been typical of officialdom. "I find it hard to suppress a shudder," he told a Town Hall audience July 13, 1965, "when I hear a top Birch Society official assert that two thousand of the Los Angeles County's peace officers are Birch members. Whether two thousand or two hundred, that frankly disturbs me more than all the reports of Minutemen training in the hills with rifles and bazookas."

When I asked him about it, Rousselot explained with a puckish grin that the total included all levels of law enforcement in the county: the police, the sheriff's department, the prosecutor's staff, and the FBI. In my opinion Rousselot was slightly padding his figure, but if "state-of-mind" Birchers were counted, as J. Edgar Hoover counts contributors to the Communist Menace, then it was well on the low side. Police departments in general and the Los Angeles force in particular have traditionally been strongholds of conservatism, and in recent years there has been a sharp increase in activism and militancy. During the 1964 presidential campaign, Los Angeles police openly drove up to the pet-food plant of Dr. D. B. Lewis—who, when he died two years later, bequeathed a million dollars to the Birch Society—and picked up pro-Goldwater literature for distribution in the streets. At the time of my talk with Rousselot, a bitter controversy had erupted over an alleged power grab by Birchers in the Santa Ana police department in adjacent Orange County.

I suggested to Rousselot that the society might well do without intemperate types such as Revilo P. Oliver, who was listed on the national council and as an associate editor of *American Opinion.* A professor at the University of Illinois, Dr. Oliver is a master at mixing classical metaphor with gutter language, with repelling results. As a sample, he had written that liberal intellectuals are "witch doctors and fakers with a sanctified itch to save the world," who, in addition, are taxing America to death for the benefit of every "mangy cannibal in Africa." Rousselot concurred that Oliver tended to overdo things. A few months later Oliver, the man whom Robert Welch had termed "an authentic genius of the first water and quite possibly the world's greatest living scholar," was eased out of the society. He apparently had outdone himself at the 1966 God, Family & Country Rally by saying that "vaporizing" the Jews was a "beatific vision."

The exit of Oliver seems to have marked an attempt by the society to tone up its image, which had been severely damaged by the effects of earlier verbal haymakers thrown by Welch himself. The society had been propelled into notoriety in 1961, when the national press picked up on portions of his opus *The Politician* portraying Dwight Eisenhower as a "dedicated, conscious agent of the communist conspiracy" and Ike's brother Milton as his "superior and boss within the Communist Party." Although Welch had hedged after the fuss began by saying his views didn't necessarily represent those of the membership, the society never had been able to live down the outrageously fraudulent statements.

Another embarrassing ally appeared on the Birch stage in the person of Major General Edwin A. Walker, who joined in 1959, shortly after the society was formed. While commanding the 24th Infantry Division in Germany, Walker had installed a compulsory "Pro-Blue" program that embraced readings from Billy James Hargis and eventuated in his forced resignation in 1961. Out of uniform, he made wild charges about communist penetration of the armed services. Given a chance to offer proof when he testified before the Senate Armed Services Committee on April 4, 1962, he instead became vague and flustered. When asked for comment as he left the hearing room, he punched a journalist in the nose. "In patriotism, loyalty, and combat, there are no moderates," he declaimed in launching a political career that abruptly ended when he was soundly beaten by John Connally in the 1962 Texas gubernatorial race. In 1963, he appeared in a Mississippi courtroom in a show of solidarity with Byron de la Beckwith, on trial for the ambush slaying of Medgar Evers (the trial ended in a hung jury and no retrial was held). Despite the fact that he has been connected with a host of other rightist endeavors, the truculent general is popularly associated with the Birch Society and has helped to drag it down in public esteem.

Nor has the satire depicting the society as composed of "little old ladies in tennis shoes" done much for its image. It began in 1964 when Stanley Mosk, at that time California attorney general, poked fun at Birchers as being mainly wealthy businessmen, retired military officers and—the part that hurt—LOLs. Thousands of tennis shoes poured in by mail to Mosk's office; the press propagated the spoof, and cartoonists, notably Interlandi, perpetuated it. "We've got them," Birch senior coordinator G. Edward Griffin conceded good-naturedly to a *San Francisco Chronicle* reporter June 17, 1970. "They're some sort of embarrassment to us, since they're sure to be quoted."

As a result, the society has become the whipping boy of the right. "Whenever brickbats are to be thrown at the right in general," George Thayer has written in *The Farther Shores of Politics*, "whether in a spirit of fairness or with malice aforethought, the John Birch Society invariably catches the

27

brunt of the onslaught." Critics come not only from the left and center but, stingingly, from the right. In 1962, William F. Buckley, the super-articulate guru of the right-wing intelligentsia, and Barry Goldwater both commented cuttingly on Welch's excessiveness. Soon afterward, FBI director Hoover, patriarch of the far right whose bulldog visage has adorned the cover of *American Opinion,* ventured to say that he had "no respect" for Welch and forbade his agents to join the society ("We still have high regard for him and the FBI," reaffirmed Rousselot). Politicians and public officials studiously avoided seeking Birch endorsement and, if they got it, promptly repudiated it. The stigma was wryly admitted in 1966 when Ronald Reagan's political ambition surfaced and he decided to run for governor. It so happened that Reagan and Rousselot were friends, and in 1962 the actor had spoken on behalf of Rousselot's congressional candidacy. So the Birch functionary felt obliged to reciprocate and privately pledged to help—with praise or condemnation, whichever would do the most good.

The image problem is compounded by internal strife centering on the personality and beliefs of the brusque Welch. He founded the society on the premise that it needed a "hardboiled, dictatorial, and dynamic boss"—namely himself. He styled it along monolithic lines and ran it in an autocratic manner, often expelling members for whimsical reasons. But many members who were able to abide the "tight ship" were turned off by Welch's fascistic predilections. He admired Franco of Spain, Salazar of Portugal, Batista of Cuba, Trujillo of the Dominican Republic, and Rhee of South Korea, totalitarians all, who undoubtedly would have agreed with him that democracy is "a demagogic weapon and a perennial swindle." And he linked up with extremist William S. Schlamm, who on a 1960 European lecture tour under the auspices of the society enraged Western Europeans and Americans alike when he averred that the United States could easily afford to sacrifice seven hundred million people to defend the West and its territorial aspirations in Eastern Europe.

As designed by Welch, the society functioned semi-secretly. Local chapters were kept small and designated by four-letter code names, and the identity of members was closely guarded. This enabled the society to wage campaigns of harassment, disruption, and letter writing that gave the illusion of spontaneity, but in time these tactics became transparent. For exampie, elected officials began to detect patterns in the volume of letters they received on controversial issues. So did business firms sponsoring programs or carrying products the Birchers disapproved of. In 1964 when Xerox Corporation footed the bill for six national television specials on the United Nations, which the Birchers call "the house that Hiss built," it received forty-five thousand letters opposing the program and only twelve thousand supporting it. An analysis, however, disclosed that the forty-five thousand letters had been authored by only eleven thousand people, while the twelve thousand had as many authors. Further research revealed that two monthly society bulletins to members had urged the letter-writing effort.

Some Birch leaders realized that although a certain number of people will always be attracted to a conspiratorial group, the road to the future lay in opening up the closed society a bit and sprucing up its public appearance. Some liberalizing changes were made, notably that the society would exert a leadership influence but leave members free to make up their own minds on specific issues. But the Birch Society still *is* Robert Welch, and Welch still is above all the business executive. Under a corporate structure that is headed by Robert Welch, Inc., and controlled by the founder and his wife, Marion Probert Welch, the society is essentially a manufacturer of ideology, taking in close to $4 million annually and paying its executives handsomely. As one right-wing leader put it, "In the sense that the JBS is a profitable business, no one is going to take it away so long as Bob Welch and his wife are alive."

But even Welch is mortal, and as of this writing there are two top contenders to take charge. One is Scott Stanley Jr., the good-looking young managing editor of *American Opinion*. The other is Edward Griffin, thirty-nine, a Los Angeles publisher as well as a Birch Society coordinator. Griffin, who resembles presidential aide Robert Finch, has that affable All-American look and is married to a former beauty queen who won the title "Mrs. California." But Griffin's affableness fades when the subject turns to politics. "This is a struggle against the forces of collectivism," he intones with the right-wing's propensity for apocalyptic language. "It's war, with the stakes no less than life and death."

Whether the society will eventually be worth inheriting is debatable. Up to this point in its relatively brief history it has remarkably paralleled the Know Nothing movement, which began in the 1840s as a chauvinistic response to the influx of Irish immigrants to the Northeast and their assimilation by the Democratic Party. The movement spread rapidly across the nation as the Native American Party, fostering a number of secret orders whose initiates answered inquiries with the stock response that they "knew nothing"—hence the name. In 1855 the Know Nothings abandoned much of their secrecy and ran their own candidates for elective office, but failing at the polls they became increasingly factionalized and gradually faded from the scene.

As it embarks upon the 1970s, the Birch Society is practically static—the membership stands only slightly above the hundred thousand mark it attained a decade ago. It may be that the organization is limited by having only a narrow appeal. Part of its radical fringe has moved on to more militant or blatantly racist groups. But the real paradox is that the society has not measurably benefited from the resurgence of the right. The partial answer is that this resurgence is quartered mostly in the blue-collar classes, while the society has always drawn heavily from the white-collar upper middle class. Another factor is the society's insistence that it is educational in nature rather than political, which means it is reduced to the role of "infiltrating" the Republican Party or, in a few areas, the Democratic Party. This has met with limited success—Rousselot and fellow California Bircher John Schmitz* made it to Congress in 1970, a few state and local candidates have been elected in conservative strongholds, and some observers credit the society with the defeat of Nelson Rockefeller in the 1964 California primary. However, the society has little political muscle of its own. It might have had more had the 1968 campaign of George Wallace gained enough votes to throw the election into the House of Representatives, where each state would have one vote. According to tabulations of the Institute for American Democracy, twenty-two state organizations of the American Independent Party were heavy with Birchers, and in New York, New Jersey, Massachusetts, Pennsylvania, Illinois, and Texas, among other states, a number of Wallace electors were members of the society. Wallace had welcomed Birch support, saying that its adherents "are some of our finest citizens and its opposition to communism is well founded." Nevertheless, the society didn't come away empty-handed in the view of the Anti-Defamation League, which maintained that Birchers used the campaign "to advance their own propaganda and fill their own ranks and coffers."

If the society is something less than a force on the national scene it has had localized impact. The society has long operated a speakers' bureau—Willis E. Stone, author of

* Schmitz was appointed, appropriately, to the House Internal Security Subcommittee. A Birch sympathizer, Philip M. Crane of Chicago, was also elected to the House in 1970. (Crane denies membership.)

the Liberty Amendment to abolish the graduated income tax; Julia Brown, a black former FBI informer within the Communist Party; E. Merrill Root, the society's poet laureate; and Cuban émigré José Norman are in the stable—that helps spread the gospel. Local ad hoc fronts keep springing up; in 1970 in Marin County, California, for instance, a group calling itself the Committee Against Socialized Housing materialized to fight successfully a ballot proposition that would have authorized a federally financed low-cost housing program, and essentially the same group, now calling itself the Save Our Servicemen Committee, showed up at a Board of Supervisors meeting to demand that a measure calling for total victory in Vietnam be placed on the ballot. "We should not be negotiating peace," the spokesman declared, "we should be dictating it!" And there have always been the standing fronts such as the Committee to Investigate Communist Influence at Vassar College. Current national projects pushed by the local chapters are TACT (Truth About Civil Turmoil), MOTOREDE (Movement to Restore Decency), and SYLP (Support Your Local Police). The emphasis on decentralization is indicated by Welch's disclosure not long ago that the society has close to a hundred coordinators, nearly a thousand section leaders, and almost four thousand chapter leaders (some of whom handle more than one chapter).

Currently a color film, *No Substitute for Victory*, is being sponsored by local Birch chapters. Narrated by John Wayne, it knocks "no-win" wars with appearances by General Mark Clark, Admiral Grant Sharp, Lowell Thomas, and Martha Raye, among others.

Any evaluation of the society must take into account its allies and sympathizers. Besides Rousselot and Schmitz in Congress, it has a collaborator in Congressman John Rarick. A former judge from Francisville, Louisiana, Rarick performs such favors as inserting items from the society's *Review of the News* into the *Congressional Record*, and in return the society helps fill his campaign war chests; in his last two campaigns a fund-raising group called American Friends of John Rarick has been chaired by Tom Anderson, a member of the Birch Council from Tennessee.* Others who often mesh efforts with the society are Billy James Hargis, Dean Manion of the "Manion Forum" and Dan Smoot of the "Dan Smoot Report," and Phoebe and Kent Courtney of New Orleans, who run the Conservative Society of America. And then there is the incomparable Lester Maddox, who while governor proclaimed August 23 "John Birch Society Day" in Georgia.

Yet another in the Birch orbit is the Reverend Paul D. Lindstrom, who is nominally a member but has risen to prominence in his own right. Pastor of the nondenominational Church of Christian Liberty in the prosperous Chicago suburb of Prospect Heights, the lanky, balding Lindstrom has exploited right-wing dissatisfaction with public school education by opening his own Christian Liberty Academy where children learn from the McGuffey readers, study "patriotic history," and are smacked with a rod called the "board of education" when they misbehave. The Lindstrom complex is burgeoning: he has set up congregations in Milwaukee, Wisconsin, and Rockford, Illinois, has his own seminary, and is drawing plans for more schools in the Chicago area. A sampling of his philosophy was quoted in *Newsweek*, July 13, 1970: "We tell them Nixon's Vietnamization policy is basically tantamount to surrender. . . . We agree with J. Edgar Hoover that Martin Luther King was the most notorious liar in the country. . . . The United Nations is a foolish attempt at world government inspired by Satan." The pastor of the church with the red-white-and-blue candles first broke into the news when, as chairman of the Remember the *Pueblo*

* Rarick, a Democrat, was stripped of his seniority after he supported George Wallace in 1968.

Committee, he called a press conference to announce, several days before the event, that the spy ship was about to be released; the scoop prompted Senator Stephen Young to charge that Lindstrom must have been tipped off by "right-wing sympathizers holding sensitive jobs in the Defense Department." Since then Lindstrom has gotten wire service coverage on several of his ventures, including an excursion to Leavenworth penitentiary to demand the release of Green Beret Captain John T. McCarthy, charged with murder.

In a 1961 progress report, Welch declared that the society had "the formula for ultimate success," but had to "grow into an army of sufficient size, fighting with facts and truth as our weapons, until the enemy with all his ruthless cunning, gigantic organization, limitless resources, and entrenched power, still cannot withstand the total impact of our unified strength and dedicated labors." To achieve victory, he saw the need for a society one hundred times larger.

A decade later it had hardly grown.

3
ORANGE
COUNTY
CALIFORNIA
the geopolitics
of conservatism

Orange County is radical in its conservatism.
                    former California governor Goodwin Knight

The significance of the Birch Society today lies not in the
minimal power it possesses but in its role as a catalyst in
propelling already conservative areas further to the right.
Orange County in Southern California is a good example.
Birch membership is still small compared to the total population of the county, but a kind of state-of-mind Birchism
pervades it, pulling the solidly conservative base along. The
situation is exemplified by State Assemblyman Robert
Badham, who during the 1964 campaign denied Birch membership but declared himself for the society's policies "99
and 44/100 percent." These political waves running in the
same direction tend to reinforce each other, crashing on the
electoral shores with considerable force. Among the reactionaries who have ridden the crest are Ronald Reagan, George
Murphy, and Max Rafferty.

    When the computers used by the television networks to
make early predictions of election winners in California are
programmed, they are usually programmed to assure that any
moderate or liberal Democrat must gain as much as a two-to-
one margin in the northern half of the state to make the
outcome close. For some two-thirds of the votes come from
south of the Tehachapi Mountains, and as these come in the
conservative candidate invariably starts coming on strong.
The most solidly conservative area of them all is Orange
County, which in 1970 gave Ronald Reagan more than a
two-to-one margin, far in excess of what he polled statewide,
and went for Senator George Murphy 263,176 to 185,204
even though John V. Tunney won the election by some six

hundred thousand votes. In tight races this kind of relentless reaction can prove—and has proved—the difference.

As an enclave of right-wing voting power, Orange County is similar to other such pockets around the country. Dallas, Texas, has long epitomized the ideological city, and Houston is not far behind it. Certain affluent suburbs of Chicago are not only predictable as voting blocs but are recognized as hotbeds of activism. Some Florida population centers—like St. Petersburg, with its large percentage of retired people—are staunchly conservative in outlook. But Orange County is something else again. With a population of 1.4 million, which is expected to nearly double in the next decade, and ranking second among California's fifty-eight counties in terms of total personal income, it is incontestably the most economically mobile and politically mind-set county in the nation.

Orange County lies in the middle of a population belt extending from Los Angeles to San Diego. Much smaller in area than either Los Angeles or San Diego county, its western border starts just south of the Long Beach oil towers and follows a gradually more rugged coastline past Newport Beach and Laguna Beach to a few miles south of San Clemente and the "Western White House" of Richard Nixon. Close to its northern border is Yorba Linda, Nixon's boyhood home. A magazine published by and for Orange Countians calls the area "Heaven on Earth," and given the picturesque coastline, sprawling beaches, colorful harbors, and rolling foothills, the comparison is not, if one overlooks the vast sea of tract homes and proliferation of neon and plastic, grossly overdrawn. The climate is mild the year round, and dense smog has pushed only into the northern fringe. There are various attractions such as Disneyland, Knott's Berry Farm, a huge game preserve, Movieland Wax Museum, and Movieland of the Air with its collection of vintage airplanes. Sports and recreation are a way of life, with surfing so popular that the police list "surfboard theft" in a separate crime category. The Laguna Beach Festival of the Arts is nationally renowned, and over Easter Week college students still gather at Balboa Beach for an all-out bash known as Bal Days.

The politics of Orange County are, as they are elsewhere, a product of demography and economics. In the early days cattle-raising was the only activity of consequence, and even when the county broke free of Los Angeles County in 1889 there were only thirteen thousand settlers. Then came the citrus industry and the vast groves of oranges and lemons. A quarter of a century ago, historian Robert Glass Cleland described the landed gentry, the growers, and the ranchers in *California in Our Time:* "They look with suspicion on Wall Street and even upon their Republican brethren among eastern manufacturers and bankers; show genuine and intelligent concern for the welfare of their employees, but decry labor unions and all forms of farm-labor organizations; regard socialism, communism, and the New Deal as synonymous, and condemn all forms of federal aid to the individual—except when such aid is needed by the citrus industry itself." These attitudes have not greatly changed.

By 1940, with agriculture still dominant, there were only 132,000 people living in the county. But World War II brought expansion. Oil derricks sprang up around Huntington Beach, and the El Toro Marine Air Base and other military facilities were rushed to completion. The first mass immigration began. But it was not until the postwar industrialization that Orange County's phenomenal growth set in. Aerospace and electronic giants such as Beckman Instruments, Autonetics, North American, Hughes Aircraft, and Philco's Aeronutronic Division moved in, spawning a cluster of satellite firms. Hunt Foods, still the largest ketchup processor in the nation, blossomed into a huge conglomerate. Now onequarter of the national military/aerospace dollar flows to California—one half of that quarter to Orange County.

In sharp contrast to the space age is the feudal Irvine Ranch, its eighty-eight thousand acres covering one-fifth of the county from the Santa Ana Mountains to the sea. In 1906, a thousand of its acres were planted with orange groves and it still markets under the Sunkist label, but it remains largely unchanged from the days of the Conquistadores. Grudgingly, the directors of the Irvine Corporation donated a thousand acres for the burgeoning campus of the University of California and sold off more for new home sites. But this is mostly the doing of Joan Irvine, a direct descendant of founder Jim Irvine, and the attitude of the directors is mirrored by what one of them thundered not long ago: "What goes on inside the Irvine company is none of the general public's damn business."

As the bulldozers cut their wide swaths through the flatlands and foothills, making way for homes and industrial parks, agricultural production went into steady decline. As late as 1955, 144,000 acres were planted; now the total is less than half that. Only in the southern part of the county can be found vast, uninterrupted expanses of lemon, orange, and avocado groves, motor-driven propellers set above them to circulate the air and keep frost from settling. Because of the rapid industrial and residential building that has occurred, the county is known as "realtors' country," and its Real Estate Association is not bashful about diving into politics. It sponsors "Realtors for America" programs dealing with "erosions of freedom," and was a prime mover in the 1964 anti–fair-housing referendum that won in the county by the unheard-of ratio of four to one. Other conservative blocs are formed by colonies of retired people—the largest is Leisure World at Seal Beach—and an inordinate number of active and retired military personnel.

The Orange County brand of conservatism bears no resemblance to the New England variety, the "you-mind-your-business-and-I'll-mind-mine" kind of native individualism that saw Vermont turn its back on Goldwater in 1964 (while Orange County was one of only two California counties to go for the Arizonan, and it went big). It is more akin to the meddling regionalism of the South, where, incidentally, much of the influx of recent years originated. But race is not a major issue, simply because there are only a handful of blacks in the county. Although demographic statistics are difficult to come by, five-year-old figures show the county is seventy-five percent Protestant, eighteen percent Catholic, over one percent Mormon, less than one percent Jewish, and less than one percent black. Perhaps more than any other place in the United States, Orange County is a WASP bastion, and a wealthy one at that since the median family income is the second highest in the state.

The daily voice of Orange County is the Freedom Newspapers chain of the Hoiles family, whose patriarch, Raymond C. Hoiles, died in 1970 at the age of ninety-one. The flagship of the chain—which also includes the adjacent *Anaheim Bulletin* and *Orange News* and dailies in backwater cities of Texas, Florida, Ohio, Nebraska, North Carolina, Colorado, and New Mexico—is the *Santa Ana Register*, which proclaims itself "Metropolitan Orange County's Watchful Newspaper." The credo printed on its editorial page hints at the extreme laissez-faire philosophy of founder Hoiles: "We believe that all men are equally endowed by their Creator, and not by a government, with the right to take moral action to preserve their life and property and secure more freedom and keep it for themselves and others." The Bible-quoting Hoiles scorned tax-supported schools as compulsory indoctrination and believed people should buy their own books rather than subsidize public libraries. He was consistent. During World War II he opposed government relocation of Japanese-Americans and in 1962 denounced the Francis "anti-Communist amendment" as one more piece of state interference (the amendment, which would have introduced the loyalty oath on a

41

100635

sweeping basis, passed in Orange County although it was emphatically rejected by the rest of the state). His objection to labor unions, he declared in a pamphlet available to visitors to the *Register*'s modern plant, is that "every man is different from every other person and thus each man's services have a different value."

To ensure the right slant on the news, the *Register* utilizes the *Chicago Tribune–New York Daily News* news service, and presents a gallery of columnists that features H. L. Hunt, Willard Edwards of the *Chicago Tribune*, and Russell Kirk of the *National Review*. Even though Orange County predictably went heavily for Goldwater in 1964 and the *Register* reported on his campaign to the virtual exclusion of Lyndon Johnson's, the newspaper refused to endorse Goldwater with the explanation: "Some of his expressed views parallel those of the *Register*. But we do not believe political action is a solution for human problems. We do not believe governmental agencies—which are based on compulsion—will ever solve human problems. Individuals can, but government can not." On a recent trip to Orange County I picked up a copy of the *Register* (July 22, 1970) to check the vox populi. One letter to the editor bitterly denounced Cesar Chavez and the grape strike with exhortations to "stand up" for Father Daniel Lyons (of *Twin Circle*) and "boycott communism; eat grapes!" Another, from a college student, urged support of Young Americans for Freedom and Voices in a Vital America, which was described as a "non-political anti-radical movement." A third railed against "Socialist Party A and Socialist Party B" in Washington and invoked the memory of victories by Generals MacArthur and Patton to urge "victory in Vietnam." The fourth was a nostalgic bit about the visit of the Prince of Wales to the United States. Since the Freedom Newspapers blanket Orange County and the several other dailies are scarcely less reactionary, the only alternative is the local edition of the *Los Angeles Times*.

Perhaps symbolic of Orange County philosophy and values is Walter Knott, who back in 1920 set up a berry stand on a road to the beaches, later expanding to sell berry pies baked by his wife Cordelia, and chicken dinners. From this humble start Knott, now pressing eighty, built a complex ringing up sales of millions of dollars annually. The restaurant of Knott's Berry Farm at Buena Park serves almost eighteen hundred dinners at a time and close to two million dinners each year. Shops and concessions are run by the three Knott daughters and their husbands, and the homespun enterprise is a true American success story.

With success, Walter Knott turned his energies and resources toward the fight against communism and "creeping socialism." Although he made his fortune under Roosevelt's "socialistic trend" administration, the folksy entrepreneur became treasurer of the Liberty Amendment to repeal the graduated income tax and a member of the advisory board of Billy James Hargis's Christian Crusade. He promoted Town Meetings for Freedom, the American Committee to Free Cuba, and a Latin America literature project of the Christian Anti-Communism Crusade. He was one of Ronald Reagan's original financial angels, and has been elected to the Republican Party Central Committee.

But Knott's pet projects are down on the Berry Farm. In a converted white farmhouse called the Freedom Center are the headquarters of his California Free Enterprise Association and Americanism Educational League (CFEA was originally part of the business, but when the IRS refused to regard it in this light Knott shifted it to the tax shelter of the league, a "patriotic public service foundation"). The executive director is Dr. William E. Fort Jr., an indefatigable speechmaker who doubles as chairman of the Patriotic Educational Committee of the California Sons of the American Revolution. On the board of trustees are announcer Harry Von Zell and retired Admiral Robert W. Berry, and the

National Advisory Council numbers such right-wing stalwarts as W. Cleon Skousen, an author of strident anti-communist tracts; Loyd Wright, prominent in the affairs of the American Security Council; Rear Admiral Chester N. Ward, a member of the ASC's National Strategy Committee; and Robert Morris, former chief counsel of the Senate Internal Security Subcommittee. One of the stated purposes of the league is to "explain our free-enterprise economy to youth, and to all economic illiterates." Activities include providing a "nationally recognized forum for outstanding speakers" and working closely with "anti-subversive forces [and] security and national defense experts to ensure adequate defense of America." The league awarded its "American of the Year" prize in 1965 to J. Edgar Hoover, and it has actively recruited personnel for the FBI. In one "S.O.S." bulletin, the league set out Bureau requirements and pay schedules and exhorted:

THIS IS A ONCE-IN-A-LIFE-TIME OPPORTUNITY FOR GOOD PATRIOTS TO PERFORM INVALUABLE SERVICES TO OUR COUNTRY DURING WHAT IS THE MOST CRITICAL TIME OF OUR COUNTRY'S HISTORY. PLEASE CONSIDER THIS A MAJOR PROJECT BY SPREADING THE WORD AMONG DEDICATED PATRIOTS AND URGING THOSE WHO QUALIFY TO ARRANGE FOR AN INTERVIEW WITH THE FBI.

The league also operates the Freedom Center on the Berry Farm, which includes a bookstore stocked with ultra-right literature and a replica of Independence Hall. The center offers speakers and motion pictures like *Communism on the Map* for civic, religious, and service clubs. The Orange County Board of Supervisors once passed a special citation commending the "exemplary work" of the center, and for farmer Knott that homegrown tribute was probably the highlight of his "patriotic" career.

Tolerance of divergent opinion is not a consistent

Orange County virtue, as Steve Allen, the television personality who styles himself a liberal Democrat, can attest. In 1964 when Allen presided over a rally for the Democratic opponent of Assemblyman Robert Badham, he found himself picketed by Birchers. In 1970 when Allen was named grand marshal of Anaheim's Halloween parade, the ultraconservative Anaheim Republican Assembly demanded that he be barred because he did not fit into the free-enterprise and patriotic mold of the parade. Allen withdrew "because of the danger that a few extremists might cause a disturbance that could deprive Orange County children of a few hours of innocent merriment."

A Long Beach State College journalism professor, Dixon Gayer, has pierced the reactionary pall hanging over Orange County with exposure and satire. In 1962, as a columnist with the Garden Grove (Orange County) daily, Gayer conjured up a gross parody of the John Birch Society called the Webster Quimmley Society "after that great patriot who chickened out on the Santa Ana Freeway." Gayer, who resembles Wally Cox, coined his group's motto "Patriotism without Panic," and entered an antique car in a Fourth of July parade carrying a sign "Insanity First."

Not everyone was amused. Gayer's phone rang at all hours, his newspaper received letters branding him with crimes ranging from high treason to sodomy, and a television station on which he had appeared got a batch of telegrams abusing it for "giving time to this Commie" (the batch was found to bear forged names). The *Santa Ana Register* ran an "exposé" about a leftist cabal known as the "Secret Six," naming Gayer as one. The exposé was in turn exposed as a hoax, and the newspaper ran a half-hearted retraction. Gayer's employer dropped his column due, he said, to a desire to "economize." (Gayer is not out of print. Since moving over to the college he has published his own monthly, *The Dixon Line*, with communiqués from the Birch battlefront.)

The Orange County ideology is reflected in its elected representatives. For many years most of the county and north San Diego County was represented in Congress by Republican James B. Utt, a short, personable man who spun around his district in a Thunderbird. Several years ago Utt startled the nation by suggesting that a military maneuver in Georgia, "Operation Watermoccasin," was in reality a training exercise for communist-trained United Nations troops about to take over the United States. Utt sponsored the ill-fated Liberty Amendment in Congress and in June 1968 was featured along with Robert Welch and Harry Von Zell at a convention of the Liberty Amendment Committee at the Disneyland Hotel. Some idea of Utt's popularity can be gained by the fact that in the 1968 elections he ran up 56,549 votes in Orange County compared to only 11,285 for his Democratic opponent, who barely managed to outpoll the American Independent Party candidate.

When Utt died in 1970 his successor was Republican John G. Schmitz, who was elected in a landslide. An avowed member of the Birch Society, the former Santa Ana College instructor had been a state senator for a number of years, during which he became noted for his "right-to-work" bills. Like Utt, Schmitz has participated in projects sponsored by Willis Carto's Liberty Lobby and a host of other right-wing endeavors. Not without humor, Schmitz once quipped that he joined the Birch Society "in order to win the liberal vote in Orange County."

Just how ideological the Orange County vote is can be judged from the registration ratio. Latest available figures give the Republicans 306,696 voters and the Democrats 243,000, which is not exactly lopsided. But the election results are. In 1968, Richard Nixon polled 314,905 votes to 146,869 for Hubert Humphrey, while the state narrowly went for Nixon; in the Senate contest, turn-back-the-clock Superintendent of Public Instruction Max Rafferty got

301,053 votes to 187,166 for liberal Democrat Alan Cranston, but Cranston won handily statewide. In 1970, when he ran for re-election as the state school chief, Rafferty was swamped by Wilson Riles but still carried Orange County.

Lately, however, there is accumulating evidence that the younger generation is not going to hew religiously to its elders' line, or even lifestyle. Racial and ethnic hangups are not as rampant in the schools as in the civic and service clubs, and the use of marijuana is probably as prevalent as elsewhere. Recently the student body president at Villa Park High refused to lead the pledge of allegiance at assemblies on the grounds that he opposed the policies of the U.S. government, and his stand was ratified by two-thirds of the students. The First Methodist Church of Garden Grove, which lost two hundred parishioners en masse several years ago when its pastor marched at Selma, Alabama, has begun classes in modern dance, writing, and black studies. A student body president from Buena Park told the *Orange News* that although he supported Nixon's Vietnam policy he favored reduced marijuana penalties, a volunteer army, and an end to school dress regulations.

In Orange County these are radical positions, and the reaction to them has been uncompromising. School bond issues are plunging to defeat. Vague "anti-loitering" ordinances are being enacted to allow the police to hassle "hippies" and longhairs, and police in two cities raided screenings of *I Am Curious: Yellow*. Noncompulsory sex education was making strides in Anaheim until the school board felt the heat from one of the vociferous little bands of traditionalists that abound in the county. The lines are being drawn through all strata of Orange County life.

Whether Orange County will enter the 1970s or retreat further into its shell is a question of more than parochial interest. Northern California, which has seen one progressive candidate after another drowned in the tidal wave of votes

47

from Southern California in general and Orange County in particular, is rife with talk of creating two Californias. For a multitude of reasons, division will not come to pass in the foreseeable future, and it may well be that Orange County, as predictable a political entity as what once was called the "solid South," will continue indefinitely as the thumb on the scale of California politics.

4
THE
KU KLUX KLAN
trapped between
white and black

God help the white man if ever the back-to-the-jungle policy of Communist tyranny is ever forced on white America! It could be you or your loved one!

                    —recruiting handbill of the United Klans of America, Inc.

Perhaps no political entity in America is in as sorry repute as the Ku Klux Klan. Its image is one of nightriders skulking about the land, and even in right-wing circles it is regarded as distinctly déclassé. To complete the picture, federal authorities have put the "heat" on it as they have on no other so-called hate group. Not only has the Justice Department placed the Klan on the attorney general's list of subversive organizations (for using force and violence to deny citizens their Constitutional rights), the House Un-American Activities Committee—now the House Internal Security Subcommittee—and the FBI, which normally are concerned with "subversion" on the left, have bedeviled and denounced it.

But simply to tag the Klan as a hate group and then proceed to chronicle its bizarre and brutal activities, as many accounts do, is overly simplistic. The Klan is a genuinely American phenomenon, a movement with deep socio-economic roots. The quintessential Klansman is a poorly educated, unskilled, low-income white trapped between a rigid white power structure above and the black masses moving inexorably up from the bottom. All of the nineteen men indicted in the "Klan assassination plot" to murder three young civil rights workers in Mississippi in 1964 were low-income southern whites, their occupations ranging from truck driver to nightclub bouncer to rural Baptist minister to small café operator to sheriff and sheriff's deputy.

The Klan began innocently enough as a Confederate

veterans' fraternity but soon was transformed into a counter-force to oppose the radical changes threatened by Recon-struction. It proliferated rapidly, but with the end of Reconstruction in 1877 it melted away just as rapidly. It was not revived until 1915, the year of D. W. Griffith's epic motion picture *The Birth of a Nation,* which depicted Klans-men as heroic defenders of the southern way of life. The second coming of the Klan was the handiwork of an Alabama preacher, William J. Simmons. Naming his organization the Invisible Empire of the Knights of the Ku Klux Klan, Sim-mons hired two publicity agents and began proselytizing. His timing was excellent. By 1925 the Klan boasted five million members and an annual income of $75 million in contribu-tions and dues.

Simmons's Klan was far more expansive in philosophy than the old Klan. In addition to black subjugation he preached hostility toward foreigners, Catholics, and Jews, the "international Zionist conspiracy" and its Wall Street finan-ciers, and all forms of permissiveness. It was Simmons who adopted the lavishly embroidered robes and peaked hoods that have become a symbol of the Klan, and he wedded these bizarre trappings to a demonic mythology. Klan-originated tales of priest-nun orgies and papist ambitions spread rapidly through the backwaters of southern sociology.

The historical importance of this Klan is that, unlike the current organizations, it had widespread political power, not only in the South but in several Midwest and border states, and even on the federal level. At various times it had a firm grip on the legislatures and/or statehouses of Louisiana, Texas, Oklahoma, Kansas, Maine, Colorado, Indiana, and Oregon, a diversity suggesting that the movement had a solid populist base. Ohio and New Jersey were strongholds. At the 1924 Democratic national convention Klansmen were among the delegates—estimates place their number around three hundred fifty—and some historians credit them with defeating Al Smith of New York, a Catholic, with the slogan "Keep the Pope out of the White House." In a show of strength, some forty thousand Klansmen in full regalia marched down Pennsylvania Avenue in the nation's capital in August of 1925, the Klan's high-water mark as it turned out.

The second Klan fell into eclipse when corruption and licentiousness on the part of some of its high leaders were exposed by incidents and investigations. By the beginning of the 1930s, membership had leveled off at slightly over three hundred thousand. Robbed of its political influence by the scandals and by declining acceptability, the Klan turned to terror tactics and strange alliances. For instance, in 1940 it joined the German-American Bund in a rally at Camp Nordlund in New Jersey during which a towering cross was burned and the martial strains of the "Horst Wessel Lied" filled the air. In a way the Nazi anthem was a swan song, for in 1944 a dwindling Klan dissolved itself rather than pay a huge judgment in back taxes.

The present Klan began in the postwar era under the leadership of Dr. Samuel Green, an Atlanta dentist. It groped along without any real impact until the school desegregation ruling of the Supreme Court in 1954—"the Decision," as it was called in the Deep South—which galvanized the entire white supremacy movement. The current numerical strength of the Klan is difficult to assess, since it is secretive and splintered into some fifteen units, some working closely together, others at each other's throats. Estimates vary. Following its 1965 hearings, the House Un-American Activities Committee (HUAC) placed the figure at about fifteen thousand. In his annual report to the attorney general at the outset of 1968, FBI director Hoover said membership was between fourteen and fifteen thousand, mainly in the South. The Anti-Defamation League has recently put the figure at thirty thousand. Other sources have ranged upward to one hundred thousand.

The largest unit, the United Klans of America Knights of the Ku Klux Klan, claims thirty-five thousand members in eighteen states. This group, an outgrowth of Samuel Green's Klan, is led by former tire-plant worker Robert M. Shelton Jr. and based in Tuscaloosa, Alabama. Shelton and his hierarchy were the main targets of the HUAC probe. After they refused to produce their records, Shelton and six other leaders were cited for contempt of Congress by an overwhelming vote of the House on February 2, 1966, and were subsequently indicted and convicted. Almost to a man, southern segregationists in the House voted for citation, and the only opposition was voiced by a scattering of liberals opposed to HUAC's tactics. The ostracism of the Klan by the respectable right was pronounced by roly-poly Joe Pool of Dallas, the late acting chairman of HUAC and a stout reactionary, who declared that the Klan record represented "the activities of sneaky, cowardly men" who indulged in "floggings, beatings, and killings for racial reasons."

The psychoses of the United Klans do not stop with the black menace. Ever since they learned that some eighty percent of Southern psychiatrists were Jews, Klansmen have been spouting anti-Semitism. They imagine the Society for Mental Hygiene and all mental health research centers to be part of a conspiratorial network run by Jews "wanting to brainwash the Americans." Among the horror stories repeated as fact is one about a secret hospital in wilderness Alaska where many Gentiles were given lobotomies and turned into communist robots for promoting racial integration. Shelton has repeatedly dredged up the old canard about the international Zionist conspiracy; in his version Jewish-dominated investment banking houses on Wall Street are at the heart of the scheme.

The second largest Klan is the National Association Knights of the Ku Klux Klan, whose chairman is aging lawyer James K. Venable of Tucker, Georgia. The NAK is actually a loose confederation of local Klaverns with a membership total of ten thousand. Although Venable says there are members in most states, and the California unit under William V. Fowler is fairly active, the bulk of the NAK is in the South. On the militancy scale, it ranks near the bottom.

Third in size and perhaps the most violence-prone and clandestine of the Klans is the White Knights of the Ku Klux Klan, which has staked out Mississippi as virtually a private preserve and has intimidated Shelton's group into withdrawing from the state. The Imperial Wizard of the White Knights was, at least until recently, Samuel Holloway Bowers Jr. of Laurel, Mississippi, who runs a coin-machine enterprise sardonically named the Sambo Amusement Company. The FBI has implicated the White Knights in a number of civil rights homicides, and Bowers himself was indicted for conspiracy in the 1964 deaths of James Chaney, Andrew Goodman, and Michael Schwerner near Philadelphia, Mississippi,* and the 1966 firebomb death of Vernon F. Dahmer Sr., who was prominent in voter registration in the Hattiesburg area.

As in the matter of campus violence, it is not clear how much of the violence attributed to the White Knights is spontaneous and how much is triggered by methods of entrapment and *agents provocateurs.* The question arose after a tragic White Knights incident in Meridian, Mississippi. On the night of June 30, 1968, police in dark clothing staked out the Meridian home of Jewish businessman Meyer Davidson, who had posted a $75,000 reward after the bombing of a synagogue earlier in the year. When a car pulled up and a man got out carrying a box, the police closed in and a gun battle erupted. When it was all over, the man, Thomas Albert Tarrants III, lay wounded and his companion, schoolteacher Kathy Ainsworth, was dead. The box contained a dynamite

---

* Seven of the men indicted were convicted. Bowers received a maximum term of ten years.

bomb, police said, adding they had expected a gun battle and had never thought either Klan member would be taken alive.

Presumably, his Klan membership was established by a notebook in Tarrants's pocket which contained the entry: "Gentlemen: I have committed myself totally to defeating the Communist-Jew conspiracy which threatens our country—any means necessary shall be used. Please be advised that since 23 March 1968, I, Thomas Albert Tarrants III, have been underground and operating guerrilla warfare. I have always believed in military action against the Communist enemy." There were also Klan membership cards in Miss Ainsworth's purse, police said—without disclosing to whom they were made out. According to the Meridian chief of police, the stakeout was set up because Davidson's car window had been shot out several nights before. Just why a Klan terrorist would carry such a notebook entry or shoot out a car window at a home he intended to bomb was unexplained.

The suspicious circumstances of the shootout piqued the curiosity of Jack Nelson, a veteran reporter of the southern scene now manning an Atlanta bureau for the *Los Angeles Times*. Digging into the case, he wrote a story alleging that the FBI "paid $36,500 to two KKK informants to arrange a trap to catch two young Klan terrorists in a bombing attempt." Whether the informants planted the notebook on Tarrants and shot out the window Nelson didn't say, but his exposé drew no denial from the FBI, though it brought an alarmed cry from the American Civil Liberties Union and the American Friends Service Committee. In a joint statement on April 7, 1970, the two organizations urged the president "to investigate the alleged unlawful actions of the FBI and the local police." The statement asserted in conclusion: "If citizens and their government remain silent about the Meridian incident, then the dreams of a Martin Luther King and a Robert Kennedy, and a host of other dreamers, will have died with them." But silence prevailed.

The White Knights have no monopoly on violence. For example, all the men charged with the slayings of Lemuel Penn, Viola Liuzzo, and the Reverend James Reeb were reportedly connected with the United Klans of America. In fact, the overall pattern of Klan bombings, lynchings, and beatings shows that no one unit can be singled out. The FBI apparently has riddled the various Klans with paid informants as thoroughly as it once did the Communist Party. The Bureau paid a huge sum to Klan insiders in order to crack the Philadelphia, Mississippi, murders, and two plants inside the White Knights testified at the trial (interestingly, one was a member of the Meridian police department, Sgt. Carlton W. Miller). A Louisiana state police undercover agent reported in 1967 that a wave of bombings in the Baton Rouge area was the work of a Klan cell trying "to give the impression that it was union strife in the capital city which spawned the bombings."

Evidently violence is the last resort of the Klan as it seethes with indignation at the sight of White Citizens Councils cornering the nonviolent segregationist market.* However, the Klan cannot be lightly dismissed as merely the occasional perpetrator of violence—some units at least are fast developing a capacity for continued violence in the form

---

* Composed of activists among the southern aristocracy and business elite, the Councils sprang up as a direct reaction to the Decision in 1954. Operating with a mantle of respectability and using the methods of economic, political, and social pressure and persuasion, the Councils fluctuate in size and activity as they respond to specific developments. Chairman of the Citizens Councils of America is Roy V. Harris, an Augusta, Georgia, lawyer and former speaker of the Georgia legislature; one of its more flamboyant figures was the late Leander Perez Sr., the feudal baron of Plaquemines Parish, Louisiana. The Council takes a share of the credit for the political fortunes of George Wallace, former governor Ross R. Barnett of Mississippi, the Arkansas phenomenon Orval Faubus, and numerous petty politicians in the South.

of paramilitary squads. Secret training programs have been held on bombing, setting booby traps, making Molotov cocktails, shooting, judo, karate, and clandestine communications. One undercover investigator recently told me about a training ground used by the Louisiana-based Universal Klans, which broke away from the United Klans not long ago. The site is in rural St. Bernard Parish some fifty miles from New Orleans. Inside a farmhouse on the site, the investigator related, there was a portrait of the Nazi "martyr" Horst Wessel flanked by candles and Nazi flags; the room contained a supply of *National Socialist World* published by the American Nazi Party in Virginia. In back were crosses wrapped in burlap, ready to be dipped in gasoline. A miniature train once used in a New Orleans amusement park transported Klansmen and Minutemen, who also used the site, across a pasture and through a copse of trees to a rifle range. A storehouse held an "enormous supply" of rifles, ammunition, dynamite, and hand grenades. In the investigator's estimation there was locally a sizable overlap in membership between the Klan and the Minutemen. He quoted one of the leaders as bragging, "We won't need the National Guard if a race riot breaks out around here. We'll wipe them out with the Minutemen."

An offshoot of the paramilitary trend is small elite squads that specialize in bombings, terrorism, and murder. Known by various names such as "the Underground" and "the Secret Six," they operate with or without the sanction of higher Klan authority. The assassination of high political figures is a subject that is seriously contemplated, and what may have been bits and traces of such a scheme surfaced after John Kennedy was assassinated. On October 30, 1963, less than a month before the Dallas tragedy, the chief of police of Denton, Texas, divulged to the Secret Service that a man had bragged, "We have something planned to embarrass President Kennedy during his visit to Dallas, Texas." Upon questioning, the man denied making the threat but admitted being a "former member of the 'Klan' in Arkansas and the National States Rights Party, and [being] presently a member of the John Birch Society." On November 14, 1963, only a week before the event, a man in custody on federal car theft charges told the FBI a similar story. According to the FBI report

> he is a member of the Ku Klux Klan. . . . During his travels throughout the country, his sources have told him that a militant group of the National States Rights Party plans to assassinate the president and other high-level officials. He stated that he does not believe this is planned for the near future, but he does believe the attempt will be made.*

A third report that came to light, by far the most specific, was supplied by an undercover agent for the Miami police department who secretly taped his colloquy with a militant segregationist. The man evidently skittered from group to group seeking an outlet for his feelings, for he mentioned affiliations with the Klan, the Constitution Party, and the small Nebraska-based Congress of Freedom. The man said he was going to form the Constitutional Party for States Rights "as a front to form a hard-core underground for possible violence in combating integration."

The man, who had inherited a small fortune and was able to move about freely, boastfully told the agent on November 9, 1963, that John Kennedy was a "marked man" and a plan to kill him was already "in the works." The

* These two reports were published in the volumes of the Warren Commission Report as Commission Exhibit 762. The Secret Service closed its file on the second one because the FBI had felt "the subject was trying to make some sort of deal with them for his benefit," and besides there was "no information developed that would indicate any danger to the president in the near future or during his trip to Texas."

instigator of the plan was said to be the late Jack Brown, a Klansman from Chattanooga, Tennessee. The details were strikingly similar to what happened at Dallas thirteen days later. The president was to be "shot with a high-powered rifle from an office building and the police would quickly arrest a patsy . . . just to throw the public off." The Miami police furnished the Secret Service with a copy of the tape, and when Kennedy visited the Florida city on November 15 extraordinary precautions were taken, even to the point of flying him to and from downtown in a helicopter rather than allowing a motorcade. The undercover agent was later to report that the man telephoned him from Dallas on the morning of November 22 and in the course of the conversation proffered, "I don't think you will ever see your boy [Kennedy] again in Miami."

The same tape also contains talk about killing Dr. Martin Luther King Jr.* The man comments of Brown, "He hasn't said so, but he tried to get Martin Luther King."

"He did?" the agent asked.

"Oh yes. He followed him for miles and miles and couldn't get close enough to him."

"You know exactly where it is in Atlanta, don't you?"

"Martin Luther King? Yeah."

* The tape was played for newsmen by the Miami police on February 3, 1967. The FBI had interviewed the segregationist participant in the taped conversation on November 27, 1963, and he had categorically denied any knowledge of the assassination. The undercover agent has been interviewed by Bernard Fensterwald Jr., executive director of the National Committee to Investigate Assassinations. In his report dated June 5, 1968, Fensterwald quotes the agent as relating that he "took the call from Dallas [on the morning of the assassination] at face value and placed a call to Mr. Charlie Sapp of the [Miami police] Intelligence Division. Unfortunately, Mr. Sapp was asleep. . . . Consequently, he called Sgt. Everett Kay of the Intelligence Division whose response was 'It's no use to tell the FBI about this because they won't do anything about it anyway.' "

"Bustus Street."
"Yeah, 530."

To go with its paramilitary capabilities there is some evidence that the Klan is penetrating the military and the police to some extent. There have been persistent reports of Klan activity in the U.S. Army, and on June 11, 1970, the Army announced it was reopening its investigation into charges of a Klan Klavern operating among forces stationed in West Germany. The announcement prompted Robert Shelton of the United Klans to puff that "we have Klan units in the Army and in the Army in Germany," although how much is behind the boast has yet to be seen. While it has been taken for granted that southern law enforcement is spotted with Klansmen and sympathizers, it came as something of a surprise when Chicago police spokesmen revealed on December 28, 1967, that a Klan cell of at least five officers had been functioning inside the department.

In evaluating the effective potential of the Klan—or any other rightist group—account must be taken of its connections with other organizations. The Klan has established contact with racist groups in South Africa, Australia, and Scandinavia. As the St. Bernard Parish setup suggests, there is a significant amount of simultaneous membership and cooperative action born of a mutuality of interest with the Minutemen, the National States Rights Party, and the neo-Nazis, to name several groups. Roy Frankhouser Jr. of Reading, Pennsylvania, rather exemplifies this fitful alliance. He is at the same time Grand Dragon of the United Klans in Pennsylvania and state coordinator of the Minutemen. "We work independently, but we also complement each other, and the lines of communication are always open between us," Frankhouser has explained. "We've got the same enemies, the same friends, and the same goals. We're fighting under different leadership, but we're fighting *together* just the same."

As for the enemy, Frankhouser expressed what many resentful whites are thinking: "If the niggers push us too far, we won't be burning crosses—we'll be burning cities." Which is why the word currently being passed at Klan meetings, "The last hope of the poor whites is the Klan," may yet rally an entirely new kind of white power.

5
ROBERT DE PUGH AND THE MINUTEMEN
the enemy is washington

Ultimately, the only pro-American, patriotic organizations will be underground organizations. All others will have been hounded out of existence.

—*internal bulletin of the* New Jersey Minutemen

We must stop pretending that the bureaucrats have a natural "right" to the wealth they take from us. They are parasites and have gained power over the people by trickery. . . . If the citizens of the United States are to regain their freedom from excessive government, they must do so by means of a counterrevolution. This may be violent or nonviolent depending on future developments.

Robert Bolivar DePugh in his Blueprint for Victory

On the early evening of July 12, 1969, two FBI agents peered over the lip of a mesa overlooking the Rio Grande a few miles south of Truth or Consequences, New Mexico. Below them was a small house with a driveway leading down to a secondary highway paralleling the river. Two men exited from the house, got in a pickup truck, and started out the driveway. The agents dashed to their car, parked nearby on a power company service road, and radioed the FBI surveillance command post. The order was given to close in. The agents drove gingerly down the rutty road and joined another FBI vehicle in forcing the pickup off the highway. Weapons drawn, the G-men took into custody a middle-aged man wearing a mustache and cowboy hat, and a younger, muscular man. Thus ended the year-and-a-half underground stint of Robert Bolivar DePugh, national coordinator of the Minutemen, and his top aide, Walter Patrick Peyson.

DePugh and Peyson had disappeared in February 1968, shortly before a Seattle, Washington, grand jury returned an indictment charging them with conspiracy to rob a bank. The indictment was the outgrowth of events capsuled in a *Seattle Times* headline January 26: "FBI SEIZES SEVEN IN PLOT TO BLOW

UP REDMOND POLICE STATION, ROB FOUR BANKS." The seven were said to be members of the Minutemen, and DePugh and Peyson had somehow—and somewhat belatedly—been plugged into the plot.

The arrest on the shoulder of the New Mexico highway posed a problem for the FBI, for it foreclosed the possibility of searching the house incidental to arrest. Four days later a swarm of G-men reappeared at the site armed with a search warrant and enough weaponry to outfit a *Bonnie and Clyde* movie set. Evidently fearing that the house was booby-trapped or that it contained armed occupants, they crawled up and surrounded it before rushing inside. They found a veritable munitions dump, including explosives, grenades, rifles, and a Belgian Fabrique Nationale automatic rifle. In his appropriations testimony the following March, J. Edgar Hoover boasted: "The Minutemen organization, which has as its purpose the training of individuals to overthrow the government of the United States when the government is taken over by the Communists, was dealt a stunning blow with the apprehension by the FBI of its fugitive leaders, Robert DePugh and Walter Peyson." This appraisal contrasted sharply with one the FBI chief had given only four years earlier when he called the Minutemen a "paper organization" with "just enough followers over the country so they can occasionally attract a headline, usually because of their preoccupation with violence or weapons of war." Had the Minutemen blossomed into a full-scale threat in those four years which included DePugh's underground stint?

The answer must necessarily involve a scrutiny of the current state of the Minutemen. The name itself has come to be a generic one, encompassing the entire paramilitary right wing, of which DePugh's faction is the best known. At one time, most of the factions were aligned in a kind of mutual-interest confederation. But in the past few years ideological rifts and personality conflicts within the leadership have generated internal rivalries and spun off still more factions, and the present situation is, to say the least, fluid. But despite his incarceration, the charismatic DePugh will doubtless remain the dominant figure of the paramilitary right for some time to come.

I first met Robert DePugh in 1966 when I journeyed to Norborne, Missouri, to interview him for an article on the Minutemen.* Norborne, a dot on the rich and rolling farmlands of northwest Missouri some seventy miles from Kansas City, is the site of the family-run veterinary medicine firm, Biolabs, Inc. Strung along State Highway 10 as it leads into town is a series of signs repeating the phrases of the Hail Mary in the fashion of Burma-Shave jingles. Norborne itself and its eight hundred fifty souls are pure Middle America. The Biolabs building, a one-story wooden structure permeated by the odor of vitamin A, is next door to the American Legion post. DePugh's wife Ramona and sons Ralph and John have kept it going on a day-to-day basis, and his brother Bill DePugh, an ordained Baptist minister, has served as manager. At the time of my visit Biolabs' net worth was reputedly $350,000, but due to DePugh's prolonged absence business has slipped and the firm is barely struggling along.

We talked in his windowless office, its wall shelves lined with the pharmaceutical and biology texts intermingled with political tracts and guerrilla warfare manuals. Despite a pallor, DePugh is ruggedly handsome, with intent dark eyes and coal-black hair receding in accordance with his age, now forty-nine. With his soft Missouri twang and his drab off-the-rack suit, he could easily have passed for a small-town businessman prominent in nothing more venturesome than the local Lions Club.

As he tells it, DePugh's political concepts crystallized while he was in the Army signal corps during World War II.

* The article appeared in the January 1967 issue of *Ramparts.*

POWER ON THE RIGHT

He came into contact with several radar scientists who seemed "not to hold allegiance to the same flag." Later, during the McCarthy hearings, he recalled those scientists and "wondered why McCarthy was being smeared for saying things I knew were true." It was apparently a classic clash of Midwestern parochialism versus global-minded sophistication. DePugh became an early follower of Robert Welch, but was drummed out of the Birch Society when he organized the Minutemen.

Legend has it that the Minutemen came into being quite spontaneously on a small Missouri lake in June of 1960. It was the height of the U-2 crisis, and ten duck hunters, DePugh among them, were speculating on the outcome. "Well, if the Russians invade us," one hunter supposedly quipped, "we can come up here and fight on as a guerrilla band." Another hunter, a Special Forces veteran, took the proposal seriously and hauled out his training manuals. In deadly earnest, the ten started to "prepare for the day when Americans will once again fight in the streets for their lives and their liberty."

DePugh only smiles wanly when asked if the story is apocryphal, and of the original ten only he and Richard Lauchli have ever been identified. Rich Lauchli, his cherubic features rimmed by a sandy brush-cut, was an ex–World War II paratrooper who ran a machine shop in Collinsville, Illinois, not far from St. Louis. It was a training exercise in 1961, run by DePugh and Lauchli in the fields near Collinsville, that first attracted press attention to the Minutemen.* Before long Lauchli had formed his own Counter-Insurgency Council of Illinois and broken with the Minutemen. "Our CIC broke with the Minutemen in 1962," Lauchli has said, "because that organization was badly managed and didn't

* In the interest of historical firsts, it should be noted that in the late 1950s Lauchli headed a small, loosely run paramilitary band called the Internal Security Force of Illinois.

have proper military security; there was no effort made to screen applicants." For his part, DePugh considers Lauchli less than guarded. "He spars with strangers for all of two minutes," derides DePugh. "Then he opens up." In fact, Lauchli had been conned into selling illegal arms several times by Treasury agents. In 1964 he was arrested for agreeing to sell machine guns, a flame thrower, aerial bombs, and other weapons to T-men posing as representatives of a Caribbean country, and spent time in the Terre Haute federal penitentiary. While in the pen he talked a fellow convict due for release into applying preservatives to a large cache of submachine guns; the con tipped off federal agents and Lauchli was no sooner out than he was in again.*

Yet Lauchli's criticism of the Minuteman structure was partially valid. Despite its military trappings, the organization was not set up with a tight military-like chain of command and control. It was more like a franchise operation, with DePugh in Norborne providing the national identity, policy directives, publicity coordination, propaganda materials, and training publications. In turn, the units in the field would remit dues and submit intelligence data. Active units sprang up in New York City, Kansas City, St. Louis, Tucson, Seattle, Spokane, San Diego, Los Angeles, New Orleans, and many other points. For security reasons, each unit functioned somewhat like a Communist Party cell, with the members often unknown to each other except by a code name or number. Despite their fanaticism, some of the unit heads

---

* In August 1963 the hapless Lauchli was among eleven men arrested in an FBI raid on a training ground near New Orleans, Louisiana. A quantity of bomb casings and dynamite was seized. Five of the men were exiled Cubans, and the group presumably was preparing for anti-Castro operations. Apparently the raid was carried out in error, however, for the men were quietly released and a cover story given out by the wife of the property's owner that a recently arrived Cuban named "José Juárez" had been given permission to use the grounds.

were not in the "crazies" category; among them an insurance executive, an Air Force reserve captain, a real estate broker, and a publisher.* DePugh loftily explained to me that the outfit relied upon "individual responsibility" to retain stability and contended that members were in fact screened, but readily admitted that there was no control mechanism over their activities. When I queried him again on this point recently, he replied: "I have never attempted or even intended to maintain a 'military type' of leadership over the organization. Such types of leadership are too easily infiltrated or supplanted by a coup d'état." His control over the Minutemen, he asserted, is ideological. "I may lose a little piece of it now and then but such losses are usually temporary. My ideological control is so strong now that it is virtually self-perpetuating. An ideological leader always has the option of exercising military-type leadership when it serves his purpose—and the safe thing is that *no one else has that option.*"

I had expressed concern to DePugh during our 1966 discussion that his ideological excesses might arouse some of the more unstable and volatile elements to act recklessly and without authorization. He had drawn up a manifesto in 1961 that was distinctly revolutionary. It proclaimed that "our diplomatic war against communism has already been lost by bunglers or traitors within our own government," and consequently the members must "prepare to take any action—no matter how brutal—that may be required to renew the protection of the United States Constitution for future generations." And in order to gain and hold hegemony over the paramilitary right, he had to sound more radical than his rivals. Indeed, DePugh's rhetoric has not lacked the inflam-

* The membership total of the hydra-headed Minutemen is anybody's guess, including DePugh's. He put it at "over twenty-five thousand." J. Edgar Hoover put it at five hundred. Defector Jerry Brooks put it at eight thousand, plus thousands of sympathizers.

matory touch. A 1963 issue of the Minuteman publication *On Target* addressed a warning to twenty "Judas" members of Congress who had voted against appropriations for HUAC; it ended: "Traitors beware! Even now the cross-hairs are on the back of your necks." He once coyly mentioned to a newspaper reporter how easy it would be to conduct germ warfare on the populace, and gave a *Playboy* journalist visiting Norborne a glimpse of a mysterious "C file," about which he confided: "Anybody listed in file C has betrayed his country to the most ruthless enemies it has ever known. The penalty for treason is death, and if the execution of the sentence is left to us—well, we accept the responsibility."

Perhaps inevitably, the Minutemen have been chronically afflicted with assassination schemes of the most bizarre sort. In 1962, a Dallas man who had been an American Nazi Party recruiter and Minuteman hanger-on came up with the notion that by periodically assassinating a member of Congress at a time publicized in advance, his colleagues who were not "voting American" would be terrorized and the Minutemen could "ultimately gain control of the government." The first victim was to be Senator J. William Fulbright, during one of his swings into Arkansas. According to Minuteman defector Jerry Milton Brooks, "he purchased a rifle with a telescopic sight, but on the day he was to depart for Little Rock, news of the plot leaked to DePugh, who blew his top." Then in September 1966 four Dallas Minutemen hatched a plot to ambush Stanley Marcus, the wealthy Jewish liberal, owner of Nieman-Marcus department store, but decided that it should be done on one of his out-of-town trips since "another assassination in Dallas would be too much." Again, DePugh got wind of it and intervened.

Attacks on the United Nations have also been on the agenda, and one scheme got as far as an overt act. It grew out of a training session in 1965 when bull sessions debated means of wiping out the occupants of the UN building in one

fell swoop. When mortars were ruled out, someone
came up with the idea of injecting poisonous gas into the
air-conditioning system, and someone else purchased a quantity of cyanide for that purpose. Again according to Brooks,
a member who was a New York state policeman was going to
use his credentials to get into the building's basement. Finally
DePugh decided to nix the plan, much to the dismay of some
of his more fanatic followers. Yet the fume infusion technique didn't really die—a former anti-Castro activist in New
Orleans told me he was present when W. Guy Banister, a
retired FBI official involved in paramilitary efforts aimed at
Fidel Castro, tossed out the possibility of pouring cyanide
into the ducting system of the Cuban premier's palace. Says
Brooks of the Minutemen's designs on the UN: "That place is
a symbol of everything they hate. They're bound to take
another crack at it some day."

The Minutemen broke into the headlines on October 30,
1966, when New York police intercepted nineteen members
garbed in hunting clothes and heavily armed who were start-
ing out, the police said, to firebomb three "liberal" summer
camps: Camp Webatuck at Wingdale, New York, Camp Mid-
vale in the Ramapo Mountains of New Jersey, and a community at Voluntown, Connecticut, run by the New England
Committee for Nonviolent Action. It turned out that the
Minuteman band had been infiltrated by the NYPD's Bureau
of Special Services (BOSS), which had kept it under surveillance for ten months. As a result, raids were mounted on
arms caches that yielded a million rounds of rifle and small-
arms ammunition, 125 rifles, 10 dynamite bombs and mis-
cellaneous materiel, as well as an impressive portable communications system. In a companion raid on the premises of a
Syracuse businessman, police seized a quantity of hypo-
dermic needles and syringes in addition to an array of
weaponry and organizational files indicating that the Minutemen were far more numerous and active in the New York—

New England region than had previously been suspected.*

In one of the more surprising developments, it was disclosed that a state policeman, one of three in a Minuteman "action squad," had for two years been spiriting heavy weapons out of armories for his comrades and tipping them off about law enforcement radio frequencies and countermoves. The three were quietly dropped from the police rolls.

Shortly after the raids the *Washington Post* quoted an official source in New York City as saying that if the assaults on the camps had succeeded, the next strike would have been an assassination attempt on James Farmer, the former CORE head who had been deemed a "top black Red." In any event, the Minutemen in the area were not idle for long. In June 1967 a band of five mounted an attempt on the life of Herbert Aptheker, director of the American Institute of Marxist Studies and a national functionary of the Communist Party. They secreted a pipe bomb with a timing device on the roof of a Bronx building over a room where Aptheker was slated to lecture on Marxist dialectics. The bomb went off tardily, severely damaging the emptied room. The bombers were swiftly apprehended and convicted. Then in August of 1968 the Voluntown, Connecticut, commune was again targeted, and again an informant alerted police, although almost too late. When the word came, state troopers surrounded the grounds, but six Minutemen slipped through and entered the main building. As one of the women there later recounted, the masked men, dressed in combat fatigues and bearing rifles with fixed bayonets, "spoke quietly, moved quietly, and seemed very self-assured." When the troopers finally realized what had happened, a gun battle opened up, leaving four raiders, one trooper, and one woman in the audience wounded. The intruders were charged with conspiracy

* Charges against some were dropped, and none had been convicted when the author last checked.

to commit arson and assault with intent to kill.

"Kooks they are, harmless they're not," a BOSS detective is quoted in a *Playboy* article on the Minutemen in June 1969. "It's only due to their own incompetence and not any lack of motivation, that they haven't left a trail of corpses in their wake." Perhaps, but along with the incompetents the Minutemen have quite a few experts and near-experts in such special fields as guerrilla warfare, clandestine communications, and detonation. One of the New York group, for instance, was a reserve sergeant in the Green Berets, and the organization as a whole is well stocked with ex-servicemen qualified in the military arts. Although the press has tended to play up the more ludicrous aspects when a case breaks—in the Seattle bank robbery affair it was the fact that members referred to each other by James Bond code numbers—the fact remains that there has been a demonstrated competence. To cite three prominent examples, ex-Marine Wally Peyson is a virtuoso with the machine gun; Rich Lauchli turned out thousands of very fine automatic weapons at his LAXCO machine shop; and DePugh himself made an FBI explosives expert look amateurish on cross-examination while representing himself at trial. The Minuteman handbook contains instructions on such subjects as "Booby Traps," "Anti-Vehicular Mines," and "Incendiary Weapons Composition" that are hardly in the Boy Scout class; its section on silencer construction observes that "the advantages of a gun that makes no noise when fired are obvious" and is clearly the work of a specialist.

In conjunction with their irregular warfare capacity, the Minutemen also conduct clandestine operations in intelligence, infiltration and counter-tactics. At Norborne there is a file broken down into geographical regions containing data on individuals and groups—such as the National Council of Churches and B'nai Brith—that are considered subversive. DePugh claimed to me that there were sixty-five thousand persons on file, including fifteen hundred "verified" as members of the communist "hidden government," but this seems exaggerated considering the lack of staff. The Minuteman chief further maintained that his members had penetrated the Black Muslims, CORE, SNCC, and various peace groups, and just recently he contended: "We started out to merely infiltrate the New Mobilization Committee and before we knew it virtually took over leadership and literature production. During the last two years we've recruited many of our best young people directly out of New Left organizations." Although this is difficult to check, one former member told me that he had seen internal Communist Party memoranda and knew of undercover Minutemen within an SDS chapter at the University of Chicago and a peace group at the University of Wisconsin. The September 1970 issue of *On Target* contained a fairly comprehensive listing of Socialist Workers Party and Young Socialist Alliance meeting places throughout the country as well as the names and addresses of national and district leaders.

The concentrated effort to infiltrate the public safety forces was at least partially successful. Minuteman Bulletin No. 8 for the New Jersey–Maryland–Delaware region, dated September 1965 and marked "For Internal Distribution Only," told of a confidential briefing given to the New Jersey National Guard at Fort Dix, which is worthy of repeating here in light of Kent State:

> The plan which was revealed by the State Attorney General (Arthur J. Sills) is that in the event of any racial riots or other civil disturbances, the New Jersey State Police would take charge of the National Guard and all local police units. A form of martial law would be declared and under this declaration, weapons could be confiscated both from stores and homes without the need for any search warrant. National Guard personnel

were told that they would not have ammunition for their weapons unless events took a radical turn. Sills's statement that "You will have unloaded weapons and it's to your benefit to take weapons that are not needed from civilian hands" met with groans and hisses and "That's what you think" from the assembled guardsmen.

The bulletless situation disturbed the Minutemen, and in the bulletin they instructed that "members in all states should make efforts to cultivate members of National Guard units if they have not already done so." In addition, the bulletin noted that anti-gun legislation was pending in New Jersey and advised members to have one "giveaway" gun with others safely hidden away. And when the gun roundup came, the bulletin cautioned, "DON'T SHOOT NATIONAL GUARDSMEN. Many of them are already in our organization, and many others are fully sympathetic with our position."

In our 1966 talk, DePugh also asserted that the Minutemen kept tabs on other elements of the right not aligned with his group, mentioning specifically the Christian Anti-Communism Crusade, Billy James Hargis's Christian Crusade, factions of the KKK, and the American Nazi Party. DePugh was the bitter rival of George Lincoln Rockwell, and he recently said that ANP member John Pratler, who was convicted of the sniper slaying of Rockwell, was actually a Minuteman plant.

DePugh boasted, too, of Minuteman provocateur techniques such as dressing in "hippie" garb, joining peace and civil rights demonstrations, and trying to put the demonstrations in a bad light by acting obnoxiously and creating friction. On one occasion, at least, the Minutemen were eminently successful in the provocateur role. During the 1966 raids in the New York area, police found a large supply of leaflets bearing the imprint of a black nationalist group in the

Bellmore, Long Island, home of Minuteman unit leader William Garrett. The content was highly incendiary—it included the exhortation "Kill the White Devils and have the white women for our pleasure." According to the district attorney, the leaflets had been tossed from speeding cars in racially troubled neighborhoods in Queens and western Long Island. The chairman of New York City's Commission on Human Rights, William H. Booth, believed that there was a connection between the paramilitarists and reported attacks on whites by blacks that led to disturbances in East New York, Bushwick, Lafayette, Bensonhurst-Gravesend, and South Ozone Park in 1966.

For his part, DePugh denies having a hand in the violent turns Minuteman "patriotism" has taken. The record is in his favor. Although he has been involved in some bizarre episodes—he was accused of holding a couple who threatened to defect captive in a large wooden box during the period of hiding from the FBI—there is no indication that he ever caused bodily harm. On the contrary, his role in aborting the reputed assassination attempt on Senator Fulbright and the United Nations wipe-out suggest that he has served as a brake on some of the membership's more violent impulses. In fact, Victor Horsfall, the man in the wooden box, subsequently told the FBI that during the hiding-out Wally Peyson proposed robbing Texas banks but DePugh countered diplomatically by saying it wasn't "the proper time." And in the *On Target* edition of November 4, 1964, he had cautioned: "We are not proposing violent action. We are not proposing that anyone grab his gun and head for the hills. We have never made such proposals. The communists are winning by infiltration, subversion and psychological warfare. We must turn our enemies' own tactics against them."

This last was written following the Goldwater debacle, as shattering to the Minutemen as to the rest of the radical right. "In all the conservative movement you cannot find another organization that worked harder than the Minutemen have to elect Barry Goldwater," DePugh wrote in a campaign post-mortem. "Literally millions of pieces of campaign literature were distributed by our members. Our members worked as volunteers in many local Republican headquarters." Recalling the original manifesto that "a pro-American government could no longer be established by normal political means," he called for a renewed recruiting drive in order to implement the irregular tactics.

Yet by the time I visited Norborne in May 1966, DePugh had reverted to politics. Just off the press was a paperbound tract, *Blueprint for Victory*, which was to be in effect the platform for his new Patriotic Party. In it DePugh presented his views with force and clarity, but he also hedged, "A new party *can* win if it serves its proper function as the political arm of a complete patriotic resistance movement." The major planks in the platform urged "pruning the bureaucratic tree from top to bottom, [eliminating] oppressive taxation, retaining the integrity of the armed forces, halting the drift toward world government, and nipping government snooping into the private lives of the people."

The Patriotic Party got off to a fairly auspicious start on July 4, 1966, when some four hundred people crowded into the U-Smile Motel in Kansas City for the founding convention. One of the principal speakers was the Reverend Kenneth Goff, who heads the paramilitary Soldiers of the Cross in Englewood, Colorado, a group with close ties to the Minutemen—membership of the two groups overlaps and they hold joint training exercises. A spare, silver-haired man who switched from communism to Gerald L. K. Smith's Christian Nationalists in the 1930s, Goff is a pulpit firebrand. "The anti-Christ totalitarianism of the Fabian Socialist one-worlders will banish God from the skies and capitalism from the face of the earth," he let loose in one burst. "We need a party in America stamped 'Made in America,' not 'in the

Kremlin.' " Attendance at the 1967 convention slipped to one hundred fifty, but DePugh was nonetheless fancying a membership of three thousand. If nothing else, the affair demonstrated the bonds the Minuteman coordinator has been able to forge with other elements of the far right. The invocation was offered by Merle Thayer, executive director of the Congress of Freedom; the Nebraska-based Congress is aligned through Colonel Curtis Dall with the Liberty Lobby of Willis Carto, with whom DePugh has maintained a stable if not intimate working relationship. Myron C. Fagan, the aged director of Hollywood's Cinema Education Guild, decried Reds in the movie industry and the international conspiracy of the "Illuminati," embodied by the Council on Foreign Relations. Richard Cotten, whose "Conservative Viewpoint," beamed over a large network of smaller radio stations, provided a forum for fulminations against the Zionist conspiracy and "mongrelization of the races," proposed that the Patriotic Party back George Wallace in 1968. And Reverend Goff was back for an encore, this time revealing that "twenty thousand Russian spies" were brainwashing American tourists visiting Expo 67 in Montreal.

One of the more intriguing facets of this convention was the role—or non-role—of William Penn Patrick, the cosmetics tycoon from San Rafael, California. A transplanted southerner, Patrick made a name for himself in ultraright circles by a quixotic campaign in the 1966 Republican gubernatorial primary against an idol of the respectable right, Ronald Reagan. After this debut, he helped finance recall efforts against liberal Senator Frank Church of Idaho. DePugh envisioned as an ideal ticket Wallace for president with moneybags Patrick as his running mate. Patrick actually flew to Kansas City for a conference with the Patriotic Party brass, and at the convention the ticket was endorsed. Two months later, however, DePugh told his membership that Patrick would have to be dropped, explaining that Patrick had been recommended in the first place "because he had promised to provide the money necessary to keep the Patriotic Party alive, to open Patriotic Party headquarters throughout most of the major cities in the United States, and to finance the printing, the transportation, the telephones, and all of the other expenses." But not a red cent had been forthcoming.

Despite its lack of finances, the Patriotic Party is still limping along. It still puts out the Patriotic Party Newsletter and it still runs a sprinkling of candidates under its own or a compatible banner. "The Patriotic Party has gained virtual control over the American* and American Independent parties," DePugh recently told me, most likely with some exaggeration insofar as the AIP is concerned. "But the Minutemen are on the verge of losing control of the Patriotic Party." The struggle for control of the party is part of the general realignment in the radical right, and will be touched upon in the next chapter. DePugh's eighty-year-old father, Ralph A. DePugh, a combat infantryman in World War I and active in the American Legion, ran in the 1970 American Party primary for U.S. Senate in Missouri, but lost. And James Kernodle, a Birch Society section leader who has long fought to exclude blacks from his amusement park near Kansas City, ran for U.S. Congress the same year under the American Party emblem.

By far the most colorful Patriotic Party standard bearer was Robert Bagwell, a gardener from Roosevelt, Long Island, who in 1970 ran for the lower house on the unique slogan "Send a Minuteman to Congress!" Originally from North Carolina, Bagwell joined the KKK at fourteen and later gravitated into the National States Rights Party (on one arm he has tattooed "NSRP" over a decorative skull). I met him in

* The American Party, on the ballot in several states, is virtually identical to the AIP.

September 1970 at the trial of DePugh in Albuquerque, where he drove with his wife and dog in a black Volkswagen with "Continental Minutemen" painted on the doors. Bagwell is short, with brush-cut black hair and horn-rimmed glasses, and he talks with a certain style. In his campaign literature, Bagwell declared that "wars are run for the profit and benefit of a few international financiers" and argued that the United States should stay out of war unless its "existence is at stake." In fact, most Minutemen are opposed to the Vietnam war. "Forty thousand boys killed in Vietnam," old Ralph DePugh once said. "We ought to bring them all home—the communists have been running wild in this country since the Kennedy administration." Yet most members believe in a potent military establishment. Bagwell asserted that we must have an "impregnable defense against would-be aggressors and develop our Armed Forces into the most powerful military force in the world."

But any grandiose plans DePugh had for the Patriotic Party were largely undermined by his difficulties with the law, which began in television-drama style in June 1965. It seems that the Minuteman leader became over-anxious in trying to recruit two women to the cause, with the result that they reported having been detained against their wills. The authorities sprung a series of raids, including one at Minuteman headquarters in Independence, Missouri. The timing was unfortunate from DePugh's standpoint; a two-week training session on surveillance and explosives had just started, and out-of-town members had gathered, including the West Coast coordinator, Troy Houghton, and his lieutenant, Dennis Patrick Mower. Tipped off that the raid on headquarters was imminent, the men fled, but in the basement the raiders found a deactivated Thompson submachine gun, which, it was learned, belonged to Mower and had been brought by him from California. This was enough to support a federal case and trigger a series of legal woes for DePugh and his compatriots.

The government tied those woes into one package by indicting DePugh, Peyson, and Houghton on a variety of counts under the National Firearms Act, which prohibits the possession of unregistered automatic weapons. One of the witnesses at the trial, which began in November 1966, was James Clark, a California attorney general's operative who had infiltrated Houghton's Minuteman group; he testified that at a field exercise near the Mexican border in August 1965 Houghton had demonstrated the use of an illegal silencer-fitted pistol. The balance of the government's case rested largely on the credibility of Minuteman defectors who said the defendants had been in possession of unregistered automatic weapons. One was Al Sommerford, a Korean War combat soldier who had once conducted phases of Minuteman training sessions and who claimed he left because "I refused to train a bunch of nuts and kooks into being assassins." Another was Raithby Roosevelt Husted, a former Marine Corps buddy of Peyson, who connected Peyson and DePugh to five machine guns found buried in northwest Missouri. The third was Jerry Brooks, an adventure seeker who had spent considerable time at Norborne and was nicknamed "Rabbi" because of his anti-Semitism. The three were convicted, DePugh receiving a sentence of four years, Houghton three years, and Peyson two. All were released on appeal.

For reasons unknown, the attorneys for the three had decided not to introduce at the trial a signed statement obtained from Ray Husted when federal agents brought him back to Kansas City to appear before a grand jury (he had disappeared some months before and joined the Air Force). In the statement furnished to DePugh, dated August 17, 1966, Husted related that he was accosted by FBI men and taken to a clinic and given shots. He remembered signing a statement for them and "taking some FBI and ATTU [Alcohol and Tobacco Tax Unit] men to a cemetery and enlisting in the USAF." Declared Husted: "It was implied if I didn't go along with them I would be put in a mental hospital."

And Jerry Brooks subsequently recanted his testimony, saying he was coerced into giving it. In an affidavit dated May 9, 1967, he said he was first contacted by Kansas City FBI agent George Arnett in December 1965. "He told me that he wanted to find out about the Minutemen and he said if I did not cooperate, I would be in some kind of trouble." Shortly thereafter, Brooks continued, he was approached by agents of the ATTU, who wangled out of him a statement and testimony concerning the possession of machine guns by the defendants. "They said I could expect to spend from ten years to life in the penitentiary or mental institution if I did not cooperate with them and do and say what they told me to." Still later he claimed he *had* told the truth in court.

On January 19, 1968, a bizarre bank robbery took place that was to cast its shadow over DePugh. First, a bomb exploded outside the city hall of Overland Park, Kansas, a Kansas City suburb, diverting the police. Then two men held up the Metcalf State Bank a few blocks away, escaping with $13,000. Police recovered quickly enough to chase one of the robbers, and in an ensuing gun battle a Kansas state trooper was killed and the robber injured. He turned out to be Henry Floyd Brown, a man with a long criminal record and only one year out of Leavenworth Federal Penitentiary. But the robbery began to take on political overtones when Brown's girlfriend allegedly claimed that proceeds from the robbery were to be used in "recruiting an army to fight communists." The story within a story developed further when the prosecuting attorney told *Kansas City Star* reporter J. Harry Jones Jr. that a Los Angeles resident who had been a criminal confederate of Brown had divulged that Brown and some accomplices had planned to exploit civil disturbances. "He said they had discussed waiting in a city while violence or demonstrations were in progress," Jones quoted the prosecutor. "Then they would bomb the local police department, making it appear that the department was bombed by the demonstrators, and during the confusion commit a bank robbery."

The propinquity of DePugh and his Minuteman headquarters to all this immediately started bells ringing. And they rang even louder a week later when the seven putative Minutemen were seized in the Seattle area as they supposedly were about to implement an elaborate plan that closely resembled the Brown modus operandi. According to Chief of Police Robert A. Sollitto of Redmond, north of Seattle, the group intended to blow up a power substation as a diversion, then rob three banks in his town and perhaps a fourth in Des Moines, a town to the south, near the airport. An informant on the inside leaked the date, January 26. That morning the seven were arrested as they sat in automobiles flanking Redmond. The vehicles yielded floor plans of the banks, camouflage clothing, brass knuckles, ten Molotov cocktails, nine sticks of dynamite, blasting caps, and a carbine with four hundred rounds of ammunition.

As yet there has been no evidence adduced that DePugh had anything to do with either the Overland Park or Redmond capers. Harry Jones of the *Star* reported that two Overland Park police officers who questioned Brown quoted him as saying he was not a member of the Minutemen but knew "quite a few" persons who were. "Brown said he was going to discuss the political situation with DePugh," one of the policemen said, according to Jones, "and if they couldn't get together and DePugh wouldn't go along with what he wanted, he'd have DePugh killed, and take over the Minuteman organization himself." Kansas City publisher Tom Leathers, who secured an interview with Brown, quoted the accused robber: "First off, I'm not a part of the Minutemen. Apparently someone's trying to tie me in with them because that big Seattle bank robbery happened just after mine. And both jobs looked alike. I understand they're after Robert DePugh for the Seattle one—but I don't know DePugh or anyone else connected with the Seattle bank hold-up. De-Pugh and I think a lot alike, but that's as far as it goes."

Pursued by the press, DePugh maintained that he knew only one of the men in custody in Seattle, a former Washington State chairman of the Patriotic Party. Could any of the others have been Minutemen without his knowledge? He conceded the possibility. Approximately a month after the arrests a federal grand jury indicted five of the seven for conspiracy—plus DePugh and Peyson. The indictment provided only one clue about what link, if any, the pair had with the Redmond seven: the date the conspiracy purportedly began. On that date, August 20, 1967, DePugh and possibly Peyson were running a two-week training camp in the mountains of Summit County, Colorado, and the FBI, according to the *Denver Post* of September 24, 1967, had kept watch. Had any of the Redmond seven attended? If so, what evidence was there that DePugh and Peyson helped hatch a conspiracy? As this is written the Redmond five have been convicted but DePugh and Peyson have not been brought to trial.

When the FBI went looking for DePugh and Peyson following the indictments, they had dropped from sight. Soon DePugh began sending "Underground News Bulletins" to news media and the membership. Bulletin Number 1 declared: "We are fugitives not because we made machine guns, or robbed banks or kidnapped little girls. We are fugitives because we dared openly to oppose those traitors in our government who have destroyed our constitutional Republic and are rapidly replacing it with a bureaucratic dictatorship. We are not criminals—we are political refugees in our own land." The FBI "WANTED" handbills (which more and more are being issued for political fugitives) didn't mention the Minutemen, but did contain the customary warning that the persons sought should be considered armed and dangerous.

DePugh later told me that during his year and a half of ducking the FBI he didn't leave Colorado and New Mexico. At Pinos Altos, New Mexico, and later at Truth or Consequences, DePugh apparently had established a headquarters-in-exile. At one time or another a number of members visited or stayed at the installations, including his son John DePugh, Robert Taylor, Joan Gourley, Janet Taylor, and Victor and Mary Ruth Horsfall. (The latter three are no longer in the Minutemen.)

During his absence DePugh had failed to appear for a hearing on the unregistered machine gun charge stemming from the raid on Independence headquarters, and federal charges of bail jumping and unlawful flight to avoid prosecution were filed against him. In a brief trial in Kansas City in January 1970, DePugh was convicted and sentenced to four years for bail jumping. It was highly ironic, for his attorney had counseled him before he went underground to keep in touch because the machine gun conviction would not stand, and indeed, shortly after the Kansas City trial, it was dismissed as without merit. Yet the four-year sentence stood, and DePugh faced still another trial in Albuquerque federal court under the Gun Control Act of 1968.

I appeared at the Albuquerque trial as an expert witness for the defense on FBI internal procedures. It was DePugh's contention that he had not been advised of his Constitutional rights until four hours after his arrest, and, more importantly, that he had never made the implicit admissions which formed the basis for the FBI's search warrant permitting seizure of the evidence against him. Upon examining the FBI documents obtained under discovery rules, I did indeed note critical inconsistencies. A reconstruction of the FBI agents' version of the arrest revealed that the agent taking custody of DePugh advised Peyson of his rights, while the agent taking custody of Peyson advised DePugh of his—an implausible situation. And the utterances attributed to DePugh concern-

ing weapons in the house had not been reported on the con-
temporaneous interview report forms, as regulations required.
Yet even though he was entitled to a court-appointed attorney as an indigent defendant, DePugh acted as his own
counsel. He was badly out-maneuvered by the U.S. attorney a
number of times. For instance, he didn't know how to cope
with objections to my testimony, with the result that most of
it didn't get into the record, yet he allowed the prosecution
to adduce the irrelevant but emotionally damaging testimony
of the Horsfalls that when they became disillusioned and
tried to bolt the Truth or Consequences house they were put
in boxes "for security purposes."

The witness room for the defense provided a glimpse of
the current state of the Minutemen. Joan Gourley, the
twenty-year-old who had been underground, acted as De-
Pugh's secretary and line of communication with the outside.
His wife, Ramona DePugh, was there from Norborne, where
she oversees Biolabs with one hand and operates the Minuteman–Patriotic Party nerve center with the other. So was un-
communicative John DePugh, also twenty, and young Robert
Taylor, a bright "libertarian" conservative, both of whom
had been at Pinos Altos. Also present were the two congressional aspirants, Robert Bagwell from New York and James
Kernodle from Kansas City, and Roy Frankhouser Jr. of
Reading, Pennsylvania, Grand Dragon of the United Klans of
America in the Keystone State as well as Minuteman coordinator for the region. Short and wiry, with a bristly
mustache, Frankhouser has been a staunch DePugh loyalist.
"Hitler had the Jews; we've got the niggers," he was quoted
in the June 1969 *Playboy* piece. "We have to put our main
stress on the nigger question, of course, because that's what
preoccupies the masses—but we're not forgetting the Jew."
Despite his firebrand language, Frankhouser is nobody's fool.
"For the first time since Huey Long," he analyzed, "the stage
is set for the rise of an American brand of fascism. Not that

right-wingers can take any credit for it. The race riots have
done our work for us; the black nationalists are our biggest
recruiting agents; I wish there were a hundred Stokely
Carmichaels and Rap Browns. After each Watts, each Detroit,
we get thousands of new backlash members—and best of all, a
big slice of them are disgruntled cops and National
Guardsmen."*

There were others in the witness room who epitomized
the multi-layered structure of the Minutemen—an activist
nucleus surrounded by a Birch-like general membership sup-
plemented by an array of sympathizers. The wife of Soldiers
of the Cross leader Kenneth Goff, a brunette slip of a
woman, testified that she had taught Minutemen at the
Colorado encampment from a U.S. government manual, "150
Questions on What Every Guerrilla Should Know." While
waiting she sternly lectured FBI agents who were witnesses
for the prosecution about the flood of communist literature
they were allowing into the country. Silver-thatched Gorden
Greb, owner of a Kansas City x-ray equipment firm and
operator of a conservative bookstore, showed up as a character witness. He displayed a reprint of a speech J. Edgar
Hoover had delivered in 1962 before the American Legion
convention in Las Vegas, pointing out its attack on "the
communists." "Didn't you read Hoover's latest testimony?" I
asked. "How he practically saved the country by arresting

---

* Frankhouser was in the news when, on October 31, 1965, one Daniel
Burros committed suicide in Frankhouser's Reading home. Brilliant and
psychotic, Burros had alternately belonged to the American Nazi Party,
the National Renaissance Party, the American Racial Fascist Party, and
the KKK. He was on the staff of George Lincoln Rockwell's magazine
The Stormtrooper, resigning in 1962 to edit *Kill!,* which was "dedicated to the annihilation of the enemies of the White People." Interestingly, too, his name and address as well as Rockwell's were in the
notebook of accused assassin Lee Harvey Oswald. Burros shot himself
when the *New York Times* printed evidence that he was part-Jewish.

DePugh?" Greb looked crestfallen. "I guess I'm not up to date," he said. Another character witness was the Reverend Robert I. Hatch, pastor of the First Bible Presbyterian Church in Kansas City (a Carl McIntire affiliate) and a Birch Society chapter leader. And so were a quartet of typical Middle America ladies, pleasant and prattling, hung up on knitting, sunflower seeds, and anti-communism. There were a few deprecatory jokes about Martin Luther King, and incessant talk about "communists" (when one witness was late in arriving, someone ventured that maybe he had been "kidnaped by the commies"). Mild-mannered Reverend Hatch ventured that the fate of the country was in God's hands, but, hedging his bet, announced that he was leading a caravan to Washington the next week to participate in Carl McIntire's March for Victory.

At trial's end, DePugh stood convicted on charges brought under the Gun Control Act of 1968 and he was later sentenced to ten years and returned to Leavenworth. It was becoming increasingly clear that the federal law enforcement establishment was every bit as dedicated to throwing the book at him and his Minuteman hierarchy as it was to socking it to the Black Panthers and SDS on the left. What also seems manifest was that the anti-Minuteman crusade was not only a propaganda ploy to give the illusion of balance in using the law as an instrument of political suppression. For DePugh had a rather singular thrust to his anti-communism—he held that the main enemy was not in Moscow but in Washington. He had once declared on a radio program that "the Liberal-Communist-Socialist conspiracy that now effectively controls our federal government will pass any laws that they have to, to effectively silence opposition to the present bureaucracy, regardless of what form it will take," which considering the Gun Control Act of 1968 was rather prophetic. He had also said, in a takeoff on Huey Long, "When fascism comes to the United States it will come in the guise of anti-communism." Thus, in the eyes of DePugh and his followers, J. Edgar Hoover and the FBI were not the towering heroes they were to most of the far right, and the CIA was not a desirable means to that all-important end, defeating communism. Rather, they were arms of an oppressive bureaucracy, and DePugh had been outspoken in saying so. So he had to go.

In taking a stand against federal law enforcement, DePugh had driven an ideological wedge between himself and other paramilitary rightists who saw the Kremlin as the symbol of all they hated, and played ball with the FBI, ATTU, and CIA. Thus the national coordinator of the Minutemen found himself opposed not only to the federal government, but to some potent factions of the right as well.

6
THE
PARAMILITARY
RIGHT
a movement in flux

*Commies, Peace Creeps and assorted racial crud! Your arch enemy, the
Iron Cross, is on the loose! If there are any doubts as to our willingness
to use a gun in defense of THE WHITE RACE, please note our several
gunfights. . . . WE, MEN OF THE IRON CROSS, shall lead our White
brothers to final, brutal and blood-soaked victory!*
                    —George Carpenter of the Iron Cross Motorcycle Club,
                    an affiliate of the neo-Nazi "Statecraft" coalition

The entire movement is in a state of flux.
                    —Robert DePugh of the Minutemen

It had been almost four years since I had seen Robert DePugh
when I talked with him in his holding cell in the U.S. Marshal's office in Kansas City in January 1970. He had been
brought there from Leavenworth Federal Penitentiary for the
bail-jumping trial, and I had been subpoenaed as a witness for
the defense. Very simply, he and his attorneys were considering putting on a technical defense to the charge—that he had
gone underground out of fear for his life. There were indications, he explained, that an opposing element of the radical
right had marked him for death, and there had been no point
in seeking protection from the FBI because this very element
cooperated closely with the Bureau.

    Although DePugh tends to be cryptic, at least with out-
siders, I presumed that he was alluding to a Minuteman splinter group that he had described as a "Nazi clique" in a telephone conversation in October 1967. There is no mistaking
DePugh's antipathy toward the American Nazi Party of
George Lincoln Rockwell, and I suspect that his remark
about fascism coming to the United States in the guise of
anti-communism was aimed in Rockwell's direction. DePugh

seemed to delight in the fact that Rockwell's assassin was a double agent—his. But he didn't downgrade the Nazi commander's organizational prowess. When I proposed that the ANP might have been a gross burlesque, given the swaggering and posturing of its central characters, he replied, "Not at all. It had the best underground in the right wing." But that takes money, I persisted. "Rockwell had it," he retorted. "One of his principal sources was Clint Murchison."*

In the 1967 phone call, we had talked about the Nazi clique that had spun off from the Minutemen in the context of the assassination of John F. Kennedy. The Zapruder film, taken by a spectator at Dealey Plaza on November 22, 1963, and the only known complete motion-picture sequence of the shooting of the president, very graphically shows, in my opinion, Kennedy being hit from both the back and the front, which means at least two people firing. Even a cursory inspection of Dealey Plaza reveals it to be an ideal site for a guerrilla-type ambush. I had broached the possibility that renegade Minutemen had been at the operational level that day. "I'm inclined to agree with you," DePugh had said.

The working hypothesis of neo-Minuteman involvement was not idle speculation. Back in 1966 DePugh had divulged that not only did his organization accept Klan members, it had recently absorbed en masse twenty members of the American Nazi Party. "We have a close understanding as to how they are going to familiarize themselves with the evils of National Socialism as preached by George Lincoln Rockwell." I doubted then—and doubt now—DePugh's ability to

---

* DePugh clarified that he was referring to (the late) Clint Murchison Sr., the Dallas oil multimillionaire. Murchison, incidentally, was especially close to J. Edgar Hoover, hosting him each August at his Del Charro Motel in La Jolla, California. Rockwell was not exactly hostile to the FBI. In explaining to reporter George Thayer why he would have the FBI round up all the Jews, he said, "Hoover is our kind of people. He talks like a pink, but when he acts, he acts like a white man."

hold tight ideological control over ANP recruits and others with overlapping allegiances.

Among the latter was W. Guy Banister of New Orleans, who had been in charge of the Chicago FBI office before retiring in 1955 to become deputy superintendent of police for New Orleans. Upon leaving the police, Banister opened a private investigative agency, Guy Banister Associates, Inc., at 531 Lafayette Place. The office doubled as a nerve center for right-wing political activities. Banister published the racist *Louisiana Intelligence Digest,* which depicted integration as part of the Communist conspiracy, and collected what were reputed to be the largest files of "anti-communist intelligence in the state. Data from the files were regularly delivered to the local FBI office.

When he "defected" from the Minutemen in 1966, Jerry Brooks, who possesses a photographic memory, recited on tape the names, addresses, and brief characterizations of a long list of persons he said were members. Included were Guy Banister and one of his investigators, Hugh F. Ward (DePugh later confirmed to me that the pair were members). Brooks added that Banister and Ward were affiliated with something called the Anti-Communist League of the Caribbean, which was involved in Latin American intrigue. He named New Orleans attorney Maurice Brooks Gatlin Sr. as belonging to the League. I checked, and there was such an organization in New Orleans with Gatlin as its attorney of record, although there was no evidence it took in members. Presumably, the name was a variation on the Anti-Communism League of America, based in the Chicago suburb of Park Ridge, with which Bannister had contact while heading the FBI office there. I also learned that Jerry Brooks himself had worked for Banister around 1962. When I finally located him, Brooks confirmed this. He said it was a brief employment, consisting mainly of clipping and sorting incoming material that went into the files and over to the FBI. Gatlin, he thought, had

considered him something of a protégé, and on one occasion
confided that he was going to Paris to deliver $100,000 to an
army clique preparing to assassinate French President Charles
De Gaulle.

In Banister's stable of investigators were David W. Ferrie
and Jack S. Martin. Both were initiates in a flockless cult
called the Apostolic Orthodox Old Roman Church, which has
a distinctly right-wing bent. But they had a bitter falling out.
It was Martin who, hours after the assassination of John Kennedy in Dallas, reported to District Attorney Jim Garrison
that Ferrie had suddenly embarked on a trip to Houston.
Questioned by the FBI on his return, Ferrie merely said he
had "gone ice skating," and although he admitted being
"publicly and privately" critical of the president for with-
holding air cover at the Bay of Pigs and admitted using ex-
pressions like "he ought to be shot," he contended he did not
mean the threat literally.

Rumors persisted that Ferrie was in the Minutemen,
which he may have joined through Banister. The important
thing, however, was his guerrilla warfare skills. An expert
pilot, Ferrie was commander of a Civil Air Patrol squadron.
One of his erstwhile subordinates revealed that he trained
some of his CAP cadets and Cuban exiles in commando
tactics and formed them into five-man small-weapons units.
Another former CAP member quoted Ferrie as saying he
"was working for the CIA rescuing Cubans out of Castro
prisons," and, indeed, Ferrie displayed to friends a long
abdominal slash he said was inflicted by a Castro militiaman.
Still another former member of the Ferrie CAP squadron
never had a chance to say much after the assassination: Lee
Harvey Oswald. When he was residing in New Orleans in the
summer of 1963, Oswald apparently renewed his acquain-
tance with Ferrie. In fact, he made a quickly corrected slip in
handing out some of his pro-Castro literature. On one piece
entitled "Hands Off Cuba" he stamped the address: 544

Camp Street, New Orleans, Louisiana. In fact, 544 Camp Street and 531 Lafayette Place were separate entrances to the same premises: the office of Guy Banister Associates.*

Now DePugh, as he marshaled his defense against the bail-jumping charge, was proposing to have me testify about the series of deaths of persons in the penumbra of the Kennedy assassination in order to justify his own flight as motivated by fear. Whatever the Minuteman leader may have had in mind when he fled, there was no denying that the incidence of death defied the actuarial charts. In the summer of 1964 Guy Banister was found dead in bed of an apparent heart attack at the age of fifty-four, his monogrammed .357 magnum at his side. That same year Maurice Gatlin fell or was pushed from a sixth floor balcony of a hotel in San Juan, Puerto Rico. On May 23, 1965, Hugh Ward, Banister's Minuteman associate who reportedly had been taught to fly by Ferrie, was at the controls of a Piper Aztec when it plunged to earth, unaccountably out of gas, near Ciudad Victoria, Mexico. Then on February 22, 1967, shortly after the Jim Garrison probe had focused on him, David Ferrie died of what was officially diagnosed as an embolism brought about by extreme hypertension.

---

* An investigative team from the *New Orleans States-Item* reported in a copyrighted story April 25, 1967, that a source close to Banister said he had seen fifty to one hundred boxes containing rifle grenades, land mines and unique "little missiles" in the office just prior to the Bay of Pigs invasion. Banister explained that "the stuff would just be there overnight. . . . A bunch of fellows connected with the Cuban deal asked to leave it there overnight." It was all right, Banister assured him, because "I have approval from somebody." Apparently, Banister was operating under the aegis of an intelligence agency, although which one is unknown. Among office papers he left behind was a memorandum to attorney Guy Johnson, an Office of Naval Intelligence reserve officer, reporting, "We apparently have cut across a CIA operation in the Taca affair," Taca being a Central American airline company.

But Jack Martin was still very much alive and, although DePugh didn't know it, had popped up with information that tended to substantiate DePugh's contention that his life had been in danger. Upon his return from covering the Clay Shaw trial in New Orleans in March 1969, Arthur Kevin, news director of radio station KHJ in Los Angeles, mentioned to me that Martin had approached him and played a tape purporting to be a telephone conversation between himself and a Denver right-winger. The tape supposedly was made while DePugh and Peyson were fugitives. "We don't want DePugh and Peyson to come back," the Denver party said, offering $7,500 each to make sure they didn't. When Martin balked at murder, the proposal switched to fingering the pair for $1,500 each. Just how Martin might be able to find the fugitives was not explained, and Kevin didn't pursue the matter. Then, a few days before the bail-jumping trial was to start, Alcohol and Tobacco Tax Unit agent Jim Moore of Kansas City showed up at my home near San Francisco to inquire why I had been subpoenaed. I had no idea, since I hadn't been in touch with DePugh or his attorneys. Moore, who once infiltrated the Patriotic Party as an undercover operative, said that he anticipated the defense would be that DePugh had fled in fear of his life. Perhaps he did, I proffered, describing the Martin tape. He agreed that in the interest of justice the tape should be obtained. When I saw him three days later at the opening of the bail-jumping trial in Kansas City he reported that ATTU men were still trying to locate Martin in New Orleans. But the matter of the tape quickly became academic, for the defense attorneys decided to forgo putting on witnesses of their own, instead attacking the government's case as unsupportive of the charge. During his instructions to the jury, Judge William R. Collison offered his opinion that DePugh was guilty as charged. DePugh scribbled "SUNK" on a slip of paper and handed it to his attorneys. The jury wasn't out long, and the judge later meted out a four-year sentence.

DePugh's future as the titular head of the paramilitary right depends not only on his ability to tread water while in jail, but on the result of current shakeouts and realignments taking place. Some splinter groups calling themselves Minutemen seem to be gathering strength. One, New Orleans–based, is headed by a retired Army colonel. Another, centered in Hollywood and Orange County, calls itself the "Real Minutemen" and functions within a church structure; one of its members, who served in military intelligence during World War II, privately claims to have a close relationship with the FBI. The main split between these versions of the Minutemen and DePugh is that they view Moscow, not Washington, as the principal enemy, and consequently cooperate with federal authorities.

But personality and factional disputes have also contributed to the ferment. Take the case of Troy Houghton of San Diego and Dennis Mower of Lancaster, DePugh's original one-two leadership in California. Despite a flair for outlandish canards—he once announced that Red Chinese troops were poised below the border in Mexico awaiting the signal to invade—Houghton was a solid organizer and kept the activity level high. In May 1967 Houghton traveled to Springfield, Missouri, as a defense witness for Mower, who was being tried on charges of transporting and possessing the deactivated machine gun seized in the raid on Minuteman headquarters at Independence. (Mower was convicted; on appeal, the court vacated conviction on charges of transporting but upheld conviction on possession.) At trial's end, Houghton drove off and has not been seen since. Some think he went underground, while others are sure he is dead. A few neo-Minutemen, DePugh complains, are trying to hold him responsible for the "murder" of Houghton.

In any event the disappearance of Houghton seems to have completed the estrangement between Mower and

DePugh which had begun when Mower dropped out of the Minutemen several years before and formed his own Southern California Freedom Councils. On Mower's calling card for the paramilitary councils is the inscription "The wages of sin is death." One of the cards was found in the wallet of Thomas Tarrants after he was captured in the Mississippi shootout, and in fact the two had met a week before. This was not unlikely, since Mower has told me he is on very friendly terms with Sam Bowers of the White Knights of the Ku Klux Klan.

My first interview with Mower impressed me with the efficiency of his group. In 1968 I went unannounced to Lancaster, on the fringe of the Mojave Desert. At his home, a lieutenant instructed me to go to a coffee shop and wait. After half an hour I was ushered to a motel room. In the room was a "security officer" whom I had noticed checking to see if anyone was tailing me. And although I had given only the name "Bill Turner," they had me pegged. "Is your middle initial 'W'?" I was asked. I nodded. "How thick is your file on me?" I inquired. "Not too thick," replied Mower matter-of-factly.

The baby-faced, impeccably groomed Mower exemplifies the cross-pollination and strange alliances—some quite fleeting—that abound on the paramilitary right. Mower is, first of all, a minister in the Church of Jesus Christ–Christian, whose reigning dignitary is the Reverend Wesley A. Swift of Lancaster.* Three decades ago Swift was part of Gerald L. K. Smith's Christian Nationalist Crusade and a rifle team instructor for a KKK group. He founded his church on the premise that members of the white race are the lost children of Israel. A spellbinding Bible-thumper, Swift has put to-

---

* While stationed nearby in the Marine Corps in 1963, Walter Peyson attended Swift's services. This was his entrée into the paramilitary movement.

gether a string of "parishes" in California and a small-station radio network reaching an estimated million listeners. The Reverend Oren Potito of St. Petersburg, Florida, is head of the church's "Eastern Conference." Potito, a one-time organizer for the National States Rights Party, was the 1962 campaign manager for retired Admiral John G. Crommelin, running for governor of Alabama, whose stock-in-trade speech is "The Hidden Force," exposing the "Jewish-Communist-Integration Conspiracy." Potito has openly stated that his church has formed "guerrilla warfare units" designed to defend the country in the event of a communist takeover.

The Swift complex includes the militant Christian Defense League (CDL), self-described in its publication *Christian Defense News* as "white Christians" united in opposition to, among other groups, CORE, the NAACP, the Urban League, the American Jewish Congress, B'nai Brith, and the Anti-Defamation League. Admiral Crommelin was listed as Eastern Regional Director of the CDL; another director was lawyer Bertrand Comparet of San Diego, who has regularly handled NSRP clients and was defense attorney for Dennis Mower at his Springfield trial. Another CDL stalwart was Conrad "Connie" Lynch, who held Minuteman number C41412, was California organizer for the NSRP, and is an ordained minister in the Church of Jesus Christ–Christian. He is most prominently a traveling black-baiter, being credited by Florida authorities with inciting mob violence in St. Augustine in 1964, and being conspicuously in evidence during the 1966 anti-black agitation in Chicago and the 1969 disturbances in Berea, Kentucky. The paramilitary side of the CDL was unmasked in 1964 when a police raid on the Cucamonga, California, home of member William H. Garland turned up eight machine guns and a supply of rifles, shotguns, pistols, incendiary bombs, and caps. Garland's explanation was that he was a "patriot" ready to repel "invaders."

One of the driving forces in the CDL in its early days was retired Lieutenant Colonel William P. Gale, who had trained guerrilla bands in the Philippines during World War II. In the late 1950s Gale formed the small, paramilitary California Rangers, which the California attorney general's office alleged was "designed as a secret underground guerrilla force . . . linked with other non-military organizations by a common ideology and leadership." Gale's strategy was to try to recruit members through veteran's organizations, but it backfired in 1963 when the *Long Beach Press-Telegram* exposed his efforts to convert the American Legion Post in Signal Hill into a Ranger front, and one of his Rangers was arrested for selling a machine gun and Sten gun to undercover agents. In 1963, when a wealthy Los Angeles benefactor put money into the CDL, Gale tried his hand at improving its fortunes (at the same time professing "the ministry of William P. Gale" from the pulpits of Swift's churches).

The CDL's activities stepped up under Gale's leadership. According to an infiltrator who later supplied surreptitiously made tape recordings to radio station KLAC in Los Angeles: "I was the security agent for the CDL national director. I guarded the security building and the files therein, the files which extended through most every state in the union. Members of the Klan, members of all other extremist groups who joined in to help make Christian Defense League the central group, the reporting group, for all of these organizations. The very sister and co-worker in this, of the CDL on the West Coast, is the National States Rights Party." On the night of June 10, 1964, he related, Swift and his associates met in Reseda with George Lincoln Rockwell to discuss "a merger for the purpose of exchanging and compiling intelligence information; to make and keep an up-to-date roster of agents, double agents and other informers," and to devise a command order. California Deputy Attorney General Thomas McDonald has advised that there has been a "real coalescence" between the Swift complex, the NSRP, and Klan-like groups in Southern California.

As for the paramilitary aspect, the infiltrator revealed: "We had occasion to have with us, from time to time, people who sold illegal guns for the rightist groups, without the proper registration procedure. In many cases these weapons were hidden in holes in the ground where they might be dug up later, in what they called defense against communism and against aggression, even by the FBI, the federal forces, or the National Guard." About this time California law enforcement encountered a rash of arms episodes. In addition to that involving CDL member Garland, an attorney general's report dated April 12, 1965 recounted:

On June 18, 1964, two self-admitted Minutemen, Willard Noble Holstine and Joseph Raymond Carey, were taken into custody by Burbank Police when found in possession of illegal weapons.

On June 27, 1964, Minutemen member Adelbert Harold Schlapia was taken into custody in the Los Padres National Forest when found to be in possession of a veritable arsenal consisting of thirty-three thousand rounds of assorted ammunition, three M-1 rifles, two M-1 carbines, two Czechoslovakian military rifles, some shotguns, a military 12-gauge riot gun, 45-caliber automatic pistol, etc., in addition to a supply of gun powder and dynamite caps. . . .

On October 16, 1964, Minutemen member Robert Romero was arrested by Los Angeles police when officers found in his home the following: seven machine guns, six rifles, four hand guns, thousands of rounds of ammunition and clips of ammunition, dynamite and dynamite caps, fuses, twenty hand grenades including smoke, gas, and explosive types, and seven booby traps.

On March 26, 1965, agents of the Bureau of CII

[Criminal Identification and Investigation] and officers of the Los Angeles Sheriff's Department seized 370 machine guns and a number of silencers from the premises of the Erquiaga Arms Company in the City of Industry, Los Angeles County. The head of the firm, Juan Erquiaga, was known to have had dealings with the above-mentioned Minutemen, Harold L. Schlapia and Robert R. Romero, and also with Minuteman Keith Dwayne Gilbert who as of this date is wanted for the theft of fourteen hundred pounds of explosives which were recovered from his residence, together with a cache of weapons and a supply of Minutemen literature. At the time of the seizure of the Erquiaga plant, the officers found a rifle left there for modification belonging to Terrel R. Eddy, [former] State Chairman of the National States Rights Party of California.

Both Joseph Carey and Keith Gilbert revolved in Dennis Mower's orbit. Not long after his arrest, Carey dropped from sight and is still being sought. Gilbert had been convicted of an unprovoked assault on a black motorist at a stop signal in 1964. In February 1965 he was arrested by Los Angeles police intelligence and charged with the possession of fourteen hundred pounds of stolen dynamite; the police said he had planned to kill Dr. Martin Luther King Jr. by blowing up the Hollywood Palladium. He disappeared when a warrant was sworn out for his arrest and fled directly to Vancouver, obtaining refuge with the British Israelites, another sect preaching that the white race is the lost tribe of Israel. Later captured in eastern Canada, he was convicted and is presently in San Quentin prison.

During the period 1963–64, closed meetings of the Christian Defense League were held at the Lafayette Place residence in Los Angeles of G. Clinton Wheat, a burly Klansman. Activity against Cuba was a major topic of discussion. One of those who attended on occasion was Loran Eugene Hall, an anti-Castro adventurer whose nom de guerre was Lorenzo Pasquillo. A swarthy man who could easily pass for a Latin, Hall was mentioned in the Warren Commission Report in connection with information supplied by a Dallas woman aligned with the anti-Castro movement. Sylvia Odio told the FBI that in September 1963 three men materialized on her doorstep seeking aid against the Cuban premier. One, Latin-appearing and using a nom de guerre sounding like "Leopoldo," introduced the third man, an Anglo, as "Leon Oswald." They had just come from New Orleans, they said, and were about to leave on another trip. Unsure of her visitors, Mrs. Odio declined to help. The next day Leopoldo telephoned her to say that Oswald had been in the Marine Corps and was an excellent shot. The Cubans "don't have any guts," Leopoldo quoted Oswald, "because President Kennedy should have been assassinated after the Bay of Pigs, and some Cubans should have done that, because he was the one that was holding the freedom of Cuba, actually."

The FBI investigated this intriguing aspect—to a point. The Warren Commission Report advises:

On September 16, 1964, the FBI located Loran Eugene Hall in Johnsondale, California. Hall had been identified as a participant in numerous anti-Castro activities. He told the FBI that in September of 1963 he was in Dallas soliciting aid in connection with anti-Castro activities. He said he had visited Mrs. Odio. He was accompanied by Lawrence Howard ... and one William Seymour from Arizona. He stated that Seymour is similar in appearance to Lee Harvey Oswald; he speaks only a few words of Spanish, as Mrs. Odio had testified one of the men who visited her did.

Although the FBI inquiry had not been completed when the

Report went to press, the Warren Commission concluded it was not Oswald at Mrs. Odio's, but expressed no curiosity over why someone would have been using his name barely a month before the assassination. As documents in the National Archives show, Hall shortly thereafter recanted his admission, and Howard and Seymour stoutly denied having been at the Odio residence. When I interviewed him in 1968, Hall continued to insist that he had not been there, but he did acknowledge the meetings at Wheat's Lafayette Place home. It was a collection point for arms and ammunition destined for free-lance efforts against Cuba, he said. Among those present at one time or another, he confirmed, were Edgar Eugene Bradley and Dr. Stanley Drennan. The West Coast representative of Dr. Carl McIntire, Bradley was indicted by a New Orleans grand jury in December 1968 for conspiracy to assassinate Kennedy, but the case was never brought to trial because Governor Reagan refused to approve extradition. Dr. Drennan, Hall said, had contributed medical supplies to his group, known variously as Patrick's Raiders and the Intercontinental Penetration Group. It had been in training on No Name Key in Florida in the summer of 1963.

Another guerrilla expert who had been on No Name Key and who cropped up in the course of the Warren Commission probe was Robert K. Brown. Commission Document number 641, an FBI report dated December 4, 1963, states in part:

> Captain ROBERT KENNETH BROWN, The School Brigade, Fort Benning, Georgia, advised that he has been active in Cuban matters for several years and during the spring of 1963, in connection with anti-Castro activity, he was in contact with the National States Rights Party in Los Angeles, California.
>
> In connection with this, he contacted Dr. STANLEY L. DRENNAN . . . North Hollywood, Cali-

fornia, who was active in the National States Rights Party. Brown stated that once while a guest in Dr. DRENNAN's home, DRENNAN stated in general conversation that he could not do it, but what the organization needed was a group of young men to get rid of KENNEDY, the Cabinet, and all members of the Americans for Democratic Action and maybe ten thousand other people. BROWN stated that he considered the remarks as being "crackpot"; however, as DRENNAN continued the conversation, he gained the impression that DRENNAN may have been propositioning him on this matter.*

Brown was no newcomer to paramilitary circles. He had once joined Troy Houghton in maneuvers near the Mexican border, and was an insider in the Miami colony of Cuban exiles and American adventurers he himself referred to as the "Soldiers of Misfortune." In addition to his occasional periods of active duty as an Army sniper instructor, Brown runs Panther Publications in Boulder, Colorado, a mail-order house specializing in texts on guerrilla warfare (e.g., *Special Forces Operational Techniques, British Textbook of Explosives*) and such hardware as commando knives and folding rifle stocks.

In August 1970 Brown was called before the McClellan subcommittee conducting hearings on domestic terrorism and given a rough time about Panther Publications (which he has since renamed Paladin Press), the complaint being that he was fostering terrorism. Brown retorted that this was not so, that he had founded the firm in 1963 simply because of the widespread interest in guerrilla warfare and related topics.

Shortly before the Senate hearings, Brown had returned

---

* Drennan reportedly was interviewed by the Secret Service on June 14, 1963, concerning remarks of this nature.

from a tour of duty in Vietnam where he had served as an intelligence officer, Green Beret team commander on the Cambodian border, and "political warfare officer." He had been severely wounded by shrapnel. He said he had requested Vietnam duty "because basically I agreed with what we are trying to do there."

When I talked to him in January 1971, Brown contended that his politics were part conservative, part liberal, but that he had approached right-wingers for aid against Castro because they had the money and the will. He reminisced that he had been pro-Castro prior to the success of the revolution, and had in fact encountered Loran Hall in Havana in 1959. In 1967, when *Life* magazine was probing the John Kennedy assassination, Brown worked with two *Life* reporters, mostly concerning the possible involvement of anti-Castro adventurers. Brown remarked that he had been a bit leery of approaching the FBI to report the Drennan incident because a year or so earlier, when he had reported talk by right-wing militants of assassinating Miami District Attorney Richard Gerstein because he was a Jew, agents treated him "as some kind of nut."

In fact, plans for sniping John Kennedy had become almost table talk among paramilitary factions in Southern California by 1963. One such plan had even been formulated in 1960 while Kennedy was still campaigning. A paramilitarist told me that he was approached—quite seriously, he believes—to fire at the candidate with a scoped .357 magnum during a scheduled visit to the Laurel Canyon shopping center at Van Nuys; the scheme called for the detonation of plastic explosives, then in vogue in the Algerian struggle, as a backup device.

In September 1963 a young man came to a Los Angeles assemblyman in a near panic, saying that he had joined a "patriotic" paramilitary group loosely known as "The White Knights of the Invisible Empire" but had been shocked when, at a meeting near Palmdale, one of its leaders ticked off names from a list of three hundred "dangerous" left-wingers who had to be exterminated. Heading the list, which included Earl Warren, Arthur Goldberg, William Fulbright, and Robert Kennedy, was the president. The young man became convinced the group would carry out their madness when they followed through on the bombing-murder of a black businessman who was "causing trouble." The assemblyman relayed the information to the Los Angeles sheriff's office, which arrested twelve men but released them for lack of evidence.

Currently, the paramilitary right in California is in a process of realignment. Clinton Wheat, at whose home Christian Defense League meetings were held, moved to rural Northern California in 1965 and then disappeared when New Orleans District Attorney Garrison issued a material witness warrant for him in 1968. A deep split has developed between Wesley Swift and Colonel Gale. After running for governor as the Constitution Party candidate in 1966, Gale seems to have settled into a clique that includes Dr. Drennan and Edgar Eugene Bradley. Dennis Mower, still headquartered at Lancaster under the aegis of Swift, appears to be on the move. Mower's main vehicle remains the Southern California Freedom Councils, spread over a wide area. He also operates a chapter of the Friends of Rhodesia. Other Lancaster-based fronts are the California Anti-Communist League and the Christian National Alliance, which publishes *Vanguard.*

Yet another Minuteman-type outfit was briefly spotlighted in April 1970 when Los Angeles police announced that an undercover operative had foiled a plot to assassinate federal judge Alfred Gitelson, who two months earlier had ruled that the city's public schools were practicing de facto segregation and ordered them integrated. Among five men taken into custody were two gun shop owners, and police confiscated several machine guns, a grenade launcher, one hundred ten rifles, one hundred thirty-seven pistols, and ten thousand rounds of ammunition. The right-wing literature in their possession included some put out by the Minutemen. But DePugh told me that the outfit is not part of his Minutemen, and that in fact the groups are working at cross purposes. "The main thing they have that we don't is money," he remarked, not without a twinge of envy. "I can't figure out where they get it all."

At this stage it would appear that DePugh's protracted efforts to centralize control of California factions in the hands of his Minutemen are largely a failure. The picture is, to say the least, a jigsaw puzzle, made no less intricate by yet another piece, the American Volunteer Groups. Named after the official designation for General Claire Chennault's Flying Tigers, the AVG was formed about 1967 by several private pilots of Boger, Texas, who installed a former Chennault aide as figurehead. As it spread, the AVG took in a number of Dallas followers of General Edwin Walker and secured a financial angel in the scion of a wealthy oil family. After Troy Houghton disappeared, a fair-sized contingent of his followers disdained DePugh and hooked on with the AVG, shifting its center of gravity west. As a countermove, DePugh maneuvered one of his loyalists, E. G. "Bud" Johnson of Dana Point, California, into the leadership position. Early in 1968 Johnson failed to return from a hunting trip—he was found, shot through the head with his 30-06 rifle; the official verdict was suicide. His successor is John Zemenik, a longshoreman of Harbor City, California, who also acts as "security officer" of the Patriotic Party but is at odds with DePugh.

At this writing, the AVG is attempting to expand its base. It held the first of a series of open seminars in Los Angeles on February 24, 1971, and attracted a hundred or so people. According to the report of someone who attended, AVG was defined as American Volunteer Groups or American Voluntary Guerrillas or Alternate Voluntary Government. Its goal was a counterrevolution aimed at "communism," which was said to mean the "left wing" personified by the hippie movement. The featured speaker, Zemenik, "condemned everything including the police, except the American flag, motherhood, and fatherhood." Zemenik stressed that every AVG local group was "subordinate to the AVG national intelligence hierarchy." My source asserted that "the main point made throughout the evening was that any and everything necessary would be used to fight communism. The only group one should join is AVG."

Zemenik's dual role in AVG and the Patriotic Party is emblematic of the tug of war now going on for control of the latter, which seems to be no more than a lively shell. DePugh remains the party's national chairman in name at least, and the *Patriotic Party Newsletter* is still published in Norborne, Missouri. The national secretary of the Patriotic Party is still James W. Freed of Dearborn, Michigan, a distinctly unfearsome white-haired man in his fifties. The national co-chairman, until recently, was Glenn Jackson of Orange, California. I first encountered Jackson when he showed up as a witness in the January 1970 trial of DePugh in Kansas City. Muscular and mustachioed, Jackson displays none of the bombast that so typifies right-wing leadership. Significantly, he was not present at the Albuquerque trial eight months later—he had been dropped from his party post by DePugh. For his part, Jackson considered DePugh too ego-bound and prone to err in the selection of leaders, naming Houghton and Mower as examples. On the other hand, DePugh detected a shift of affinity on the part of Jackson toward the AVG and John Zemenik.

The power struggle—if it can be called that—has now assumed a third dimension with the entry of a group called the Provisional National Government of the USA. The PNG is the latest in a series of organizational permutations presided over by Ken Duggan, whose Manhattan office places him in the midst of the "Jewish Wall Street Banker International Illuminati" cabal. "There are two types of occult politics on our planet today: nationalist and internationalist," Duggan wrote in his *Illuminator* magazine in May 1968, theorizing that "great political power lies rooted in the occult." Under the umbrella of his C.E.D. Associates, Inc., Duggan set up the Industrial Enterprise Foundation and the Interplanetary Nationalist Society, only the latter of which has surfaced to public view. The Interplanetary Nationalists, he recounted in his article, "developed a full line of witchcraft and attracted right-wing nationalists into their fold. Incantation, use of incense and potions, multi-colored candles, magic circles, pentagrams, and other devices became part of the I.N. repertoire."

In 1967 the Interplanetary Nationalists ran a candidate in the 66th Assembly District of New York, where the building of the "chief internationalist organ," the Council on Foreign Relations, is located. In 1969 Duggan ran for city council under the banner of the Patriotic Party, which he was eyeing as a rallying point for the splintered right. "C.E.D. Associates, Inc., has long studied and evaluated the activities of the right-wing nationalist movement in the United States," he declared in a flyer. "We have searched for a plan that would unite all nationalist activities under one banner. We feel that the PATRIOTIC PARTY has the BLUEPRINT FOR VICTORY ." The defeat of the Illuminati coalition, he resounded, "must become a RELIGION to us."

The flyer urged readers to join the Patriotic Party via Duggan's office or that of James Freed in Dearborn. Duggan negotiated a pact with Glenn Jackson in California, but that soon fell by the wayside. Part of the problem evidently was disagreement on running candidates, Jackson holding that "the Patriotic Party may de-emphasize the direct political approach in favor of more emphasis in the direction of other kinds of meaningful action." Dissolving his C.E.D. Associates,

Inc., Duggan created the Provisional National Government as "a move that would not only unify all nationalists and patriots, but would also get to the heart of recognizing that our country is an occupied land, run by alien forces having no interest in Americans." A closed national organizing convention was held in New York City in June 1970, and an insider discloses that "PNG has lots of money and is growing fast," but it is too early to tell what impact, if any, the PNG ultimately will have.

Another question mark is the fate of Rockwell's American Nazi Party, whose membership never was very large. Some of the members were assimilated by the Minutemen. Remnants still operate under ANP authority in Michigan, Wisconsin, and Arizona. Matt Koehl, a Rockwell lieutenant since 1962, has formed his own National Socialist White People's Party as a lineal descendant of the ANP. In California, James K. Warner, long a traveler of the far-right byways, made a bid to take over in opposition to Koehl. An old admirer of Rockwell and a National States Rights Party campaigner, Warner runs an outfit called Sons of Liberty and is high priest of the Odinist Religion and Nordic Faith Movement, which preaches a mystic brand of Aryan supremacy. In 1966, Warner transplanted his operations from Alexandria, Virginia, to Los Angeles. A special issue of *Action*, a publication of the ANP in the Los Angeles area, announced: "On January 1, 1968, a Conference of the American Nazi Party was held at Nazi Headquarters in Los Angeles. In view of the imcompetant [sic] leadership of the National Socialist White People's Party, I, Dr. James K. Warner, assumed by popular Nazi acclaim the leadership of the American Nazi Party." Whether Warner, who signs off his correspondence with "Heil Hitler!," will be able to extend his jurisdiction beyond the Los Angeles city limits remains to be seen.

The fluid state of affairs is further illustrated by the relatively new Statecraft movement, which identifies itself as

113

"an affiliation of American patriotic action groups." The affiliates listed thus far: Michigan Statecraft Enforcers, Centerline, Michigan; Iron Cross Motorcycle Club, Montrose, California; Nathan Bedford Forrest AIP, Fayetteville, Arkansas (site of the University of Arkansas); and Statecraft of Florida, Rollins College. The Michigan group is headed by young Patrick Tifer, a Wayne State University graduate who wears his hair brushed over his forehead and is fond of posing holding a scoped rifle or the Statecraft thunderbolt flag. Tifer founded *New Right* magazine, which achieved a fairly wide circulation on college campuses, and he was, briefly, chairman of the National Youth Alliance, successor to Youth for Wallace. Although he ran for local office in 1970 as an AIP member, he claims also to be a member of the Patriotic Party, which "has similar aims and goals." He has formed "Public Safety Committees" to "fight against the Left-front in our nation's schools, in the streets, in time of riots, and wherever they may be." Tifer and Statecraft have already earned a measure of notoriety in the Detroit area through television coverage of their staged counterdemonstrations and heckling sessions, and threaten to take the play away from Donald Lobsinger and his highly publicized Breakthrough, a right-wing pressure and demonstration group. Statecraft labels Breakthrough a pawn of the Anti-Defamation League.

As a movement, Statecraft seems to be held together by its "journal of political education" called *Statecraft*, published in Alexandria, Virginia, "ten minutes from savage-controlled, liberal-occupied Washington, D.C." *Statecraft* is a rare experience in screeching journalism. One letter to the editor in a recent issue asserted, "I agree wholeheartedly with you that a dynamic, popular action front is needed to save Western Culture from the Distorter! Two hundred fighting-mad Carolina Whitemen can do more to liquidate liberalism by burning out a few school buses used to mongrelize their schools than twenty thousand sewing circle conservatives can ever accomplish by 'educating' the people." There was a cartoon showing two elongated black basketball players with white coaches. "These blacks sure have livened up basketball," remarks one coach. "Yea, the winners get to eat the losers—just like in Africa," replies the other. Among the display ads was a Patriotic Products offering of a self-defense spray with the pitch, "If you are tired of being molested by wild savages and don't have a spear, use SQUEEZE PLAY." Another ad touted *The Militant's Formulary*: "If you can read this you can make bombs, MACE, incendiaries, impact ignition fire bombs, etc. Simple. Illustrated. Sources of supply." Potential takers should be cautioned, however, that the purveyor is Don "The Hook" Sisco, who once lost a hand when a bomb he was fabricating accidentally exploded.

Operation Unicorn, another paramilitary outfit somewhat different from the rest, is worthy of mention here. Its spokesman, who identifies himself as "Captain Alexander Chandler" of the Chicago area, has stated on television and radio that the group was formed half a dozen years ago at Fort Ord and Van Nuys, California, by former military officers. According to Chandler, two former FBI men head intelligence and security for Operation Unicorn, and each applicant is carefully screened. Minutemen have not been accepted, and the group, unlike others in the paramilitary right, advocates strong gun-control measures. Chandler claims that Unicorn has close to four hundred instructors, and that paramilitary training sessions are conducted at Camp Carson, Colorado, and three smaller camps in that state, as well as at Camp Ridley, Minnesota. And, said Chandler, Unicorn attempts to infiltrate left-wing groups—his own first assignment was in SDS.

Yet another new group in the paramilitary right calls itself the Legion of Justice. On December 20, 1970, Bernard Gavzer of the AP reported an anonymous interview with two of its young leaders. Gavzer quotes the two as saying that assassination of "traitors" is a prime goal of the Legion. One of the men told Gavzer that members had paid "a visit to the SDS headquarters in Chicago where they liberated a notebook, made copies of it, and then put it back." (The "notebook" was an address book said to be Cathy Wilkerson's.) The League, which is centered in the Midwest, claims to have two hundred members nationally. As one of the leaders said, "We intend to keep it small for security purposes and for effectiveness. That's all you really need in a highly trained guerrilla band."

Despite its minuscule numbers compared with the general population, and a propaganda output so wild and shrill as to have little credibility, the paramilitary right poses a clear and present danger because of its capability with arms and its possession of a huge stockpile of weapons and munitions. From Virginia to Oklahoma to California and at points between, the fortuitous discovery of a number of arms caches merely hints at the huge supply still hidden away, ready for Der Tag. As one supplier to Texas paramilitarists has put it, "Their problem isn't getting or paying for guns. It's finding places to store them."

In addition, there is always the possibility that these intrigue-driven men with their grim determination to rid the country of what Spiro Agnew calls "radic-libs" may be behind some of the bombings and other terrorist acts commonly attributed to the left. Could it be that a Minuteman team or two spells it Amerika? Or that some of the rocks pelting establishment politicians are thrown by infiltrators? At the very least it can be said that the paramilitarists' expertise with bombs and their claimed infiltration of leftist groups merit more than a casual scoff.

7
ONWARD CHRISTIAN SOLDIERS
the bible-thumpers

Progressive and liberal are Satan's pet words.

—Reverend Carl McIntire in Author of Liberty

My guess is that Mr. Bundy's "American Way of life" is anything Mr. Bundy believes in, and he has always been to the right of Joe McCarthy. If that's the case, his files ought to be bursting the walls of his Wheaton office, since millions of Americans probably have views that he considers subversive.

—Columnist Mike Royko of the Chicago Daily News

On October 3, 1970, the much heralded "March for Victory" coursed down Pennsylvania Avenue from the foot of Capitol Hill on its way to a rally and a spate of speeches demanding a military solution in Vietnam. At its head was a tall, amply fleshed man pressing a Bible to his breast: Reverend Carl McIntire. On his left was a plain-looking woman holding an American flag: his wife, Fairy. On his right was a younger man, with horn-rimmed glasses and cropped gray-black hair, carrying the flag of the McIntire church: Congressman John Rarick, the archsegregationist from Louisiana.

As the stream of marchers formed an ever-widening pool for the rally, messages of congratulation were read from Senators Strom Thurmond and Barry Goldwater and Memphis Mayor Henry Loeb, who as a gesture of solidarity had proclaimed it "Peace with Victory Day" in Memphis.

It was to have been McIntire's finest hour, a fitting climax to his three dozen years of dispensing fundamentalist religion mixed with ultranationalism. The march had been conceived as a counterdemonstration to the antiwar rally the year before that had drawn two hundred fifty thousand, and the preacher was predicting a turnout of half a million in "a

great gathering of hawks, to take out after the doves." But
this was when the star attraction was still Vice President
Nguyen Cao Ky of South Vietnam, the cocky flyer-politician
once dubbed "that natty little Hitler-lover" by the *St. Louis
Post-Dispatch.* In a burst of enthusiasm following Ky's acceptance of his invitation to be the principal speaker, Mc-
Intire raved that the Saigon vice president was "another
Agnew," and would "out-Agnew Agnew" in calling for all-
out victory. But in the end Ky succumbed to behind-the-
scenes pressure from U.S. officials and bowed out.* So it was

* Ky's about-face has an interesting history. When Spiro Agnew was in
Saigon in mid-1970 he urged Ky to return his visit shortly. McIntire
decided to follow up by extending his invitation to Ky, who agreed
almost immediately. Consternation reigned in the U.S. State Department and the White House. "U.S. officials," the Associated Press reported, "fear Ky's appearance could touch off antiwar demonstrations
and also prove embarrassing politically only a month before the November 3 congressional elections." Senator Gordon Allott, chairman of the
Senate Republican Policy Committee, called McIntire's rally "kooky"
and "subversive" in disclosing that the Nixon administration was trying
to dissuade Ky from coming. The preacher fired back, "That's the
commie line used against us for years." The Reverend Dr. Kenneth
Neigh, a vice president of the National Council of Churches, contended
that Ky's acceptance of the invitation "clearly identifies the Saigon
regime with radical right groups in the United States." The administration's fears seemed to be confirmed when various antiwar groups announced plans to make a citizens' arrest of Ky "for being a war criminal," and the Yippies declared the rally site a "free fire zone."
Meanwhile, McIntire was trying repeatedly to get in to see Nixon, and
he wired Agnew that Ky's rhetoric likely "will be similar to yours as he
pleads for his people and desires that we hasten the day of victory."
Then came a bulletin out of Saigon that Ky was reconsidering. Where-
upon McIntire flew to the South Vietnamese capital and back again to
tell a press conference that Ky's date still stood. Out of the preacher's
briefcase came a copy of the *Reader's Digest* for August 1964, which
contained an article by one Richard M. Nixon entitled "Need in Vietnam: The Will to Win" and urging all-out victory. Finally, presidential
aide Henry A. Kissinger was dispatched to Saigon, and Ky caved in. The

left to John Rarick to fire up the rally. "A people with the intelligence, the skills, the financial resources and the organizational ability to place astronauts on the moon—not once but repeatedly," Rarick told the crowd, variously estimated at fifteen to forty thousand, "is surely capable of achieving military victory over a minor, backward, disorganized, fourth-rate dictatorship."

Despite the loss of his star attraction, McIntire garnered a good deal of mileage out of the affair. Not only did he get wide press coverage as events unfolded, he came off as a sort of martyr to government power politics, thus solidifying his hold over a significant segment of Christian soldierdom. He has cut such a wide swath through the religious right that his complex pulls in some $3 million a year, well over double that of his nearest competitor in the pray-for-pay field, Billy James Hargis's Christian Crusade, and approaching the John Birch Society's bracket. In the face of multiplying internal troubles in his complex, the irrepressible McIntire marches on, no doubt spurred by the Ky publicity windfall.*

South Vietnamese leaked an explanation that Ky had mistakenly assumed that McIntire's International Council of Christian Churches was the reigning Protestant body in the United States, but this was refuted by the protracted period during which he insisted on coming. In the end, Madame Ky agreed to fill in for her husband, but the Air France plane on which she was en route from Paris to Washington turned back due to engine trouble and the South Vietnamese Embassy announced she was too fatigued to catch another.

* However, an encore nationwide rally on March 20, 1971, fell slightly flat. "No retreat, no compromise, no surrender. Victory is our banner," keynoted McIntire in calling for a military victory in Vietnam by July 4. But only sparse crowds showed up for demonstrations in Washington and various state capitals. The inevitable Lester Maddox led the Georgia contingent, while Edgar Eugene Bradley, McIntire's West Coast representative, organized the California demonstration. "We're not warmongers," declared Bradley. "The people who are stretching it out and not letting us win are the warmongers."

It was fairly early in his ecclesiastical career that Mc-Intire recognized the marketability of combining Satan with the Red Menace. Born in Ypsilanti, Michigan, in 1906, he grew up in a strait-laced Presbyterian environment before going east to enter Princeton Theological Seminary. There he met J. Gresham Machen, a leading fundamentalist scholar of the time. With Machen, he set up the Independent Board of Presbyterian Foreign Missions, which proved so schismatic that the General Assembly of the Presbyterian Church issued a mandate interdicting the Independent Board from soliciting any more funds within the conventional church structure. The two refused to comply. As a result, both were expelled from the church in 1936 after formal charges were brought and upheld by the church ruling bodies.

But McIntire wasn't out on the street. In 1934 the stoutly fundamentalist Collingswood Presbyterian Church in the suburbs of Camden, New Jersey, with a hefty congregation of twelve hundred, had asked him to become pastor. Collingswood was a good place for him, with its blue laws and its ban on sales of liquor and "smutty" literature (to this day, *Playboy, True Romance,* and *Teen Confessions* are forbidden on newsstands). In 1937 the New Jersey Presbytery successfully sued to reclaim the church building, but most of the flock followed its fire-and-brimstone preacher to temporary quarters in a tent and, eventually, a $600,000 edifice. When Machen died, McIntire founded his own Bible Presbyterian denomination.

The essential McIntire is, to borrow from Spiro Agnew, a "nabob of negativism." In 1941 he founded his own mirror image of the National Council of Churches, the American Council of Christian Churches, which has spent a good deal of its energy tearing down the traditional body as an exponent of leftist modernism, and when the World Council of Churches came into being in 1948 he set up the International

Council of Christian Churches to stand in opposition to it. Whatever the National Council is for, McIntire is dead set against. Over the years he has fired away at the United Nations, the peace and civil rights movements, and the ecumenical drift—he terms it selling out to Romanism.

An interesting commentary on this philosophy has been delivered by McIntire's son, C. T. McIntire, a college assistant professor who remains theologically conservative but sees the "American way of life" as "a spiritually totalitarian force." Writing in the December 1970 *Vanguard,* the modish-appearing son declared that the "American army overseas, joined by American corporate industrial presence, is a missionary body winning converts by the sword to the secular American democratic faith."

Although his ACCC nowhere near approaches the National Council in size, McIntire tries to give the illusion of near parity. One strategem is to hold ACCC conventions at the same time and place as those of the National Council in the hope of equal treatment by the press. In 1963, McIntire got more than he bargained for. John Kennedy was scheduled to address the National Council in Philadelphia in December, which seemed to further reduce McIntire's tolerance for the group, since he also held a strong antipathy for the president. Undoubtedly this was based in large measure on his attitude toward the Roman Catholic Church, which he dislikes nearly as much as communism. In 1945 he had branded Catholicism "the harlot church and the bride of the Anti-Christ," adding that one "would be better off in a communistic society than in a Roman Catholic fascist setup." After Kennedy was elected, he decried the manner in which the presidential office "was used to advance the Roman Catholic Church in the United States as it has never been advanced in all the years of its existence." And when Kennedy and Billy Graham played golf together, McIntire turned his wrath on the evangelist for associating with "persons whose fidelity to something other than the scriptures is evident." So it was not unexpected that when Kennedy's appearance at the Philadelphia convention was announced, McIntire swung into action. Scoring the event on his radio outlets as a violation of the doctrine of separation of church and state, he booked an ACCC meeting the same night in Independence Hall with General Edwin Walker as featured speaker. When Kennedy was assassinated, the press backlash was ferocious and the Walker appearance was gingerly dropped.

McIntire's bleak message has drawn him a faithful he estimates at two hundred twenty thousand, which sends him money through several funnels. The chief one is the Twentieth Century Reformation Hour, a tax-exempt radio series started in 1955, which is now aired for half an hour daily over six hundred thirty-five stations, most of them small.* McIntire, whose mind is remarkably facile, broadcasts extemporaneously, working from notes, newspaper articles, and the like. He holds his taping sessions each morning at six o'clock in a small studio on the top floor of the Twentieth Century Reformation Hour Building two blocks from the Bible Presbyterian Church in Collingswood. The preacher opens with a Bible verse, and as he moves through his delivery his point-making sentences are punctuated by a resonant "Amen" voiced by the Reverend Charles E. Richter, an assistant pastor at the Collingswood church who has become known to the listeners as "Amen Charlie." The finale is a

---

* As a point of comparison, the well-known ultraconservative broadcaster Dan Smoot is heard over about sixty-four radio stations and seen on about twenty-five television outlets with his weekly program, and grosses about half a million annually. However, Smoot, a former FBI agent, has attracted moneyed supporters, including H. L. Hunt, who once sponsored his program, and D. B. Lewis, the Los Angeles Bircher who remembered Smoot in his will. The "Dan Smoot Reports" are currently sponsored by Holiday Magic cosmetics, a firm run by William Penn Patrick, prominent in his own right in ultraconservative circles.

pitch for contributions and remembrances in wills. Then the tape is duplicated and mailed out to stations throughout the United States and Canada. The audience is estimated at twenty million, most of them distributed across a rural belt from Florida to Washington State. The broadcasts rake in a gross of about $3 million annually, with costs believed to run under $1.5 million.

A supplement to the radio program is the *Christian Beacon,* a weekly newspaper listing McIntire as editor. Promoted on the radio, the *Beacon* has enjoyed a steady rise in circulation to the hundred thousand level. One technique employed by the paper is to reprint articles from other sources either in agreement or disagreement with the Mc-Intire viewpoint, in the latter case accompanied by a stinging rebuttal. For instance, the *Beacon* will often reprint an item from the *Daily Worker* as evidence of the Red Menace at work. When the *Worker* runs something on the civil rights situation, the *Beacon*'s rebuttal invariably incorporates the phrase "the Negro Revolution," with the word "Revolution" underlined. And the old enemy Roman Catholicism comes in for regular attack. In the course of one book review the Roman church was tagged "one of the most pernicious influences in life on earth today," which seems to say it all.

The books reviewed by the *Beacon* and other "selected readings for reformation emphasis" as well as audio-visuals and recordings can be purchased from the Twentieth Century Reformation Book Store in the Collingswood headquarters. A recent listing included titles in the categories of "Historic Development of Conflict for the Faith in This Century" and "Communist Subversion of Our Freedom," with McIntire's *Servants of Apostasy* and J. Edgar Hoover's *Masters of Deceit* among the offerings.

Other components of the McIntire complex are Faith Theological Seminary in Elkins Park near Philadelphia, Highland College in Glendale, California, Shelton College in Cape

May, New Jersey, and two hotels in the resort city—the Christian Admiral, in which Shelton College is housed, and the Congress Hall. McIntire purchased the rundown Admiral Hotel in 1962 for $300,000 and sunk over $1 million into renovating it. In all, his Cape May holdings, sheltered under the tax-free wing of Christian Beacon Press, Inc., have a market value in the neighborhood of $3 million. The Christian Admiral bears the inimitable McIntire touch. Picture postcards term it "a year-round Christian and patriotic conference center with 333 bedrooms, American plan, dedicated to the glory of God." The rooms display such names as the General MacArthur Room and the John Birch Room. There are no cigarette holes in the carpeting, and, of course, no bars. Three double-decker London buses shuttle back and forth between the Christian Admiral and the Congress Hall, carrying guests and Shelton College students. One of the annual happenings at the Christian Admiral is the summer Bible conference, which has in the past billed such secular figures as Strom Thurmond and General Walker, and, in 1969, the leading religious fundamentalist of Northern Ireland, the Reverend Ian Paisley.

The alliance between McIntire and Paisley is, in fact, quite solid. Paisley is on the executive board of the International Council of Christian Churches, and when he has come to the United States in the past several years on fund-raising tours he has been squired around by McIntire, preceded by promotionals on the Twentieth Century Reformation Hour. Paisley reciprocated the hospitality when McIntire went to Northern Ireland in August 1969 to make tapes for his program. The two staged a protest in Belfast against the disarming of the all-Protestant B-Specials—the special police force accused of overzealousness in handling Catholics during the disturbances. With his blind side on the Catholic issue, McIntire saw no civil rights problem in Northern Ireland and offered his opinion that "the Communists are using the

Catholic hierarchy to further their aims."

On the stump, McIntire comes off as a latter-day Billy Sunday, complete with gesticulation, finger-jabbing, and an Oklahoma twang that disappears as the voice flares into righteous indignation. At a "Gene Bradley Defense Fund Rally" in Pasadena in January 1968, the preacher so stirred up a crowd of a thousand with cries identifying "the Devil ... Communism ... enemies of the Cross" as the forces behind District Attorney Jim Garrison that a photographer from the *Los Angeles Free Press,* which had been sympathetic to Garrison, was manhandled and beaten. McIntire himself has been known to fly off the handle. When he announced that a "March on Trenton" led by Strom Thurmond to protest a state agency's challenge to Shelton College's accreditation would draw thirty thousand, and the senator and twenty-eight thousand five hundred didn't show, he screamed at reporters: "They're making fun of me! But that's all right—I've got God on my side!"

In fact, not all is going swimmingly for McIntire lately despite his pretension of business as usual. Nineteen charges against Shelton College were filed by the State of New Jersey Department of Education, among them inadequate records, unqualified faculty, and failure to teach advertised courses; Shelton was forced to release its academic dean and vice president, Richard Coulter, after the press disclosed that he possessed none of the five academic degrees he listed in the catalogue. On January 15, 1971, the college's license was revoked, and McIntire is appealing. Still bedeviling McIntire, who has railed against sex education in the schools, is a 1965 Shelton scandal precipitated by fifteen girls dormitoried in the Christian Admiral. In affidavits, they charged the hotel manager, Clayton Bancroft, with various instances of improper sexual conduct. In the furor, Shelton's president, Dr. Arthur Steele, resigned (he later became president of

Florida's Clearwater Christian College),* but Bancroft stayed
on despite criticism from such friendly quarters as evangelist
Dale Crowley, editor of *Capitol Voice,* published by the
National Bible Knowledge Association in Washington, D.C. "I
cannot and will not fire this man," insisted McIntire, perhaps
with the emphasis on "cannot." Bancroft is said to be the
only man who grasps the details of the preacher's intricate
financial empire, and is treasurer of his International Christian Relief—which came in for its own share of attacks during
the Biafran struggle. Even the staunch conservative Fulton
Lewis III chimed in, pointing out that the $50,000 receipts
of a fund appeal were assertedly earmarked for a town that
had been occupied by Nigerian federal forces for over a year.
"Until the ICR officials are able and willing to document
satisfactorily that the funds in question are used, as stated, to
send relief goods to the people in the Republic of Biafra,"
Lewis commented on his "Top of the News" program on
May 9, 1969, "I would hope that they would stop raising
money in that name." However, no criminal charges have
been brought against McIntire following Lewis's allegations.

McIntire has also experienced trouble from the FCC
under the "fairness doctrine." There are three radio stations
under his aegis, WINB and WGCB in Red Lion, Pennsylvania,
and WXUR in Media, Pennsylvania. WINB is a fifty-
thousand-watt short-wave station, owned by Twentieth Century Reformation Hour, which beams the McIntire message
to Europe, much to the confusion of the Europeans—who
assume it is, like their electronic media, an arm of the government—and to the dismay of the FCC, which is helpless to do
anything about it. WCGB is licensed to the Reverend John M.

* McIntire named himself president and brought in Gordon V. Drake as
dean. In 1968 Drake resigned and joined the staff of Billy James Hargis,
from whence he has become the far right's ace spokesman against sex
education.

Norris, who is closely aligned with McIntire. The FCC drew a bead on WXUR, which is also a McIntire property. The complaints centered on a series called "The Strange Tactics of Leftism" and the refusal of the station to grant equal time to those it attacked (one of the complainants was author Fred J. Cook, who, in his *The Warfare State* and *The FBI Nobody Knows,* had lit into two McIntire idols, the Pentagon and J. Edgar Hoover; another, the Institute for American Democracy, which publishes reports on extremism). The battle raged back and forth, with McIntire staging rallies in Constitution Hall in Philadelphia and picketing FCC headquarters in Washington, and a bevy of civic groups opposing him. In the end the WXUR license was revoked by the FCC—the first time a station has been so sanctioned for violation of the fairness doctrine. McIntire is currently fighting through the courts to have the license reinstated.

But the external forces of darkness are not the only source of woe for McIntire. For some time now there have been internal convulsions triggered by his cult of personality, dictatorial ways, and predilection for mixing theology with politics. The American Council of Christian Churches was chartered so that McIntire appointed representatives to it rather than the member churches electing representatives, and in 1960 the ACCC rebelled at what it termed the "undemocratic leadership." At the 1968 convention of the International Council of Christian Churches, held in August at the Christian Admiral, some members of McIntire's most trusted inner circle pulled a *coup d'église* and gained control of the ACCC. The real target was perhaps the ACCC's Audio-Film Commission, which had just been bequeathed $100,000. The loss of control of the ACCC obviously has McIntire thoroughly rankled. He and a loyalist band showed up at the group's annual convention in Pasadena in 1970 and attempted a parliamentary ploy to recapture the ACCC, and an unseemly pushing and shoving match ensued.

The loss of the ACCC was grievous, since it claims one and a half million members distributed over fifteen sects. But the rest of the complex remains in McIntire's hands, and he goes sailing on, helped by the breeze of publicity attending the Ky episode. In 1971 he acquired a small Baptist college in El Cajon, California, renaming it Southern California Reformation College, and the Cape Kennedy Hilton Hotel in Florida, now the Freedom Center Hotel, which will house another college, a retirement center, and a museum. There is nothing in the wind to indicate he won't be able to navigate the rough waters.

Interestingly, three Christian rightists whom McIntire helped get started are doing quite well on their own. It was the dean of Collingswood who first brought "the amazing Aussie communist-hunter," Dr. Fred Schwarz, to the lotus land of the United States, and Schwarz has since flourished. At last count the Christian Anti-Communism Crusade was pulling in some $350,000 annually, although the operation of late appears to be rather static. The career of Billy James Hargis was given a tremendous lift in 1953 when, with the assistance of McIntire, he launched hundreds of balloons tagged with Bible verses to float behind the Iron Curtain. And Major Edgar C. Bundy of the Church League of America once was a public relations agent for the ACCC when it was under McIntire domination.

Hargis is perhaps the most colorful of the God-and-flag orators, as the balloon caper suggests. A roly-poly 270-pounder, he is what his fellow Oklahomans dub a "bawl and jump" evangelist who flails wildly at the air as he shouts his doomsday homilies and winds up limp and hoarse. "Any time I fail to ask for an offering, you'll know I must be sick," he has said. "And any time the people don't come up and buy my books after I have finished talking, I know I have failed to put my message across." He rarely fails. Into his institutional coffers flows over $1 million a year, the fruits of his labors as a writer, lecturer, artifact huckster, and solicitor of gifts. When his Christian Echoes National Ministry, Inc., was denied tax-exempt status in 1965, he erected the corporate Church of the Christian Crusade, which has built a modern $525,000 "cathedral" in Tulsa, and satisfied the Internal Revenue Service that it should be tax-free. But Hargis lost no time in superimposing politics on the religious base. In a mail-out plea for money, he boasted that the country's "changing mood can be traced [in part] to the work of the Christian Crusade," and tucked in a "Confidential Opinion Poll," which, accompanied by a check, would permit the recipient to indicate what issues the organization could "do the most good for America and Christianity by resisting." Among the holy-war issues: high taxes, a "slanted" news media, the United Nations, and the disarmament peril.

Although the balloon stunt gave Hargis his start, he remained just another theological anti-communist crisscrossing the Bible belt until two breaks came his way. One was in the person of L. E. "Pete" White, a promoter extraordinaire who had made a huge success out of Tulsa evangelist Oral Roberts and who agreed to take on Hargis. The other resulted from the work of one Meyers Lowman of Cincinnati, Ohio, who headed an organization called Circuit Riders, Inc., devoted to compiling records on Protestant ministers and college instructors who had ever been associated with groups thought to have a red taint. Hargis incorporated some of Lowman's research into a couple of his pamphlets and concluded that the Protestant ministry was riddled with communists. The pamphlets were later quoted in an official Air Force manual, and in 1960 Hargis became a national bone of contention when newspapers discovered the quotes. "The Air Force Manual squabble was the best break we ever got," White recounted. "The membership and the contributions nearly doubled."

Like many of his colleagues on the circuit, Hargis has

not found his lack of a doctor of divinity degree from an accredited college any real handicap. He spent a year and a half at a Bible school in Arkansas in the early days, but dropped out for financial reasons. He possesses three honorary D.D.s—from the late anti-Semite Gerald Winrod's Defender Seminary in Puerto Rico, from all-white fundamentalist Bob Jones University in South Carolina, and from Belin University (whose president was convicted of mail fraud). For a while he was on the roster of the Disciples of Christ, but he was removed in 1957 due to philosophical differences. No matter, since religion seems merely to provide a backdrop for Hargis's political enterprises.

A key sector of his operation is the National Anti-Communist Leadership School, which is held periodically. For a registration fee of $100, dilettantes can attend five days of sessions taught by a "faculty" that has in the past included Birch Congressman John Rousselot, the ubiquitous Revilo P. Oliver, and R. Carter Pittman, the eminent segregationist from Georgia. Perhaps naively, Hargis has warned against the "wild, unfounded, bigoted statement" that could "submarine our whole program," and he cringed when Pittman maintained that the difference between blacks in the Congo and in this country is that "in the Congo they eat more people than they do in the United States." From the school's students, Hargis recruits the corps of "associate evangelists" who have spread over the nation armed with anti-communist profundities and reams of Hargis-approved literature. An adjunct of the school is the annual Christian Crusade Leadership Conference. In McIntire fashion, Hargis scheduled the 1969 conference for Tulsa the same week as the World Council of Churches was slated to meet there; he provided the theme: "To Mount an Offensive Against the Religious Heresy and Degenerate Marxist Political Philosophy of the World Council of Churches–National Council of Churches." The WCC convention, Hargis told his faithful in a promotional piece, will bring "many outright communists" to Tulsa, a sure lure for anyone who had never seen a live red. Tuition for Hargis's conference was $100.

The Hargis hard line is also propagated over two hundred radio stations daily and Sunday, and a traveling troupe featuring the Reverend David Noebel, who "uncovered" a communist plot to brainwash young people through rock music, and baritone Charles Secrest (Hargis's brother-in-law) ranges the country. The Crusade also owns a circa-1910 resort hotel near Colorado Springs, Colorado, where regular youth versions of the Hargis school are held. The Crusade-sponsored American Christian College has just opened in Tulsa with an enrollment of two hundred. Hargis publishes two periodicals, the *Christian Crusade* magazine and a newsletter, the *Weekly Crusader.* A few years ago, according to Harold H. Martin in an article in the *Saturday Evening Post,* Hargis made a deal with the maker of a vitamin tablet, Nutro-Bio, whereby he would get half the profits of vitamins sold through endorsements in the magazine and by Crusade members, but it all ended up, Hargis says, with the communists smearing him for handing out equal doses of vitamins and religion.

Hargis is a tireless promoter. Recently he joined his American Christian College choir on the road with a production called "An Evening with Billy James Hargis and His Kids." He also sponsored a tour of the Holy Land with an option to take in apartheid firsthand in South Africa and Rhodesia.

The yearly conventions of the Crusade have presented some of the biggest names in the right wing. Recent lineups have included George Wallace, Curtis Dall of the Liberty Lobby, Birch council member Tom Anderson, Governor Lester Maddox, General Edwin Walker, and Brigadier General Clyde Watts (ret.), who is both secretary of the Defenders of the American Constitution, Inc., and an attorney for Walker in his bouts with the federal government.* At the 1970 convention, Hargis attacked Senators Edward Kennedy, Mark Hatfield, J. William Fulbright, and George McGovern, saying: "These liberal politicians of both parties, and their liberal counterparts in church and educational circles, are America's fifth column during World War III, in which we are presently engaged." Hargis thought he perceived a majority of Americans "switching to the right or conservative position, which demands a military solution in Vietnam and a get-tough-with-communists policy internally."

The suave Major Edgar Bundy of the Church League of America is not nearly as well known as McIntire and Hargis, but in his own way he probably swings a comparable amount of weight. The league, also known as the National Laymen's Council, was formed in 1937 by the late Frank J. Loesch, chairman of the Chicago Crime Commission, and two associates who feared the "court-packing of Roosevelt and his New Deal." For two decades the operating director was George Washington Robnett, an advertising man whose Institute for Special Research is in reality a private file on suspected communists and sympathizers. After he took over as executive director of the Church League in 1956, Bundy gave the files priority attention.

Born in 1915, Bundy attended Oglethorpe College in Atlanta and graduated from Wheaton College in Wheaton, Illinois. After a stint as a newspaper reporter, he entered the Air Force in 1941 and served as an intelligence officer in every major theater of war, receiving Nationalist China's

* An interesting sidelight is the appearance of General Watts before the Warren Commission to testify about a rifle shot taken at Walker in the study of his home in April 1963. Watts had sent two of his investigators, former police detectives, to Dallas to look into the affair, and they reported back that the chief suspect was a former aide to Walker. However, the Commission ruled that Lee Harvey Oswald had taken the shot that missed, although the evidence was meager.

highest aviation decoration and the Bronze Star from Major General Claire Chennault, the famous Flying Tiger commander who later headed up the 14th Air Force. In 1949 he wangled an invitation to testify on the Far Eastern situation before the Senate Appropriations Committee. Arguing against the foreign aid bill, he propounded his own domino theory, predicting that China would fall and South Korea would be invaded. The predictions were read into the *Congressional Record* by Senators Styles Bridges and Pat McCarran, two of the most redoubtable reactionaries of that time, and when they shortly came true Bundy became an overnight seer on Far Eastern affairs. As such, he traveled the lecture circuit, and when the Church League opening occurred he saw it as an ideal base of operations.

The energetic Bundy has been active in a variety of organizations, including the American Legion, the Sons of the American Revolution, and the Air Force Association. He is an ordained minister in the Southern Baptist Convention, although he has never held a pastorate. Under his ambitious direction the Church League's income has soared to nearly $300,000 annually. Like McIntire and Hargis, he has zeroed in on the National Council of Churches, taking every opportunity to revile it on his thirty-station radio hookup and in his monthly newsletter *News and Views* (its motto: "Eternal Vigilance Is Forever the Price of Freedom"). The stock of literature, tapes, and films the Church League offers for sale also reveals its aversion for the council. Bundy himself wrote two thin volumes, *Apostles of Deceit* and *Collectivism in the Churches,* the Church League is the publisher of *The Record of the National Council of Churches,* and in 1968 the League released the film *What About the National Council of Churches?* During the same year, with the Reagan-for-President movement on, the league reissued a motion picture, *Ronald Reagan on the Welfare State,* which was billed as "a hard-hitting exposé of the drive to substitute State Welfarism for the American Free Enterprise System." A sample of Bundy's tape productions was the ponderously titled 1964 release "How the Communists and Religious Liberals Hate Barry Goldwater (By Their Fruits Ye Shall Know Them)."

Bundy has also boosted the apartheid nations of Africa. Rhodesian Prime Minister Ian Smith was the scheduled feature speaker at Bundy's "International Symposium on Communism" in Chicago in March 1967. When Smith was denied a visa, J.D. Vorster, brother of the prime minister of the Union of South Africa, filled in. Of late, Bundy has been conducting tours of Rhodesia and South Africa. Promotional literature contends that the two nations "hold the key to freedom" on the African continent.

A prominent phase of the league program is the "Counter Subversive Seminar" held around the country and locally sponsored. For a tax-deductible ten dollars per person, groups of at least fifty hear Bundy and his retinue expose the latest communist thrusts and techniques. The seminars are based on a Church League text, *A Manual for Survival*, which describes the nature of the menace and what can be done about it. As part of the solution, it recommends reading periodicals such as *Christian Beacon, Human Events, Dan Smoot Reports, National Review,* and, of course, *News and Views,* which at one time or another has taken a swipe at the Americans for Democratic Action ("Today's Trojan Horse"), Billy Graham, the PTA, and Pete Seeger. Another suggested recourse is to "locate a few experts with former FBI, Army, Navy, or other intelligence experience and form a small study and action group." And it urges readers never to allow anyone within earshot "to slur the FBI, the House Committee on Un-American Activities, the Senate Internal Security Subcommittee, the Church League of America, the American Council of Christian Churches, or any other organization which you know to be fighting subversion."

If all this sounds like an innocent means of catharsis,

Bundy's blacklisting system and infiltration efforts do not. "The Church League files contain nearly three thousand three-by-five cross-indexed cards on individuals, organizations, and publications which serve the communist cause in the U.S.," a 1967 brochure boasted. In a letter to "Every Dedicated Anti-Communist" the same year, Bundy put it another way: "As you know, the Church League of America has been amassing data for thirty years. Our files (over twenty *tons*) are bursting with material—much of which can never be replaced." The letter announced that the league had acquired the "massive files on communism" of the late J. B. Matthews—once a research assistant to Senator Joseph Mc-Carthy—who was believed to have appropriated a good portion of the Wisconsin witch-hunter's data.* The new acquisition, Bundy declared, had given birth to "Project Anti-Communist," which would "merge the Matthews files with our own" and "computerize the new files for instant reference." This data bank, he went on, would be thrown open to anti-communists everywhere: "local police, government committees investigating the conspiracy, public officials, anti-communist groups, private citizens doing their part in the crusade to save our freedoms, and those foreign governments that are, at this moment, standing strong against the communists at the exposed salients of the free world."

The combined files, Bundy declared, "will be the world's most complete reference source on *all* leftists and their groups, apart from the FBI files—which, of course, are not open to the public." Forseeing the day of J. Edgar Hoover's retirement and the dismantlement of Bureau files by liberal politicians, he emphasized that "then our own files will become *the last major repository of anti-communist*

* In turn, much of McCarthy's data came from the FBI. The Bureau abstracted pertinent security files and turned the abstracts over to Roy Cohn, the senator's chief counsel.

data." Quoting from Romans 12:11—"The night is far spent, the day is at hand: let us therefore cast off the words of darkness, and let us put on the armor of light"—Bundy exhorted the letter's recipients to contribute, even if only the "hallowed widow's mite," to the J. B. Matthews Memorial Library. Contributors of twenty-five dollars or more would be entitled "to six complimentary reports from PROJECT ANTI-COMMUNIST on any person or organization."

Bundy evidently raised the estimated $108,000 needed for the "maximum-security library, plus equipment" and the $100,000 for the "additional staff to collate the data and program the computer," for the Matthews library has been added to the league's rambling colonial-style headquarters at Wheaton, and Matthews's widow Ruth heads a staff of some two dozen minding the file store. And recently, prospective users have been told that the league has also obtained the files of former FBI agent John G. Keenan, who upon resigning in 1945 joined with two other Bureau alumni in forming American Business Consultants (ABC), a "research" group looking into communist influence in the entertainment and broadcast industries. During the McCarthy years, ABC published a periodical, *Counterattack,* which listed persons affiliated not only with organizations on the attorney general's list but with ones it deemed "ought to have been listed," and a directory, *Red Channels,* which carried the names of 151 suspected reds. Much of the industry used the ABC publications as a blacklist, such was the chill of the McCarthy times, but actor Frederick March and his wife Florence Eldridge sued, and *Counterattack* settled out of court.

With the incorporation of the Matthews and Keenan files, Bundy places the number of index cards at close to seven million, which is a million more than the American Security Council* claims to have. While much of the data is

* See chapter 10.

surely outdated, the league keeps squirreling away fresh material gleaned from union publications, government committee reports, and the *National Review.* It even includes the names of persons who have signed full-page ads in the *New York Times* on behalf of liberal causes, and anyone in any medium "attacking or ridiculing the American way of life." In promotional brochures, Bundy claims that the league has established a "working relationship" with a number of "leading law enforcement agencies" and a "network of independent sources," all of which supply information. He also maintains that league agents have penetrated New Left and Black Power groups, specifically mentioning SDS, which was laid bare after "months of intensive research and writing following infiltration of their organization, conferences, and demonstrations by Church League undercover agents." Bundy spreads the word that the league has somehow secured the mailing lists of SDS, the Revolutionary Action Movement (RAM), the Black Panthers, and other "troublemaking groups."

While these claims are unverified, Bundy does seem to have enough information to satisfy his clients. In a mail-out to manufacturers and businessmen, he points out that an applicant's educational and professional background can be easily verified, but his "philosophy of life" cannot. "Our work forces include more than a few radicals, socialists, revolutionaries, communists, and troublemakers of all sorts," the mail-out asserts. "The colleges and schools are educating thousands more who will soon be seeking employment." For as little as five dollars a name, the league will check its files for information reflecting an improper philosophy of life. Special inquiries are offered at $150 per day plus expenses, and an infiltration attempt can be ordered at a fee in the $200-a-week range. Lately, the league has informed potential clients that in addition to *News and Views* they will receive an enigmatic periodical called *Information Digest,* published by something called National Goals, Inc. Recipients of the *Digest* receive intelligence on such things as black caucuses in the auto industry, moves planned by trade unions, and SDS summer work-in schemes. E. Edgerton Hart, executive vice president of the Illinois Manufacturing Association, recently told the *Chicago Sun-Times* he considered the league's service a "very worthwhile thing," and he endorsed it in a bulletin sent to the association's fifty-four hundred member firms. And while denying that there was an exchange of information, Chicago police lieutenant William Olson, who heads the Red Squad, was quoted by the *Sun-Times* as saying: "We know [Bundy] very well, and he knows us. We feel the work he is doing is very good."

One of the most venerable figures on the Christian right is Gerald L. K. Smith, a ruggedly handsome spellbinder whose flame still flickers in the Christian Nationalist Crusade. Smith is semi-retired, spending most of his time in Eureka Springs, Arkansas, where a huge statue of "Christ of the Ozarks" looks down from the highest hilltop and the air is filled with Tennessee Ernie Ford hymns issuing forth from a battery of loudspeakers. Each year a passion play is staged on Mt. Oberammergau at Eureka Springs under the auspices of the Elna M. Smith Foundation. The play is given in what is popularly known as the "anti-Semitic text of 1850." "Of course, the text is not anti-Semitic," Smith literature rebuts. "That's the definition the Jews give to any statement which reveals accurately the Jewish conspiracy that was hatched in order to effect the crucifixion of our Lord."

The main base of the Christian Nationalist Crusade is now at 1259 South Brand in Glendale, California. The co-ordinator is thin, purse-lipped R. L. Morgan, former secretary of the CNC pressure group called the Citizens Congressional Committee. Working alongside him are Opal Tanner White, a long-time Smith aide, and Charles F. Robertson, the "manager of printing enterprises," who is a brother of

Morgan's wife. Robertson's principal responsiblity is the monthly magazine *The Cross and The Flag,* which has a circulation of thirty thousand. A sampling of the CNC's gallery of heroes and demons is provided by the January 1970 issue of the magazine. The cover story was "J. Edgar Hoover Speaks," a reprint of the FBI director's pronouncements on everything from the "New Left movement" to Chicago police behavior at the 1968 Democratic convention. An editorial in the magazine foresaw an epidemic of private school openings and a crackdown on the "age of consent operating with the instrumentality of the press." A "Smith Missile" column decried the musical *Hair* with the comment, "Depravity is destroying us." And there was a warning by Francis Capell declaring: "The establishment of a 'Jewish State' is only one part of the Zionist program. Other parts include the reconstruction of the 'Jewish Temple' of Solomon" and the appropriation by the Jews of other Muslim religious sites. Among the "Crusading Literature" offered for sale by the CNC are "Jews Rule America," "Jewish War Crimes in Palestine Genocide," "Talmud Unmasked," and the discredited pamphlet "The Protocols of the Learned Elders of Zion." The Crusade describes itself as a movement and campaign which "carries on inside the Congress of the United States and inside the governments of the various states. It functions without compromise and is recognized as one of the most influential and effective movements in America." To which the founder himself adds: "Why not donate some money to help us carry on this fight?"

Until recently, the dean of the fundamentalist broadcasters was Howard E. Kerschner of Buena Park, California, whose "Living Issues" program was heard weekly over some two hundred stations under the banner of the Christian Freedom Foundation, Inc. The program is still aired, but the man at the mike now is H. Edward Rowe, who also writes a syndicated column "It's Up to You" with the septuagenarian

Kerschner. Another Kerschner medium is the tabloid *Christian Economics,* whose two hundred fifteen thousand readers are dosed with "free market economy and the faithful application of Christian principles to all economic activities." Another right-wing religious fixture is C. W. Burpo, whose Bible Institute of the Air emanates from Mesa, Arizona. Burpo, whose style is reminiscent of Hargis and McIntire, is heard over three powerful stations, two in western Mexico and one in San Francisco.

Yet the Big Three Bible-thumpers remain Carl McIntire, Billy James Hargis, and Edgar Bundy. For the present at least, theirs is the power and the glory in the service of Christ the Destroyer who thundered, "I came not to bring peace, but the sword."

8
THE
LIBERTY LOBBY
patriotism for sale

Where the American National Revolution takes political form, its inspiration will come from the same ultimate source as the European [Nazi] Revolution of 1933.

—Francis Parker Yockey in Imperium, *published by Willis Carto of the Liberty Lobby*

The vision of a fascist future may seem idle, but Willis Carto, now in his mid-forties, is working every day to make it come true. And more frightening than the remote possibility Carto will realize his dream is the current power of the apparatus he has built to bring himself and his ideas into power.

—Joseph Trento and Joseph Spear in "How Nazi Nut Power Has Invaded Capitol Hill," True *magazine, November 1969*

On the evening of January 25, 1969, a number of business and professional men mingled with younger compatriots at a gathering at Conley's Motel on the Pennsylvania Turnpike near Pittsburgh. The room where the meeting was held was decorated with swastikas and other Nazi trappings, and a hi-fi set blared German marching tunes. With the playing of the Horst Wessel song, the meeting came to order. A short, darkly handsome man wearing a bow tie began to lecture in a choppy style about the revelations of the book *Imperium.* When he had finished, a long-distance connection with Dr. Revilo Oliver at the University of Illinois was amplified, and Oliver repeated the "vaporization" diatribe that had been too much even for the John Birch Society.

All was not ritual and rhetoric, however. By meeting's end the dapper man in the bow tie, Willis A. Carto, had added one more component to his Liberty Lobby complex. The older men in the group, who had referred to each other by code number, were members of the elitist Francis Parker

Yockey movement, the youthful ones delegates to a regional session of the National Youth Alliance, originally the Youth for Wallace of 1968. In a neat power play (described below) Carto had captured the NYA, lock, stock, and barrel. By this maneuver and similar ones over the years, the man who is dismissed by some as a caricature Führer has assembled an ideological empire that runs through a budget of $850,000 a year. At his Washington headquarters more than forty employees feed the Lobby's computerized mailing list of a quarter million subscribers and churn out its propaganda.

Carto's forte is his uncanny aptitude for mining several strata of the conservative money lode at the same time. One right-wing leader who exchanges favors with Carto told me, "He is a much better businessman than most right-wingers, although money per se is hardly his ultimate goal." While no one downgrades his business acumen, there are some who question his indifference to money. Morris A. Bealle, publisher of the "nonconformist" and ultraconservative *Capsule News*, has been taking potshots at Carto from nearby Arlington, Virginia, for years. In his January 1969 issue, for example, Bealle alleged that Carto's modus operandi consists of obtaining conservative mailing lists—"sucker lists," he calls them—and sending out letters "begging for money" on the plea that the Liberty Lobby "would go before committees of Congress and urge favorable reports on this, that, or the other bill then up before Congress. And in some cases 'save the nation' by overwhelming Congress with their 'testimony' before committees." Despite an ineffectual record on the legislative front, Bealle asserted, the letters "didn't fail in bringing in the sheaves—of greenbacks."

Whatever the motive behind it, this is in essence the Carto technique. He sets up fronts with a magician's sleight-of-hand, then promotes them by mail order. Thus he has been able to bring into the Liberty Lobby sphere of influence thousands of respectable conservatives who would have no truck with the dark side of the movement, the white-supremacy Yockey cult. And Bealle notwithstanding, Carto has made inroads on Capitol Hill. A former Liberty Lobby employee has claimed that some eight members of Congress are initiates of the inner cult, and in any case at least a score have openly acknowledged some degree of affinity with the Liberty Lobby. If the Lobby's batting average on bills it has supported is not big league, there is no telling how many others it has successfully opposed, helping to have them tabled or bottled up in committee. Both Julien G. Sourwine, chief counsel of the Senate Internal Security Subcommittee, and Otto Otepka, appointed recently to head the reactivated Subversive Activities Control Board, are said to maintain warm relations with the Liberty Lobby.

Any attempt to understand Carto and his philosophy necessarily requires knowing something about Yockey and *Imperium.* Some have gone so far as to term the rambling tome with its super-race thesis the Bible of the far right, but Robert DePugh is probably more accurate in describing it as "an essential building block of the right-wing philosophy in America." *Imperium* is the product of the brilliant mind of the man whose torch Carto has picked up.

Francis Parker Yockey was born in Chicago in 1917 and graduated with honors from the Notre Dame law school in 1941. Entering the army, he was given a medical discharge two years later with the diagnosis "dementia praecox, paranoid type." Part of his anxiety apparently rested on his distaste for the war—he had become addicted to Oswald Spengler and his *Decline of the West* prognosis and felt, according to the wife he would shortly divorce, that "communism was the big danger and that the war should have been with Russia."

The Yockey legend has it that his political thoughts crystallized when, after a stint as a prosecutor in Detroit, he became a minor cog in the Judge Advocate General's team prosecuting accused Nazi war criminals at Nuremberg. His briefs were so patently sympathetic to the defendants that he was pressured to resign. In 1947 he withdrew to Brittas Bay in Ireland, where he spent the winter pouring out the torrent of words composing *Imperium.* The moody dissident was given to mysticism and symbolism, as his choice of a pen name, Ulick Varange, indicates. Ulick is a Gaelic word meaning "reward of the mind," and Varange suggest the Varangians, a ninth century Norse expeditionary force that conquered part of Russia. Thus was signified a wedding of Western and Eastern intellects that would produce a third political force combining the extremities of right and left and dominating by the autocratic use of power.

An exercise in Weltpolitik, the book combined a pseudo-anthropological argument for Aryan supremacy with a kind of chess-move design for the survival of the West. The authoritarian elite that Yockey envisioned taking power could only prevail by "the complete cleansing of the Western soul from every form of materialism, from rationalism, equality, social chaos, communism, liberalism, leftism, of every variety of money worship, democracy, finance-capitalism, the domination of trade, nationalism, parliamentarianism, feminism, race sterility, weak ideals of 'happiness' and the like." In his florid prose he concluded that the "soil of Europe rendered sacred by the streams of blood which have made it spiritually fertile for a millennium, will once again stream with blood until the barbarians and distorters have been driven out."

Imperium was published in a very limited edition by a British house in 1948, but it was not until after Yockey's death that it was printed in the United States. The publisher was Carto, who perhaps perceived the potential mystique not only of the book but of its author. After finishing the manuscript, Yockey had dropped into a nether world, flitting between Europe, South America, and the United States with spurious passports and cropping up in the company of leading figures in the international fascist movement. There is some belief that he was a courier in contact with fugitive German Nazis in South America, but whatever his role no one, not even the FBI, dismissed him lightly.

The beginning of the end came in 1960 when he debarked in San Francisco from a South American trip and found that one of his suitcases was missing. The airline traced the luggage to Fort Worth, Texas, where it was opened to verify ownership. Inside were three passports, all with Yockey's photograph but with different names, and seven different birth certificates. The FBI arrested him in the apartment of a Jewish businessman in Oakland where he was staying—hadn't his sister always insisted that he was not anti-Jewish, just anti-Zionist?—and held him on $50,000 bail. Whatever his clandestine game, the government obviously sensed it was being played for high stakes.

In San Francisco County Jail Yockey was hardly a model prisoner. He attempted a jail break, hurled epithets at his jailers, and tried to smuggle out messages to Cuba. One of his last visitors was a dapper little man in a bow tie, Willis Carto. On the morning of June 16, 1960, the creator of *Imperium* was found dead in his bunk, poisoned by cyanide mysteriously acquired.

In 1962 Carto, who had eulogized Yockey as a "great creative genius," brought out an edition of *Imperium* through his Noontide Press of Sausalito, California (since transplanted to Los Angeles). In an introduction, Carto termed the book "prophetic" and took the opportunity to air his own opinions. Of the embryonic space program he wrote: "Our venture to infinity will be very short-lived if we come home to an earth peopled with a rapidly degenerating human species; to nights that crawl with the prowlings of depraved, raceless savages." He went on in this turgid vein: "The ultimate expression of this militant water-pistol imperialism is the hilarious yet deeply symbolic 'Peace Corpse,' the true expression of the Zeitgeist."

In Carto's movement, *Imperium* has become the basis for a kind of fleshless cult of personality drawing the believers together, for he himself for his own reasons has elected to remain a shadow figure. He dodges the public spotlight, designating himself simply as treasurer of the Liberty Lobby and using others as spokesmen for the organization. Of his private life little is known. While in Washington he dwells in a sealed-off basement apartment in the rickety Liberty Lobby building that intimates allude to as "der Führerbunker." His entire career, in fact, is one of behind-the-scenes manipulation. His first known affiliation was with the Congress of Freedom, which when organized in 1954 listed him as a director and secretary. He drew some notice in 1956 when he opened a "Conservative Republican Headquarters" at the Republican convention in San Francisco, the purpose of which was to cope with the "good possibility that Ike planned to withdraw from the race at the last moment, throwing his support to a Trotskyite like Earl Warren." By 1957 he was on record as a regional vice president of We, The People!, a strident Chicago group. In 1959 he was employed briefly in the John Birch Society headquarters in Massachusetts—he managed to write two articles for *American Opinion*—until dismissed by Robert Welch, reportedly for leaning too heavily on Jewish matters.

It was hardly a blow to Carto, for he already had his own modest organization called Liberty and Property which functioned from a postal box address in San Francisco. Its monthly newsletter, *Right,* championed "Constitution, Freedom, and Nationalism," and some idea of what these platitudes meant to Carto can be gleaned from excerpts from *Right*: "The Bolshevik conspiracy was hatched and led by Bronx Jews and financed to a great extent by Wall Street Jews." "That the United States was on the wrong side in the last war is a fact so revolutionary to our accustomed modes of thought that it is automatically denied by most Americans."* "First of all comes loyalty to the White race and Western Civilization." The newsletter commended the National States Rights Party and the American Nazi Party to its readers as outlets for their energies.

It is precisely Carto's operating premise that he not compete with other groups and factions for the allegiance of a few but instead provide the kind of special service that draws support from the many. This was the raison d'être of the Liberty Lobby which he launched in 1957 by mailing a prospectus to "some seven hundred patriots" and shortly announcing the names of a sixteen-member advisory board. One of the respondents was novelist Taylor Caldwell, who deigned to contribute an article, "Unify with the Liberty Lobby," for publication in *Right*. Among those bodies pledging support were the Congress of Freedom; We, The People!; Gerald L. K. Smith's Christian Nationalist Crusade; and the *Santa Ana Register* of Orange County, California.

For a time, the Liberty Lobby remained mostly a paper organization. The first year's budget was a meager $10,000, and Carto's announcements about expansion plans proved premature. Nevertheless he opened a Washington "research department" on July 4, 1958, observing the conservative propensity for choosing significant dates, and "the first voting records ever prepared and published by a conservative group" soon appeared. In 1960 he formed a National Trade Policy Committee, which opposed increased foreign trade and advocated the return of "the tariff-making power to Congress."

Still, Carto remained in San Francisco, where he had

---

* In a letter to a fellow right-winger, Carto wrote: "Hitler's defeat was the defeat of Europe and America. How could we have been so blind? The blame, it seems, must be laid at the door of the international Jews. It was their propaganda, lies and demands which blinded the West to what Germany was doing."

repaired after his falling out with Welch, and the late Colonel Eugene C. Pomeroy of the Defenders of the American Constitution acted as the Liberty Lobby's Washington representative. Carto worked from a small office bedecked with Nazi symbols and pictures of Hitler and cluttered with Birch Society and British Israelite literature. In one issue of *Right* he continued his anonymity by writing a "guest editorial" under the name of a "scholar" called E. L. Anderson, a name he evidently had appropriated from the deceased uncle of an unpaid helper. (The helper, Norris B. Holt, who serviced Carto's postal boxes while he was on his frequent trips to Washington, the South and other waypoints, told me this.)*

The year 1962 marked the opening of a permanent office in Washington, the incorporation of the Liberty Lobby, and its registration as a lobbying group.† Some time earlier, Carto had proclaimed the importance of the nation's capital to his designs: "Washington, D.C., is an occupied city. It has been captured by an aggressive coalition of minority special interest groups [and we] must compete with these pressure groups on their own terms until such time as the entire pres-

* Holt grew disenchanted and resigned on October 21, 1963. When *True* magazine ran its article on the Liberty Lobby in the November 1969 issue—much of it based upon previous Drew Pearson–Jack Anderson columns—Holt was characterized as "an extreme right-wing leader in Sausalito, California." The context was that a defector from the Liberty Lobby had found copies, undated, of letters from Carto to Holt, one of which rambled on scurrilously about the Jews and cautioned Holt not to do anything about the Joint Council for Repatriation of Negroes Back to Africa "until we get a good, strong group behind us." Outraged, Holt denied he ever had been a leader of anything and insisted he had received no such letters.

† The office has moved several times. Currently it is at 132 Third Street S.E., a stone's throw from the Capitol; the back door is used as a mailing address because it is more symbolic: 300 Independence Avenue.

sure group system can be eliminated and government re-established in consistency with American principles." The outfit's professed purpose was "to formulate and promote programs leading to public education in basic principles of good government, liberty, civil rights, free enterprise, property rights and the national interest of the United States." A brochure put it more bluntly: "Liberty Lobby stands for Constitutional law, Americanism, and individualism. It opposes bureaucratic dictatorship, give-away internationalism, and collectivism."

The 1964 presidential campaign seems to have generated momentum for the Lobby. Early in the year Carto hired W. B. Hicks Jr., a former executive of the right-wing tabloid *Human Events*, as executive director, and the full-time staff was doubled to about twenty. Carto's strategy was to avoid the futility of third-party movements and concentrate on attaining leverage within the Republican Party, and to that end he began subtly to advance the Goldwater cause. The journalistic hand of Hicks was manifest in *LBJ: A Political Biography*, an expertly done personal indictment of the incumbent widely distributed by the Liberty Lobby and Goldwater partisans. By its own count, the Lobby "was directly responsible for the distribution of over twenty million pieces of literature during the election period."

For its efforts the Liberty Lobby evidently picked up a sizable bloc of Goldwater followers, for the circulation of its newsletter *Liberty Letter*, which is the sole gauge of numerical strength since there is no membership as such, more than doubled, putting it in the fifty thousand bracket, and by August 1965 it had spurted further to a hundred fifty thousand. Financial support increased, no doubt spurred by a glittering marquee of far-right stars on the Liberty Lobby's expanded board of policy. Among them: retired Air Force General George E. Stratemeyer, former USAF commander in Korea; Karl Prussion, a former FBI counterspy active on the right-wing lecture circuit; Tyler Kent, convicted of passing information to the Germans while a code clerk in the U.S. Embassy in London during World War II; Judge Tom P. Brady of Mississippi, the eminent theorist of segregation; and Kenneth Goff of the Soldiers of the Cross. Although it had been on previous committees, Carto's name was conspicuously missing from the board. The chairman is Colonel Curtis B. Dall, once married to Franklin Roosevelt's daughter Anna. A Philadelphia securities broker, Dall ranges far and wide as a Liberty Lobby spokesman. He has held press conferences on a number of subjects and appeared before congressional committees. In 1962 he told the Senate Finance Committee, in opposing the Trade Expansion Act, that "in this case, the real center and heart of this international cabal shows its hand, namely the Political Zionist Planners for Absolute Rule via One World Government."

Under Hicks's guidance publications have apparently replaced outright contributions as the Liberty Lobby's main source of income.* The bread-and-butter periodical is *Liberty Letter*, which sells for a dollar a year and has achieved a circulation of over two hundred thousand—three times that of the Birch Society's monthly *Bulletin*. It is written in a shrilly urgent style with such headlines as "FLOOD OF LEFTIST LEGISLATION IN HOUSE" and "'BLACK REVOLUTION' IS RED REVOLUTION." As the occasion demands, "emergency" editions are put out; one just before the vote on the civil rights act warned: "FINAL DEATH NOTICE OF OUR REPUBLIC, Civil Rights Passage Would Insure Dictatorship." In 1968 the newsletter roused thousands of readers to fire off letters to Congress condemning the confirmation of Abe Fortas as chief justice, after which Liberty Lobby representatives

* In 1969 Hicks went into semi-retirement in Florida; he died a few months later in a boating accident. To date, no successor has been named.

appeared at the hearings.*   Now *Liberty Letter* is in the midst of a sustained attack on public school sex education; the September 1969 issue carried a cartoon depicting a hook-nosed man labeled "SIECUS" (Sex Information and Education Council of the U.S.) pushing "filth, smut, and pornography" through a school portal. Carto has even sent out "Libertygrams" on yellow paper simulating a telegram, as for example this text: "URGENT. THE HOUR IS LATE. FORCES OF EXTREME LEFT PLANNING NEW LARGE SCALE ATTACK ON CONGRESS. LIBERTY LOBBY NEEDS YOUR HELP TO COUNTER ATTACK. YOUR FINAL COPY LIBERTY LETTER SENT LAST MONTH. SEND TWO DOLLARS RENEWAL NOW TO COORDINATE EFFORTS."

Another publication is *Liberty Lowdown,* described as a "Confidential Washington Report" mailed to regular financial donors. Every two years a *Liberty Ledger* is issued rating members of Congress on their voting records.

The flow of publications was added to in 1964 with the debut of the monthly *Washington Observer.* Among the causes the *Observer* has espoused is that of Mario Kohly, an anti-Castro leader who served time in a federal prison for supposedly counterfeiting $50 million worth of Cuban pesos in order to sabotage the island's economy. In a series of 1966 articles, the periodical contended that its staff had dug up evidence proving that Kohly "was the victim of CIA entrapment and that he was railroaded to prison on trumped-up charges and arbitrarily denied the right to call witnesses in his own defense." He was framed, the *Observer* charged, after a 1961 meeting in which "CIA agents offered Kohly $500,000 in American currency if he would induce his forty-five thousand–member underground organization in Cuba to join

---

* This Liberty Lobby "crisis project" was kicked off by Colonel Dall at the 1968 "God, Family & Country" rally of the Birch Society. Despite the estrangement between Carto and Welch, Dall is a member of the JBS and the Liberty Lobby regularly participates in the rally.

in the abortive Bay of Pigs invasion." Kohly was said to have refused because he feared that Castro agents had infiltrated the leadership of the venture.*

In August 1968 the *Observer* scored a neat "scoop" with an article on the U.S.S. *Pueblo* affair bylined by A. Lee Roberts, probably another Carto nom de plume. The piece disclosed that the electronic spy ship's captain, Commander Lloyd Bucher, had put in a request for self-destruct gear but had been denied it, thus enabling the North Koreans to capture the ship intact. The data obviously had been leaked from somewhere in the government. Saying this constituted evidence that the loss of the *Pueblo* was deliberate, the *Observer* demanded, "Who are the traitors entrenched within the Executive Department who are working—almost openly now—to surrender the United States to the Soviet Union?"

Carto has also taken over publication of the venerable *American Mercury*, which has passed through progressively more reactionary hands since it was the platform for populist muckraker H. L. Mencken. The magazine is the end product

* Richard M. Nixon quite likely played a behind-the-scenes role in the Kohly case. According to the *Observer* (October 1,1966), Nixon as vice president in 1960 "at the request of the late Senator Owen Brewster (R., Maine) asked the CIA to help the Kohly organization overthrow the Castro regime and for a while the CIA actively cooperated with Kohly." In any case, Nixon went to bat for Kohly after he had been imprisoned. By letter on March 9, 1965, on the letterhead of the New York law firm of Nixon, Mudge, Rose, Guthrie and Alexander, the former vice president pleaded on Kohly's behalf, specifically for a favorable ruling on his "application for suspension or reduction of the sentence imposed," to U.S. District Judge Edward Weinfeld. Nixon declared that Cuban exiles had from time to time "been encouraged and aided by the United States in efforts to overthrow the Cuban Government, and such efforts, in the nature of things, have been covert and sometimes extralegal. The patriotism, courage and energy of the exiles in attempting to mount a counterrevolution have been in the past, and may in the future again be regarded as advantageous to the interests of the United States as well as those of Cuba."

of a series of mergers among Carto's publications. In 1962 his Noontide Press began *Western Destiny,* which amounted to a running anthology of Yockey writings and philosophy. *Western Destiny* in turn incorporated *Northern World* and *Folk,* American vehicles for the international fascistic Northern League.* In 1966 *Western Destiny* was merged with *American Mercury* when Noontide Press acquired the latter. Shortly thereafter *American Mercury* absorbed the readership and writers of *Drake's Freedom Press,* whose founder, William H. Drake, is now a contributing editor.†

The masthead of *American Mercury* reads like a blue book of the far right. Taylor Caldwell, billed as "the most widely read living author in the world," is listed as a contributor. So are Ned Touchstone, editor of the Louisiana White Citizens Council organ *The Councilor,* and William K. Shearer, California chief of the American Independent Party. Although circulation now stands at less than seven thousand, the magazine is a coffee-table piece in rightist society.

The Liberty Lobby has also published a number of tracts on current topics. In 1963, in conjunction with its affiliated Americans for National Security, it attacked the test-ban treaty in a volume called *The Moscow Treaty,* calling it a "great betrayal of our national security." In 1964 it assaulted the Republican leadership with *Conservative Victory Plan,* which blamed the election debacle on Goldwater

* According to the *First National Directory of Rightist Groups,* the U.S. branch of the Northern League is now in Lakeland, Florida. It publishes *Eddas,* whose title is drawn from a collection of skaldic poetry and mythology. The international periodical of the Northern League is *Northlander,* which reaches a readership in North America. The April–June 1969 issue, for example, took after the British Broadcasting Corporation as "ever the source of the jungle culture in the matter of 'music' and 'dancing.' "

† Carto claims that *American Mercury* is owned by a non-profit organization and that he is not even a director.

for running a disjointed campaign and proposed that black nationalism might be exploited to "draw the votes of many hundreds of thousands of Negroes"; the proposed overall strategy was to build a "party within a party"—the Republican Party. One of the latest is *The Great Tax Fraud,* written on commission by Dr. Martin A. Larson, who has put out his own book arguing against tax exemption for churches. *Tax Fraud* is tied to the Lobby's tax equity plan, which would "place a tax burden on all income-producing, tax-exempt organizations—foundations, churches, and the like—and would plug up the loopholes for those multimillionaires who pay practically no taxes."

Currently the Lobby has a three-man lobbying team on Capitol Hill. While it is difficult to assess its impact, the degree of acceptance and support the team has attained for the Lobby suggests it is not inconsequential. Back in 1962–63 the Lobby aired a weekly radio program, "Congress Calling," which managed to attract as guests such conservative powers as Senators Karl Mundt, Frank Lausche, John McClellan, and Everett Dirksen (the sonorous solon didn't know it but he would soon be lampooned as a Lyndon Johnson stooge in the Lobby's tract *The Ev and Charlie Show*). As a gesture of appreciation, congressional guests and speakers at Lobby-sponsored functions have been awarded "Statesmen of the Republic" laurels, and at one time or another that lofty title has gone to Congressmen John Dowdy of Texas, E. Y. Berry of South Dakota, Joe D. Waggoner Jr. of Louisiana, W. J. Bryan Dorn of South Carolina, the late James Utt of California (a former Utt aide, Philip Brennan, was simultaneously on the Liberty Lobby's payroll), and John Bell Williams of Mississippi, now governor.*

One of the Lobby's warmest supporters is the crusty

---

* It is *possible* that some of these men did not know of Carto's pro-Nazi ideology but regarded him merely as a conservative.

chairman of the Senate Internal Security Subcommittee, James O. Eastland, who has been quoted as saying that "Carto is a great patriot who has worthwhile ideas, and the Liberty Lobby is doing a great service to all Americans." Eastland's chief counsel, Julien Sourwine, concedes he frequently "passes information to Liberty Lobby officials in the never-ending struggle to clean up the communist elements in this country." One of these "officials" evidently is Warren S. Richardson, the Lobby's general counsel. Richardson told a *True* interviewer for the November 1970 issue that he had recently been in the offices of the Senate subcommittee commiserating over the rejections of Clement F. Haynsworth and G. Harrold Carswell with one of the staff. "We asked him pointblank what had happened on those two nominations," Richardson recounted. "He said, 'It was nothing but politics. Haynsworth and Carswell had nothing in their records.'* This man has been a member of that committee's staff for twenty years. He has access to both the secret and public files." Other Lobby boosters have included Senator Strom Thurmond and Congressmen L. Mendel Rivers and John Rarick. Congressman Albert W. Watson of South Carolina went so far as to mail out one hundred thousand letters plugging the Liberty Lobby and soliciting subscriptions to *Liberty Letter* as "a good way to keep abreast of these perilous times on Capitol Hill." His colleague Otto Passman of Louisiana obliged in similar fashion.

One lure the Lobby holds out on the Hill is campaign contributions. For the 1968 elections Carto erected a front called United Republicans of America whose letterhead displayed twin Republican elephants and the letters "GOP."

---

* Which may have been technically true. *Life* magazine dug up Haynsworth's conflict of interest and a university student working part-time as a radio reporter discovered Carswell's 1948 racist speech, both of which were missed or overlooked by the FBI in its investigation.

The implication of official aegis was reinforced when he intimated that URA was *the* Republican political action committee and stated that it was the "only Republican committee that could be depended on to pass the money on to conservative candidates." Using a collection of mailing lists that he had bought, begged, or borrowed over the years, Carto mailed out a pitch for contributions, saying the money would pay handsome dividends later. The take reportedly was $464,000. Touching all bases, he launched a parallel solicitation named United Congressional Appeal, which, using the signature of former Dallas Congressman Bruce Alger, well respected in ultraconservative circles, raked in $123,321.04. The disbursement of the funds is somewhat murky:* $227,925 went to a Lobby official who may or may not have shelled all of it out to the war chests. Token contributions totaling $28,000 went to forty-four candidates as a goodwill gesture. The largest single handouts, of $4,500 each, were given to obscure candidates trying to unseat two leading doves, Senator George McGovern of South Dakota and Senator Frank Church of Idaho. Checks in the amount of $2,500 were sent to Max Rafferty in California, who failed to defeat the liberal Democrat Alan Cranston, to the crude racist Jim Johnson in Arkansas, who was unable to dislodge Fulbright, and to Edward Gurney of Florida, who did beat former governor LeRoy Collins, a moderate. Asked about it, Gurney replied, "Carto is no Nazi. I have seen no evidence to the effect that he is. He has given my office valuable help as well as those of other senators and congressmen."

For 1970, the United Congressional Appeal set a goal of $250,000, urging prospects to give $5,000 or whatever they could afford on the premise that U.S. troops in Vietnam "get a boost out of conservative victories." For this campaign, the Lobby was taking special aim at Senators Edward Kennedy,

---

* The author does not wish to imply that there was any embezzlement.

Edmund Muskie, Philip Hart, Harrison Williams, John Pastore, and Frank Moss, whose notions on Vietnam victory were quite different. The appeal fell short, and only $65,000 was distributed—to, among others, Congressman Rarick, Howard W. Pollock of Alaska, and Louis C. Wyman of New Hampshire.

Where the carrot will not suffice, Carto also brandishes a stick. He has reputedly built up a "Kosher Konservative Kongressmen" file containing the connections of dozens of members of Congress with the KKK, White Citizens Councils, the Yockey movement, and other groups they would prefer not to admit openly.

As critical issues arise the Lobby frequently couples its pressure on Congress with well-financed propaganda campaigns. Two such issues were the nomination of Abe Fortas for chief justice and the consular treaty with the Soviet Union (in the latter case display ads were taken in major newspapers warning about "The Communist Next Door"). While there is considerable doubt that the Lobby tipped the scales in these instances, even though it took a share of the credit, there is no dispute that it played a significant role in the resurrection of Otto F. Otepka.

Otepka was the State Department's chief security evaluations officer in 1962 when he openly charged laxity in screening procedures and overnight became a hero of the archconservatives. Then, when he flaunted regulations by slipping Julien Sourwine documents from the files and was shunted to a minor post, he became a right-wing *cause célèbre.* Despite the best efforts of Senators Eastland, Dirksen, and others, he was not reinstated and soon drifted out of government. In 1967, with the affair quieted down, the Liberty Lobby produced a film, *The Otto Otepka Story,* which cast the witch-hunter as himself the victim of a communist-liberal conspiracy. The featured "actors" included Colonel Dall, Senator Thurmond, Congressman Utt, and

Robert Morris, predecessor to Julien Sourwine. The Otepka clamor began to rise again. Shortly after taking office Richard Nixon appointed Otepka chief of the Subversive Activities Control Board at a salary of $36,000, three times what he had made at the State Department (moves are now afoot to make SACB a superboard taking over screening for all government agencies). In an interview with Joe Trento of Wide World News Service, Otepka made it clear that in his view the only subversion is on the left. "Be realistic. There are no Nazis. That is just the pink, communist method for slandering good Americans." Benefactor Carto was one of those good Americans. "The Liberty Lobby is a respectable organization—patriotic. Willis Carto is no Nazi. He believes in the fine tradition of American life, and to me that is important."

Although Carto still envisions a "party within a party," he perceived the strength of the Wallace movement in 1968 and moved in on the action. His primary target was the Youth for Wallace campus branch. According to John D. Acord, who was national head of Youth for Wallace and until recently a Liberty Lobby promoter, Carto was the sub rosa treasurer and financial angel. Thus his takeover of the National Youth Alliance, née Youth for Wallace, at Pittsburgh was merely a matter of calling in his chips. What Carto got was an organization with fewer than three thousand members but a valuable fifteen-thousand-name mailing list.

However, the Pittsburgh coup brought to a head a bitter struggle for control between Carto and a faction that included Acord. The young Acord had been awards chairman of the United Congressional Appeal, executive director of the American–South African Council (a spinoff of the Liberty Lobby's Friends of Rhodesian Independence), and chief of the National Youth Alliance. Just what precipitated the fight is obscure. The Acord forces later contended that the Pittsburgh ritual was the brunt of it, while the Carto camp held that the dissenters were opportunists and profiteers.

As a result, Acord was stripped of his positions in the NYA and UCA, and Louis T. Byers, a thirty-seven-year-old former Birch Society coordinator who had been put on the Liberty Lobby payroll, took over the NYA. The youth of the NYA are now inspired by five of the oldest hands on the right-wing circuit, who compose their advisory board: Revilo Oliver (sixty); Admiral Crommelin (sixty-nine); retired Lieutenant General Pedro del Valle of the Marine Corps (seventy-six), who looms in the Defenders of the American Constitution and is on the Liberty Lobby board of policy; Austin J. App (sixty-three) of the Federation of American Citizens of German Descent; and Richard Cotten (fifty-one), formerly of Bakersfield, California, who now runs the National Documentation Institute to contest "Zionist domination" of the airwaves. In a solicitation letter dated June 28, 1969, Cotten quoted Oliver as saying: "*Imperium,* and through it the National Youth Alliance, for the first time tells the elite of young Americans what they have so long and doubtfully waited to hear. . . . It speaks to them of honor, loyalty, race, and Western man's *will* to conquer or die." His organization, Cotten announced, "is undertaking a major effort to support the National Youth Alliance, and *Imperium,* this particularly important publication. We are well aware that the Hidden Hand must do all that is possible to prevent the growth of the former, and *Imperium*'s acceptance. We are on a collision course with destiny."

Yet all is not roses. When Byers put out a mail solicitation to try to cure the NYA's financial ills, he used the Liberty Lobby's huge list without Carto's permission or knowledge. In the meantime, Carto had warned his addressees against other appeals because he suspected that a new rival, the American Lobby, had a copy of the list. The NYA appeal fell flat.

The rival American Lobby sprang up as a result of the

Pittsburgh coup. Acord's role in it, if any, is unclear. The head man is Leo Phillips, a thin-faced young man who quit Liberty Lobby in March 1969 to open his own advertising agency, and the director is Harold Shifflet, who was ousted from the Liberty Lobby staff. Under the American Lobby umbrella now are the American–South African Council, whose chairman is R. G. Van Buskirk, and the American Education Lobby, headed by another erstwhile Liberty Lobby employee, Lee Dodson, and concerned mostly with school integration and busing.

The American Lobby operates like its estranged parent. It has evidently acquired long mailing lists with which to make fund appeals keyed to the issue of the hour. One American Lobby front, named with apocalyptic urgency the "Committee to Save America," duns prospects to help support "a reliable research organization which will provide Conservative Congressmen with information which will enable them to counter Liberal propaganda." When the movement to impeach Justice William O. Douglas gained momentum in 1970, the American Lobby put out a mailer repeating comments of anti-Douglas leaders Gerald Ford, H. R. Gross, and William Scherle, and urging, "You can be part of this drive to remove Douglas by joining the American Lobby today and contributing generously to make this project successful." The American Education Lobby climbed aboard an amendment to reassert local control of schools introduced by Senator James Allen of Alabama. When he learned that the AEL was implying his endorsement in its money quest, Allen angrily inserted a disclaimer in the *Congressional Record.*

So far the American Lobby does not seem overly prosperous or in a position to challenge the Liberty Lobby's preeminence. Nevertheless, *Statecraft,* the tabloid in which Carto has bought a degree of editorial control, has become absolutely paranoid about the American Lobby, charging that it is secretly controlled by the Anti-Defamation League, which in turn is "a creature of the Communist Party." Meanwhile the Liberty Lobby goes sailing on, steadily if not serenely. In November 1969 it sponsored a West Coast "Sex Symposium" at the International Hotel in Los Angeles featuring announcer Harry Von Zell and Colonel Dall; lurking in the background, unintroduced, was Willis Carto. Also on the agenda was John Steinbacher, a reporter for the *Anaheim Bulletin*, part of his Freedom Newspaper chain which helped Carto get his start.

When the Reverend Carl McIntire staged his "March for Victory" in Washington in October 1970, the Liberty Lobby took advantage of the influx of right-wingers by holding a seminar and "Congressional Banquet" with John Rarick and Daniel J. Flood, a Wilkes-Barre, Pennsylvania, Democrat, as featured speakers (Flood became ill, so his remarks were read). Richard Cotten of the National Documentation Institute was on the program, along with Ivor Benson, a South African journalist who has stumped the United States and Canada imputing a common design to the anti-apartheid struggle in South Africa, the Quebec French separatist movement, and the efforts of militant black groups in the United States.

The National Economic Council, with offices at 230 Park Avenue in New York, headed by long-time right-winger Merwin K. Hart, is a Liberty Lobby affiliate. Carto publishes NEC's newsletter *Behind the News*, which deviated from its usual economically oriented content in February 1970 to plead the case of jailed Minuteman leader Robert DePugh.

Another spoke in the Liberty Lobby wheel is Americans for National Security, which in pushing for a tough military posture has held out for more than a "half-a-loaf" ABM system. The chairman is the Reverend Stanley M. Andrews, a member of the Liberty Lobby board of policy and a columnist in *Liberty Letter.* Directors include General Richard B. Moran, who is tied to Billy James Hargis and his Christian

Crusade, and Admiral J. W. Reeves, identified with the American Security Council. Energetic John Rarick has been the chief booster of AFNS in Congress.

The ability of Carto to work in harmony with other groups was illustrated in a recent attack on the Ford Foundation. In October 1969, selected subscribers to *Liberty Letter* received a pamphlet blasting the foundation for its grants to organizations "ideologically oriented from liberalism to militant communism"—the National Students Association, the Center for the Study of Democratic Institutions, and the Urban Affairs Foundation, to name three. All at once there materialized in Los Angeles a group call FORD: Families Opposing Revolutionary Donations. Ford auto dealer showrooms were picketed with such signs as "Ford had a better idea! Violence! Riots! Civil Disorders! Anti-Americanism! Paid for by the Ford Foundation through Ford sales!"

It turned out that the FORD project was directed out of the Hollywood and Vine offices of something called the American Center for Education, opened in 1969 as a supposedly non-partisan organization. But ACE's leadership might have presaged what kind of axe it would grind. The central figures were Hurst Amyx, a well-known rightist in Los Angeles, and George Todt, who had aired his ultraconservative views in a column on the editorial page of the *Los Angeles Herald-Examiner.* ACE's first undertaking was a "survey" of the political leanings of the area's daily press, the results of which designated the *Los Angeles Times,* run by staunch Republican Norman Chandler, a leftist newspaper. In announcing the FORD project, Amyx revealed that ACE had underwritten the cost of a book on the Ford Foundation and its subsidiaries. Indeed, ACE did not seem to want for money. Contributions, including a substantial sum from Sun Oil Company patriarch J. Howard Pew, also a Liberty Lobby donor, were channeled through Robert Morris's University of Plano near Dallas, and subsequently Pepperdine College of

Los Angeles, both right-wing academies.*

Because Carto is the Howard Hughes of right-wing personalities, the argument undoubtedly will rage on and on over what makes him tick, money or motivation. But tick he does, as even his archenemy Robert Welch finally acknowledged Carto's existence with an admonition to his followers to stay clear of Carto. The Birch leader quoted right-wing columnist James J. Kilpatrick's rumination that the Liberty Lobby elite "dwells in a shadow world, a hundred miles to the right of Robert Welch," and added his own note that "any of these men who were once friends of ours have long since become quite hostile to the Society and myself, because of our refusal to go along with their racist views."

The little man in the bow tie had finally arrived.

* Pew made contributions to the colleges and subsequently the colleges made contributions of the same amount to the ACE.

Carto sued *True* magazine for $400,000.00 in Oklahoma, charging defamation in their 1969 article. Among twenty-nine points, Carto denied: "working every day" to make a "fascist future" come true in America; that he "published books that mocked Jews"; that the real insiders in Carto's apparatus belonged to an explicitly Nazi group called the Francis Parker Yockey movement; that Carto took his philosophy from Yockey; that he was "personally" fired from the John Birch Society by Robert Welch; that Welch "found out about Carto's anti-semitic activities"; that he owned *Right, Western Destiny, American Mercury,* etc.

Rather than contest the suit in far-off Oklahoma, *True* made a token settlement. In November 1970 *True* published an interview with Colonel Dahl, Liberty Lobby spokesman. Dahl did not deny any of the charges in the *True* article; instead, he blamed all the world's woes on the "Rothschild complex" and their associates.   —ED.

9
PATRICK J. FRAWLEY JR.
right-wing moneybag

I made $10 million by the time I was thirty.

—Patrick J. Frawley Jr.

Corporate opinion-molding power makes him No. 1 man on the right.
—Institute for American Democracy

He looks like a typical detective chief of the New York police department: ruddy Gaelic face, glacial blue eyes, graying sandy hair, three-button suit, and rep tie. And he is as obsessed with "fighting communism" as the most perfervid member of a police Red Squad. The weapon that Patrick J. Frawley uses is money. As chief executive officer of companies ringing up some $200 million a year in sales— Eversharp, Schick, and until lately Technicolor—he commands a fortune far beyond the dreams of the most venal cop. And he is quick on the draw in firing his own and company money into his crusades.

Among his beneficiaries are the Christian Anti-Communism Crusade, the American Security Council, the Roman Catholic–oriented Twin Circle Publishing Co., and Edward Scannell Butler, who describes himself as a "conflict manager" specializing in breaking up radical and liberal campus groups and who founded a propaganda outfit called the Information Council of the Americas. Among the politicians on Frawley's favored list have been Governor Ronald Reagan, former senator George Murphy and former California superintendent of public instruction Max Rafferty.

All told, Frawley's firms subsidize conservative causes— through grants and sponsorships—to the tune of an estimated $1 million a year. This is in addition to his own out-of-pocket gratuities to political campaigns such as Reagan's. The Institute for American Democracy ranks him "number one man on the right" and places him at the center of "an ideological apparatus of unprecedented scope."

Like many men of great wealth, Frawley is personally reclusive. He has appeared publicly only rarely—on the radio program, "Life Line," sponsored by H. L. Hunt's H.L.H. Products, and at the "anti-communism" rally staged by Twin Circle and the Cardinal Mindszenty Foundation in St. Louis in March 1970. His biography in *Who's Who in America* consists merely of his year of birth, his corporate affiliations, and an address of the Schick Safety Razor Company in Culver City, California. Only the campaign scandal surrounding payment of a $20,000 per annum "consultant's fee" to George Murphy drew him out in the open—to defend Murphy hotly as worth every penny of it.

The modern, closely guarded headquarters of the Schick Safety Razor Company at 5933 Slausen Boulevard in Culver City serves as the never center not only for Frawley's business empire but also for his ideological complex. Listed there are branches of Twin Circle and the American Security Council. The steady traffic of businessmen is interrupted frequently by the appearance of one of Frawley's stable of right-wing luminaries.

In fact, Frawley seems incapable of divorcing business from politics. Aides have been reported to say his business discussions are indiscriminately laced with ideology, to the point where they tend to become chaotic. The corporation boards are weighted with directors named for their political persuasions rather than their business acumen. The Eversharp board includes—in addition to Frawley, who is chairman, his father, and his wife—J. Fred Schlafly Jr., an Illinois attorney who is past president of the ultraright Defenders of American Liberty; retired General Thomas S. Power of the American Security Council; and Dr. Alton Ochsner, a physician who is president of the New Orleans–based Information Council of the Americas. In 1966, former heavyweight boxing champion

Gene Tunney, who was about to quit the board himself, disclosed that at least three of the Technicolor directors who resigned that year did so "because [they] didn't want Frawley to stay involved with Schwarz and the Anti-Communism Crusade." Said Tunney: "Patrick has some execs who don't agree with him politically, but they don't last long."*

In many ways Frawley's career parallels that of H. L. Hunt, the Dallas multimillionaire who has become symbolic of right-wing sponsorship. Both struck it rich in swift strokes, Hunt as an oil wildcatter, Frawley in mass merchandising of ball-point pens. Both bring religion to their politics, Hunt as a Catholic-shunning Southern Baptist, Frawley as a fundamentalist Roman Catholic. And both use their firms to advance their views. But Frawley is much younger than the Texas octogenarian, and his network is wider spread.

Frawley was born in 1924 in Managua, Nicaragua, to an Irish father and an American mother. His father had been a professor of English literature, then prospered as the owner of a bank, insurance company, export-import business, and heavy construction equipment dealership in the Central American country. After completing high school in San Francisco, young Frawley returned to Managua to join his father's firm. It is part of the legend that his father paid him a $4,000 bounty for not going on to college.

As a business entrepreneur, Frawley was an instant success, negotiating a $300,000 contract between the U.S. Rubber Company and the Panamanian government at the age of eighteen. His budding career was interrupted by service in the Royal Canadian Air Force, but afterward he settled in

* Quoted by Peter Galt in a *Wall Street Journal* article June 24, 1966. It was Tunney's son, John V. Tunney, who beat George Murphy out of his Senate seat in November 1970. The younger Tunney did not exploit the Technicolor fee-plus-amenities that became an issue through the insistence of the press.

San Francisco with his new wife and opened an export-import shop. His big break came in 1948 when he decided to back a garage inventor with an ink that would not leak from a ball-point pen. The upshot was the revolutionary Paper-Mate pen.

The technical breakthrough did not alone spell success, however. That came with Frawley's compulsive drive and venturesome spirit. Borrowing $40,000, he set up a mass manufacturing operation. But not until he had stood behind the counter in Macy's department store in San Francisco for two weeks feeling the pulse of the public as they test-scribbled did he launch a nationwide advertising blitz. Paper-Mate sales took off. By 1955 the company had reached a sales volume of $26 million and had a virtual stranglehold on the ball-point market.

That year, with a reputation as Boy Wonder of industry, Frawley sold Paper-Mate to the Gillette safety razor people for $15.5 million. After staying on with the new owners briefly as a consultant, he hooked up with Eversharp, a competing producer of writing instruments, then barely struggling along. By early 1958 he had become president and chief executive officer of Eversharp, Inc., which now also boasted a wet-shaving subsidiary, Schick Safety Razor Co. Acquisition-minded, he subdued Technicolor in 1960 by threatening a proxy fight, and in 1965 added Schick Electric, Inc., a previously unrelated manufacturer of electric razors and accessories.

At this point the pyramiding empire was chalking up sales of some $200 million a year and Frawley was voicing ideas about merging them to create a billion-dollar conglomerate. The merger has not materialized for several reasons. For the past several years Schick Electric has been operating at a substantial loss in a highly competitive market (in late 1970 the New York Stock Exchange suspended trading in its shares due to its sorry record). And Eversharp was forced by the Justice Department to enter into a consent decree to divest itself of either Schick Electric or the wet-shaving subsidiary; in 1970 it sold the latter to Warner-Lambert Pharmaceutical, although Frawley remained as president. Also in the landmark year of 1970 Frawley himself became the victim of a Technicolor proxy fight engineered by British film producer Harry Saltzman. Charging that the company had shown "a dismal record" under its boss, the Saltzman group forced the resignation of sixteen directors, including chairman Frawley, then-Senator Murphy, and Dr. Robert Morris, former chief counsel for the Senate Internal Security Subcommittee and one of the most ubiquitous figures of the right wing.

The criticisms of Frawley's managerial ability seem to have merit. From all reports he is a peerless promoter and generous boss but a fitful administrator. One aide described him as having a "coruscating mind," which is perhaps a way of saying he is brilliant but erratic. Until he terminated a two-decade bout with the bottle in 1964, Frawley kept such unpredictable hours that he was largely inaccessible. Even now executive conferences are likely to take place in such impromptu locations as his yacht *Gerry Ann* (named after his wife), his home screening room where Technicolor reels roll, and the family swimming pool.

The financial woes of his companies tend to confirm Frawley's inability. Eversharp has been performing poorly, having paid its last dividend in 1967. Schick Electric is, as we have seen, in trouble, and Schick Investment, a holding company, has yet to show a profit. The impact of Frawley's political crusades on the balance sheets is difficult to assess. The (recently discontinued) sponsorship of conservative radio commentator Paul Harvey may well have been profitable, since Harvey has a wide and dedicated following. And in 1967, Frawley subsidized *Freedom's Finest Hour* for TV, narrated by Ronald Reagan, which seems to have been the kind of fare that would draw customers. On the other hand, full-page Schick color ads in such small-circulation journals as the *National Review* hardly seem justified for mass consumer products. The $175,000 spent on televising the Freedom Foundation Awards Ball in 1965 was mostly money down the drain, since there was no advertising. The same seems to be true of expenditures of $150,000 for the "Up with People" troupes and $100,000 for the Schick Business Citizenship Award contest staged by the American Security Council. What is certain is that absolutely none of Schick's annual advertising budget of $8 million goes into politically "wrong" directions. "I won't advertise in *Playboy*," Frawley told the *New York Times* (July 14, 1970). "I don't like seeing the average American girl pictured as a prostitute. I have daughters. If they want to print that stuff, they've got to get their money somewhere but from me."

Obviously, such considerations are not going to boost the balance sheet into the black—a point on which company spokesmen have issued conflicting statements. Following the sponsorship of a telecast of a Fred Schwarz extravaganza in the Hollywood Bowl in 1961, a surge in sales was claimed. After a television special on Castro in 1966 called "Hitler in Havana," Frawley raved that it was one of "two programming highlights" for the year that "won the company inestimable customer loyalty." But in their 1968 annual report Schick complained that the sharp drop in net profits the previous year was due in part to a political boycott "in retaliation for [Schick's] support of political programs."

Certainly the acquisition of institutions specializing in combating alcoholism, another Frawley crusade, has been a drain on Schick-Eversharp's cash flow thus far. Following his conversion to teetotalism, he became as obsessively anti-liquor as he has been anti-communist. Schick-Eversharp purchased Shadel Hospital and Seattle Psychiatric Institute and formed a subsidiary, Enzomedic Laboratories, which has been trying to develop a drug that will cut down on the craving for alcohol.* As usual, Frawley's beliefs dictated the project. The notion that excessive drinking is a mental problem is the "left-wing approach," he was quoted as saying in *Fortune* in February 1966. "The conservative approach is that alcoholism is a *physical* problem." He expanded on this philosophy in the *Times* interview, advancing the theory that people of some races and nationalities—Irish, Scots, Scandinavians, American Indians, and black Africans—are more easily addicted to alcohol than others. "Mediterranean people like Italians and Spanish and Jews" are less susceptible, he said, with the comment, "You bring your genes with you wherever you go." Jews, he went on, have a weakness for gambling, and he proposed to have a Jewish associate write a book warning his fellow gene-bearers of their vulnerability.

Despite his corporate troubles, the political Frawley seems unaffected. He is so well off personally that he has, he says, donated ninety percent of his $90,000 Schick-Eversharp and $95,800 Technicolor salaries to charities. The terms of the Technicolor settlement left him with millions more in liquid assets. And his political endeavors have always been centered about Schick. Some of this burden was shifted in 1970 when he formed Pat Frawley Enterprises, which took over Twin Circle Publishing and sponsored the Bob Hope–Billy Graham "Honor America Day" telecast from Washington on July 4, 1970.

Oddly, Frawley's plunge into the political deep waters is fairly recent. In 1956 he put a probative toe into the pond by donating twenty-five hundred dollars to the Republican National Committee, but he didn't get immersed in the far

---

* Some premature claims were made for the drug Enzopride, which has not received FDA approval as yet. According to Standard & Poor (October 1, 1969), Eversharp has spent nearly $1 million annually on Enzopride research but plans to shut down the laboratories and reduce the outlay to $200,000.

right until 1960, when he somehow got on Fred Schwarz's mailing list. Frawley recounts that he was jarred by what he read about the extent of the communist menace, but his alarm was compounded by the fact that the Castro regime had just expropriated his Cuban properties. He impulsively wrote out a check to Schwarz for five thousand dollars.

Although his interests have spread, Frawley still supports Schwarz's Christian Anti-Communism Crusade. His initial donation won him a post on the steering committee of the Crusade's Southern California School of Anti-Communism, which anchors a number of such "schools" held regularly around the country. At the August 1961 session Frawley led off the fund-raising segment with a $10,000 handout; in 1962 Schwarz acknowledged that the industrialist contributed in the neighborhood of $50,000, making him the largest single donor. "Dr. Schwarz will not lack for money as long as I'm around," Frawley vowed, and indeed he hasn't.

A long-time Frawley aide, Edward E. Ettinger, is also active in the Crusade, of which he is a life member. As the executive vice president of Schick-Eversharp, the effusive Ettinger serves as his boss's front man and spokesman, handing out pens and razor blades to visitors. He is credited with originating the traveling "American School Against Communism," which in the view of some labor leaders is also against labor and for "right-to-work" laws. Ettinger denies this, saying, "I am not politically minded. I try to stick to the main problem—what communism is and how it operates."

The soaring moment of Frawley's relationship with Schwarz undoubtedly was the October 1961 Hollywood Bowl rally billed as "Hollywood's Answer to Communism." With fifteen thousand persons roaring approval, Ronald Reagan, George Murphy, and Roy Rogers did their thing; Schwarz and the Birch Society's Cleon Skousen provided the verbal pyrotechnics. "Russia go home!" Skousen cried. "And take your spies with you!" A videotape of the spectacle was shown on network television, sponsored by Schick and Technicolor, with Richfield Oil picking up part of the tab in the Los Angeles area.

There was surprisingly little backlash to this spectacle. A large wholesaler announced he would take Schick products out of the four hundred supermarkets he served in the New York City area, but a company spokesman countered that Schick was no longer buying television time for Schwarz even though "we still think very highly" of his work (the cessation proved only temporary). And at a 1962 Technicolor stockholders' meeting a question was raised about Frawley's rumored membership in the John Birch Society, which brought a strong response from George Murphy, then Technicolor's vice president, who "emphatically denied the reports and said that Mr. Frawley had publicly repudiated Robert H. W. Welch Jr., founder of the ultraconservative group." Frawley had indeed. In his quest for a temperate image, he had seized upon Welch's famous blooper about General Eisenhower being a Communist agent. But Frawley's mixing of business and politics was generally unchallenged.

Frawley is ecumenical in his practice of theological anti-communism. He points with pride to his support of the American Jewish League Against Communism, a creation of Roy Cohn, former aide to Joe McCarthy, which was headed in Los Angeles by the late Rabbi Max Merritt. Schwarz's Crusade, of course, represents Protestantism. And Frawley has been unstinting in helping groups oriented toward his own religion, Roman Catholicism. One is the Cardinal Mindszenty Foundation, headed by Eversharp director J. Fred Schlafly and his wife Phyllis, and a second is *The Wanderer,* a venerable publication opposing renewal trends in the church. As an aide explained, Frawley "does not believe the free enterprise system can exist except in a religious environment which acts as a restraining force."

Frawley's Catholic anti-communism is now concentrated in the Twin Circle Publishing Co., which was created in 1967 expressly for the Reverend Daniel Lyons, a Jesuit on leave from ecclesiastical duties. Lyons is a compelling personality in his own right. Nearing fifty, as is Frawley, Lyons formerly lectured in industrial relations at Gonzaga University, a Jesuit school in Spokane, and is a registered labor arbitrator. He is not exactly pro-labor. "The answer is not to be found merely in another public works program, or in retraining, or in education," he wrote in an article on automation and unemployment in the May 1965 *Catholic World.* "The private sector of the economy is so much bigger than the government that proportionately more help should come directly from it." From 1965 to 1968 he wrote a column for *Our Sunday Visitor,* the traditional weekly that is found in the vestibule of almost every Catholic church. The column, called "Right or Wrong" (later changed to "Father Dan Lyons, S. J., Views the News"), had previously been written by Father John E. Coogan, a member of the board of the National Right-to-Work Committee. Some samplers from Lyons: "It is time we buried the idea that colonialism was an unmitigated evil. . . . The Europeans [in Rhodesia] have worked hard for everything they have" (April 9, 1967). "I cannot understand how Catholic people . . . can continue to back such groups as SNCC and CORE, or get behind such persons as Martin Luther King. They are disloyal to their country and traitors to their people" (May 7, 1967).

It was Lyons's hawkishness on the Vietnam war that first arrested the eye of Frawley. In 1963 Lyons served as Catholic chaplain aboard the ship-borne University of the Seven Seas, and it so happened that another faculty member was Dr. Stephen C. Y. Pan, an official of the Free Pacific Association who was a close friend of South Vietnamese President Ngo Dinh Diem. Pan and the Free Pacific Association have long advocated U.S. intervention in Asia, and the association evidently whetted Lyons's interest in that sphere. In 1965 the priest became U.S. secretary-general of the Free Pacific Association, and in 1966 he coauthored with Pan a paperback, *Vietnam Crisis*. Published by the Free Pacific Association's East Asian Research Institute, the book lauded Diem and his brother Ngo Dinh Nhu as "two patriotic and dedicated fighters against communism" who had established "the only stable regime that South Vietnam ever had." Anticipating the quagmire of a land war, the authors declared that our "real superiority is on the sea and in the air. There is where America can escalate and the enemy cannot."

As Lyons tells it, Frawley "sent a copy to every priest in the United States, together with a letter from himself" soliciting their views. The poll indicated, according to Lyons, that the Catholic clergy overwhelmingly favored a win-the-war policy in Vietnam and the reliance on U.S. military might to "keep the peace" rather than "Soviet promises."*

Twin Circle was initially set up as a subsidiary of the Schick Investment Company, a holding company jointly owned by Schick and Technicolor, but in 1970 Frawley transferred it to Pat Frawley Enterprises. The president is the Reverend Daniel Lyons. Originally, headquarters were in New York, but they were recently moved to Frawley's Culver City offices. The principal outlet is a weekly tabloid, *Twin Circle,* styled after *Our Sunday Visitor* and bearing the official-looking legend "The National Catholic Press." Listed as "special guest columnists" are the Hearst house Catholics, Jim Bishop and Bob Considine, and the *National Review*'s William Buckley. Phyllis Schlafly is a regular contributor, as is Gina Manion, wife of Birch official Clarence Manion.

A prime target of *Twin Circle* was the California grape

---

* It should be pointed out that only a fraction of the priests responded. It is not likely that anywhere near a majority of priests today favor a win-the-war policy.

boycott, which hurt the big growers in their pocketbooks. In early 1969 the tabloid ran a series of articles by Jesuit Cletus Healy attacking Cesar Chavez and his United Farm Workers. When Archbishop Timothy Manning of Los Angeles attempted to mediate the strike, *Twin Circle* lit into him, too.

The Vietnam war has naturally been a major concern of *Twin Circle*. In 1969 Lyons junketed to South Vietnam in the company of Congressman Donald "Buz" Lukens of Ohio, another relentless hawk, and page one of the tabloid soon blossomed with a picture of the priest chatting with General Creighton W. Abrams, commander of the U.S. armed forces there. Lyons's position had been summarized in a statement before the House Foreign Affairs Committee on February 16, 1966: "I oppose any kind of negotiations with the Viet Cong. Any war should end up with negotiations, but the negotiations must be based on the fact that the other side is willing to admit defeat." After the whirlwind tour of Vietnam, Lyons and Lukens voiced their opinions in the role of self-proclaimed Vietnam experts.

Lyons's views on other topics are equally reactionary. "The current decline in the number of converts to Catholicism in this country is due more to false notions of ecumenism than to anything else," he averred in one recent *Twin Circle* column. In another he lashed out at priests running for Congress in the 1970 elections, saying that it had "taken two hundred years to build up the good name of the priesthood in this country. Why must it be lowered by 'modern' priests who want to give up the noblest of all professions to descend to the level of politics!"

Other publishing ventures of Twin Circle are a monthly newsletter, *Catholics Concerned,* which supplements the tabloid, and a series of books including a reprint of *Vietnam Crisis* and a paperback original, *Danger on the Left,* by Anthony Bouscaren and Lyons; it is, says Lyons, "the first paperback book-of-the-month club." Reprints of *Twin Circle* articles are also available, such as Lyons's "Mini Skirts and the Rise in Crime" and "The Arrogant Mr. Fulbright." With its circulation at a hundred thousand and growing, *Twin Circle* not long ago made a pass at acquiring *Our Sunday Visitor,* but the deal fell through. Instead it picked up the well-established *National Catholic Register* with its readership of one hundred twelve thousand, and the editorial slant was converted from mildly liberal to dogmatically conservative.

Lyons reaches his widest audience through a daily five-minute radio program, "Twin Circle," broadcast over six hundred fifty stations, and a television version aired in forty cities. The most usual format is for the priest to field questions posed by Tom Davis, former Birch Society eastern representative, which is something like Spiro Agnew appearing on William Buckley's "Firing Line." Lyons also manages live scenarios. One of his major efforts, called "Communism on Trial," was held in conjunction with Young Americans for Freedom in Washington in 1968. Among those pronouncing communism guilty as charged in the mock trial were the shopworn former FBI counterspy Herbert Philbrick, New Left defector Philip Abbott Luce, the American Security Council's Dr. Stefan Possony, and Major Edgar Bundy of the Church League of America. Another Lyons special was the Twin Circle–Cardinal Mindszenty Foundation rally in St. Louis in March 1969 that featured Frawley, along with Birch figures Clarence Manion and George Schuyler, and was highlighted by messages of greeting from Spiro Agnew and J. Edgar Hoover.

Perhaps inevitably, Lyons has come under fire for implied anti-Semitism. In the December 1969 *Twin Circle* he editorialized that Spiro Agnew was correct in his attack on the news media and added that "Protestants and Catholics, who comprise over ninety-five percent of our population, are represented only very slightly on the boards of the big TV networks." Challenged by columnist Lester Kinsolving,

Lyons said on' "Twin Circle" that the network directors "don't give a damn about Biafra. The only thing they care about is if Israel is threatened—that's different." How did Lyons know the boards were Jewish-dominated? "Mr. Frawley went up and talked to the boards," he replied. "He has met them all. He's met with them a lot because he spends $18 million a year. . . . he knows that ninety percent are Jewish. That's what he knows." Besides, said Lyons, all three network chiefs were Jewish. "And this is what Agnew said: 'a very tiny group.'"

This blooper and his continued assault on Catholic clergy involved in the California grape strike ended in Lyons's demotion. In August 1970, as the direct result of strong protests by bishops that he had grossly misrepresented their role in the strike settlement, he was eased out of the editorship of *Twin Circle,* although he remains as president and continues to write for it and handle the radio and television programs. His successor as editor was Robert Morris, an Eversharp director active in the American Security Council.

The jingoistic American Security Council, examined in the next chapter, is one of Frawley's chief secular interests. He is also a trustee of Americans for Constitutional Action, which rates lawmakers on their "pro-Constitution" and "anti-socialist" voting records. Through Lyons and Twin Circle he is a benefactor of Young Americans for Freedom, and Schick ads appear in the YAF organ *New Guard.* In 1963 Frawley was named "American of the Year" by the Americanism Educational League based in nearby Orange County. And he is a trustee of the Freedom Foundation at Valley Forge, whose awards have gone to such troglodytes as Dr. George Benson of Harding College, Arkansas, which produced the *Communism on the Map* propaganda film, and J. Edgar Hoover for his "writings against communism"; when the FBI chief won the award in 1962, Technicolor filmed his acceptance speech and made it available to anti-communist organizations.

What seems to be Frawley's political protégé has materialized lately in the person of boyish-looking Edward Scannell Butler. Born in 1935 in New Orleans, Butler at one time or another has been a male model, a Fuller Brush salesman, and an Army public relations man. His political predilections led him to toy with the Birch Society and to speak before White Citizens Councils. In 1960 he became executive director of a New Orleans anti-Castro group called the Free Voice of Latin America. "This young man's ultra-right-wing views were not only embarrassing but in my opinion dangerous," a former Free Voice official recalls. "He could think of nothing but the danger of some globe-encircling communist conspiracy and that it was the primary goal of the Free Voice to forewarn the people of Latin America."

Ousted from the Free Voice, Butler formed the Information Council of the Americas (INCA) and persuaded several Free Voice directors to join him. Dr. Alton Ochsner, a prominent New Orleans ultraconservative who heads the widely known Ochsner Clinic, was installed as president, and other civic lights accepted lesser posts. INCA literature blossomed with an International Advisory Committee that included Herbert Philbrick, retired National Air Lines chairman Dudley Swim, and Earl A. Emerson, once chairman of Armco Steel. And Frawley has lately been added. In 1965 Butler and INCA were lauded on the floor of Congress by Louisiana's Hale Boggs, and Senators Karl Mundt and Everett Dirksen later followed suit. As the Free Voice official put it, "I am continually amazed by Butler's Orwellian use of conceptual words and by his uncanny ability to impress his odd definitions on men of high office."

One phase of INCA's efforts is the preparation of multimedia "documentaries" called Truth Tapes, Fact Films, and Eyewitness Albums. An INCA release describes Truth Tapes as "full-length radio programs featuring the eyewitness testimony of refugees from Red Heaven [Cuba]." Beamed by INCA's "cooperating network" of more than one hundred thirty stations in sixteen Latin American countries, the tapes assertedly "help deprive the communist minority of vital mass support."

Butler's tour de force was an Eyewitness Album, "Oswald: Self-Portrait in Red," that incorporated a taped radio debate between Butler and Lee Harvey Oswald barely three months before the assassination of John Kennedy. In the course of the debate, broadcast over WDSU in New Orleans, Oswald delivered a rote-like argument in favor of Castro and told Butler, "I am a Marxist." Portions of the incriminating tape were aired nationally on the night of the Dallas tragedy, implanting from the start the notion that the accused assassin was a frustrated leftist.

It was the Fact Film "Hitler in Havana" that brought Butler under Frawley's aegis. Impressed, the industrialist had Schick sponsor a television version of it over a nationwide hookup.* Shortly thereafter Butler left New Orleans and settled in Westwood, near the Frawley mansion. Shedding the conservative business attire of his New Orleans days, he dressed mod and started a youth-oriented monthly, the *Westwood Village Square.* Carrying full-page Schick ads, the magazine has a claimed circulation of one hundred sixty thousand. In it Butler promotes a "Square Movement" complete with beach towels with square insignia, buttons, bumper strips, and "Peace Through Victory" posters. The articles run the gamut from an exposé of alleged Communist atrocities in Vietnam and a call to remember the *Pueblo,* to

* In a review on August 28, 1966, *New York Times* television critic Jack Gould panned "Hitler in Havana" as "the crudest form of propaganda," saying its tone carried "the mounting hysteria and tension and the disregard of facts that the program was shrilly denouncing in the case of Nazism and Castroism."

an anti-smoking essay by Dr. Alton Ochsner. The cover story in the Summer 1968 issue was "The Great Assassin Puzzle," in which Butler kept up his drumbeat that Oswald was a Marxist loner; in 1969 a television special based on Butler's theories was shown on the West Coast, with Schick picking up the tab. Another publication is *Aware: The Square Newspaper,* which appears sporadically. Butler also has a weekly television show, "The Square World of Ed Butler," sponsored by Schick over a syndicated network. Opening with the salute "Thumbs Up, Squares!," he has hosted a variety of guests ranging from Frawley, Lyons and John Wayne to John Kay of the Steppenwolf rock group and Yippie Jerry Rubin.

Butler is attempting to put together a viable counterforce to the campus New Left through the Square Movement and INCA. In an interview with Gary Wills quoted in *The Second Civil War,** Butler disclosed that "one year before Watts" he formed the activist core which he terms "private masters of agitprop—professional conflict managers." He explained that the "conflict manager will infiltrate troublemaking groups, try to divert them from their goals, break up their structure, create internal dissension." As for unruly mobs, "You sometimes only need a few people to break up a riot—for instance, by dropping tear gas grenades in their midst and shouting it is poison gas. Or you can have people mix with the mob, pretending to be part of it but actually clubbing its leaders." Wouldn't this be usurping the duties of the police? Not at all, Butler replied; the conflict managers would also be "professionals," and besides, "we the people" are the ones who must ultimately "provide for the common defense." To that end he has set up a paramilitary arm, the "Square Circles."

* The New American Library, 1968. Wills contributes to the *National Review,* among other publications. Butler has put all his counterrevolutionary schemes together in *Revolution Is My Business,* a paperback published by Twin Circle.

With Butler based in Los Angeles, INCA headquarters in New Orleans is overseen by Richard Warren, a former Army intelligence agent. With Butler and Lee Edwards, a veteran right-wing publicist, Warren has formed "Americans for Peace Not Surrender." But the accent is on youth. INCA has a news service on many campuses, and in 1968 organized an annual National Student Conference on Revolution. Frawley was the main speaker at the second conference in June 1969 at Lake Forest College in Illinois. It drew front-page notice when some fifty delegates picketed SDS headquarters in Chicago. Then in October 1969 Butler materialized in Washington, leading a counterdemonstration to the Moratorium March. The 1970 conference, in Philadelphia, was in danger of being totally ignored until attorney William Kunstler showed up to take exception and was engaged in a torrid verbal bout by Chicago attorney Luis Kutner, who is close to Lee Edwards.

By his ability to wield corporate power Frawley has acquired considerable personal clout. An unforgettable example came during the 1961 Hollywood Bowl spectacle. Shortly before the event, *Life* magazine deprecated Fred Schwarz's evangelical road show as a "revival meeting" that sowed the seeds of distrust in the land. Frawley picked up the phone and called the publishing empire's chieftain, Henry Luce, then hopped on a plane to confront him in his New York office. Luce saw the light, no doubt aided by Schick's heavy advertising schedule in the magazine. C. D. Jackson, then *Life*'s publisher, flew to Los Angeles in time to step before the Hollywood Bowl throng and deliver a remarkable *mea culpa*. "It is a great privilege to be with you tonight," he said, "because it affords me an opportunity to align *Life* magazine in a very personal way with a number of stalwart fighters . . . against the most implacable foe our country has ever had—imperial, aggressive communism."

More recently, Frawley exercised veto power over a nominee for United States attorney in Los Angeles. In 1969 the Nixon administration submitted the name of Samuel Potter III, a loyal Republican, to the Senate for confirmation. The customary FBI background check turned up no derogatory information. But a second FBI check was ordered, and it provided a pretext for withdrawing the nomination. Frawley and his allies had objected to Potter in the strongest possible terms.

The reason for the objection lay in the deep antipathy of the ultraright wing of the party in California to former senator Thomas H. Kuchel, a moderate. Potter's sin was that he had supported Kuchel in the 1968 primary, which he lost to the darling of the ultras, Max Rafferty. Kuchel had been under relentless attack from the ultras, and in 1963 had replied from the floor of the Senate with a searing speech that opened, "Mr. President; we face the fright peddlers." In 1965 the feud took a sordid turn when the senator discovered an affidavit circulating among members of Congress and newsmen that falsely accused him of being involved in a homosexual incident. A Los Angeles grand jury eventually indicted four men for criminal libel: two former policemen, Francis A. Capell of the ultrarightist *Herald of Freedom,* and Schick public relations man John F. Fergus. Dennis Mower of the paramilitary Southern California Freedom Councils was implicated but was not prosecuted in return for his testimony. All pleaded no contest. Under oath, Frawley disclaimed any knowledge of the character assassination plot, explaining that Fergus had been hired merely "to make speeches on free enterprise and against communism at local groups." But when the purge of Kuchel was consummated in the 1968 Republican primary, Frawley was instrumental, having thrown his support to Max Rafferty, the glib pedagogue who was superintendent of public instruction. (Rafferty lost the election to Democrat Alan Cranston.)

As the Potter affair intimates, Frawley swings considerable weight not only within the Republican Party of California but on a national level as well. In fact, he seems to have had his own private solon in the person of George Murphy, who was dubbed "the Senator from Technicolor." When Murphy's days as a film tap-dancer ended, he moved over to Technicolor as vice president for public relations at $40,000 per year—plus ten thousand shares of stock. Frawley defends the retention of Murphy as a solid business move. "When I took over Technicolor," he told the *New York Times* (July 14, 1970), "I knew nothing of the motion picture business and I hired Murphy as someone who did know about it."

When he took up his Senate duties, Murphy remained a Technicolor director and, with the approval of the board, was redesignated on the payroll as a consultant at $20,000, or half salary. In addition he was given use of a company air travel card and the use of a company-rented apartment in Washington for half rent. This raised a potential conflict of interest, since Technicolor does a brisk business with the government, notably at the space facility at Cape Kennedy. When this arrangement broke into the news in early 1970, Murphy adopted the air that this was the first time in his career that his integrity had been challenged and he intended to "make certain that my good name and the good name of my family is preserved." He disclosed for the first time that Chairman John C. Stennis of the Senate Select Committee on Standards and Conduct had looked the situation over some months before and "resolved once and for all" that there was no impropriety.

So the question arose as to what Murphy did to justify the $20,000 plus amenities. In the *Times* interview Frawley explained that in 1969 he sought Murphy's counsel as to whether it would be advisable for Schick and Technicolor to sponsor the telecast of a Bonds for Israel rally at the Hollywood Bowl, and Murphy thought that it would. The *St. Louis Post-Dispatch* had a different answer in an editorial March 24, 1970: "Mr. Murphy is Mr. Frawley's man in Washington and we have no doubt he would be bounced from the Technicolor payroll in short order if he presumed to deviate from Mr. Frawley's right-wing line."

When Murphy made his Senate run in 1964 he turned down Frawley's managerial assistance, apparently on the premise it would be more gutty than cerebral, but he mustered no resistance to his boss's bankroll. Frawley was left to devote his campaign energies to the Barry Goldwater putsch. He became Pacific Coast vice president of American Businessmen for Goldwater-Miller, and his wife was a Goldwater delegate to the Republican national convention. By cover letter on Schick letterhead dated October 14, 1964, Frawley mailed some forty thousand copies of Phyllis Schlafly's *A Choice Not an Echo* to Catholic clergymen, warning that the news media were trying "to destroy Senator Goldwater before he can be fairly judged by the American people." In a burst of messianic fervor he concluded, "I am convinced that how we Catholics vote on November 3 will decide not only the future of America but also the future of five million Catholics and of the whole free world."

Then, four days before the election, Schick paid for ads in major newspapers to promulgate Fred Schwarz's analysis of the Sino-Soviet split: "The greatest threat to the continued existence of a free America comes from the subtle, clever, integrated program of Russian communism." The ads were a thinly disguised pitch for Goldwater.

Frawley has played an equally important role in the political career of Ronald Reagan. The actor's candidacy was in fact launched by Frawley and three of California's craggiest conservatives: Henry Salvatori of Western Geophysical, an oil exploration firm (now merged into Litton Industries, of which Salvatori is a director), auto dealer Holmes Tuttle, and the late A. C. Rubel of Union Oil. The trio had been active with Frawley in the Goldwater campaign, and now they perceived in Reagan the man to pick up the torch. Reagan had wide recognition as an actor, and had achieved instant political identification through his TV speech on Goldwater's behalf, "A Time for Choosing." The path to the nomination was cleared well in advance when Thomas Kuchel, still a senator and considered the strongest moderate contender, pondered the capture of the state GOP machinery by the ultras and dropped out with a bitter assault (without naming names) on the "fanatical, neo-Fascist political cult, overcome by a strange mixture of corrosive hatred and sickening fear, recklessly determined to control our party or destroy it."

The Reagan finance committee was spearheaded by Salvatori, who had raised over $1 million for Goldwater. A dour multimillionaire, he has a long track record of aid to ultraconservative causes. Among groups receiving contributions have been the Christian Anti-Communism Crusade and the Anti-Communist Voters League, and he poured money into the fight to get a loyalty oath on the books in California. A close crony of Frawley, he also sits on the National Strategy Committee of the American Security Council. During the 1966 campaign, I talked with George Christopher, the former mayor of San Francisco, who had run against Reagan in the Republican primary and been trounced. Christopher recounted that he had asked Salvatori why his group was backing Reagan. "We want to win, that's the point," was the reply, with an allusion to Reagan's popularity as an actor. When Christopher pointed out that Reagan was totally lacking in governmental experience, Salvatori retorted: "I'll tell him what to do. He's got to listen."*

Besides Frawley, Salvatori, Rubel, and Tuttle, the fi-

* After the Reagan victory, Salvatori et al. became known among the Sacramento press corps as the "Kitchen Cabinet."

nance committee included Walter Knott of Knott's Berry
Farm in Orange County, active in right-wing causes; Loyd
Wright, another member of the American Security Council's
Strategy Committee; Fritz Burns, a Birch Society contributor; William Coberly, a Birch endorser; C. C. Mosely, on the
national advisory board of H. L. Hunt's Life Line Foundation; and E. S. Harwick, a sponsor of the Manion Forum. A
large portion of the war chest they filled went to the
Spencer-Roberts public relations agency—to disguise the extremist tendencies that had made Reagan so attractive to his
backers in the first place. Political satirist Arthur Hoppe has
tagged Reagan "a former left-winger right-winger." His swing
to the far right began when, as president of the Screen Actors
Guild, he guided the witch hunt in Hollywood and appeared,
with George Murphy, as a "friendly witness" for HUAC. It
reached full arc when he married Nancy Davis, whose father,
a prominent Chicago surgeon, got him to do promotional
stints for the American Medical Association's drive against
Medicare. Of late he has served on the national advisory
board of Young Americans for Freedom, made campaign
appeals on behalf of Bircher John Rousselot and oilman-
segregationist Charlton H. Lyons (who ran unsuccessfully for
governor of Louisiana in 1964), joined with Birchers in 1964
in an effort to keep the tabloid *Human Events* solvent, and
narrated a film, *The Welfare State*, produced by Major Edgar
Bundy's Church League of America. Appropriately, the
theme of Reagan's campaign, "The Creative Society," was
thought up by the Reverend W. Stuart McBirnie, a right-wing
radio preacher from Glendale who participated in some
"brainstorming" sessions.

Frawley was sufficiently buoyed by Reagan's landslide
victory in the general election of 1966 to help promote the
abortive Reagan-for-President move in 1968. When Richard
Nixon manipulated the nomination Frawley was initially
cool, but Murphy convinced him that Nixon wasn't that dead

center and he started writing checks. When Reagan came up for re-election as governor in 1970, Frawley kept writing.

Frawley's lone departure from supporting reactionary Republicans came during the 1969 mayoralty race in Los Angeles when he fell in behind reactionary Democrat Sam Yorty. The contest is non-partisan, with the result that the two top vote-getters in the primary were incumbent Yorty and City Councilman Thomas Bradley. Yorty, an irresponsible red-baiter,* had bolted the Democratic ranks on several occasions to support Republicans, including Reagan over Brown. Salvatori acted as the mayor's campaign manager and Frawley played his usual behind-the-scenes role. At one stage, according to Bradley insiders, the pair became frantic, not only because the polls showed Bradley, who is black, with a substantial edge, but because there was talk of a Ted Kennedy-Tom Bradley ticket for 1972. The campaign wound up with a barrage of racial innuendoes aimed at Bradley and an attempt to smear him because his campaign manager had years ago allegedly flirted with the Communist Party. Yorty squeaked through to victory.

Frawley and his wife contributed generously to Reagan's successful 1970 re-election campaign. So did Salvatori, who came under attack from challenger Jesse Unruh as symbolic of the moneyed special interests behind the governor. Salvatori also contributed significantly to the campaigns of James Buckley, George Murphy, and others

---

* For instance, Yorty called Governor Edmund "Pat" Brown a communist dupe while running against him in the Democratic primary in 1966 on the sole basis of an article in the rightist *Intelligence Digest,* published in Britain. And within hours of the shooting of Robert F. Kennedy, Yorty was on national television implying that Sirhan Sirhan was a communist because his car had been spotted parked near a hall used at times by the W. E. B. DuBois clubs. What Yorty didn't say was that the car was just as close to the Fez Club, an Arab hangout where Sirhan's brother played in the band.

who strongly backed the Nixon position on the war.

So Frawley sits in his hillside mansion with his nine children, occasionally entertaining in his own fashion a Bob Hope or George Murphy or Loretta Young, essentially a frightened man trying desperately to halt the creeping socialism overtaking the vast land outside. After I wrote a profile of him for *The Progressive* of September 1970 he told the *Santa Monica Evening Outlook* that he felt I was "complaining that a gradual, imperceptible change in our form of government has been interrupted by concerned citizens across the country, and that as a result of this, the New Left has lost confidence in the gradualism being practiced and is instead resorting to the naked fist." The article, complained Citizen Frawley with a touch of paranoia, was "just setting me up to be assassinated—that's all."

In my opinion Pat Frawley is the most visible, resourceful, and possibly the wealthiest, of a breed that exercises more enduring impact on news channels and opinion than Spiro Agnew. It is these men of wealth and power that are doing so much to shape elections and influence the appointments of the public officials whose right-eyed myopia lies at the bottom of many of this country's most urgent problems.

10
THE AMERICAN
SECURITY
COUNCIL
free enterprise
wages the cold war

The cold war is a psychological hot war, waged by communism to shape and influence the actions of free men.
                                                        —American Security Council brochure.

Despite the official ring to its name, the American Security Council is not "the other league" to the National Security Council, nor does it have any formal government status. It is a pressure and propaganda group, funded by blue-chip corporations, which promotes a tough military stance based on hard-line anti-communism. In its field the ASC may be just as influential in shaping U.S. policy as the National Security Council. After the seesaw legislative battle of 1969 over the Safeguard ABM system, President Nixon acknowledged in writing that the "American Security Council played a major role in achieving that victory." Since the margin of victory for the pro-ABM forces was one vote, it is conceivable that the ASC played a decisive role. In any event, the ASC is one of the most powerful mainsprings of the right.

I first became aware of the ASC in 1962 when I noticed some of its literature on the desk of another former FBI agent who was a security officer at the University of California's Lawrence Radiation Laboratory. In exploring further, it turned out that the ASC is a kind of FBI offshoot. It was founded in 1955 by former G-men, and the initial service it offered member firms was a dossier system modeled after the FBI's, which was intended to weed out employees and prospective employees deemed disloyal to the free enterprise concept.

The Joseph McCarthy virulence and the cold war were both at their peak when the ASC began as the Mid-American Research Library. The impetus was provided by the late

General Robert E. Wood, then board chairman of Sears, Roebuck & Co. Along with the cantankerous Colonel Robert R.
McCormick of the *Chicago Tribune* ("the world's greatest
newspaper," the colonel used to trumpet, and its radio station's call letters are still WGN), Wood had been a prime
mover in the isolationist America First Committee and a
prime adversary of the trade union movement. With the
growing preoccupation of industry with "security," the
establishment of a private body that would provide corporations with a blacklist service and loyalty review board was
almost inevitable.

Expanding rapidly, the Mid-American Research Library
was renamed the American Security Council in 1956, when
former FBI agent John M. Fisher, who had come to Sears as a
"personnel consultant" with J. Edgar Hoover's blessing in
1953, was installed as president and executive director.
Before long Fisher had surrounded himself with Bureau-
trained men. Jack E. Ison was appointed operating director
and William K. Lambie Jr. research director; both had put in
a few years with the FBI; both are still in those positions.
W. Cleon Skousen, who was named field director, had been
an agent from 1940 to 1951 and is well known in right-wing
circles as the author of *The Naked Communist* and *The Communist Attack on U.S. Police.* Skousen left the ASC in 1960
to become a John Birch functionary, and is a perennial figure
on the society's lecture circuit. In time, retired FBI assistant
director Stanley J. Tracy was brought in to sit on the strategy
staff. Among the non-staff officers with a history under
Hoover are Senior Vice President Kenneth M. Piper, "director
of human relations" for Motorola; Vice President Stephen L.
Donchess, a U.S. Steel executive; and Vice President Russell
E. White, a General Electric security consultant.

For the first few years, the ASC devoted itself to amassing the dossier system housed in the "Research and Information Center" in the executive offices at 123 North Wacker

Drive in Chicago. In 1958 it purchased a collection of one million names from the estate of Harry Jung, publisher of *American Vigilante* and described by the *Chicago Sun-Times* at the time as "one of Chicago's most notorious purveyors of anti-Semitic propaganda during the late 1930s and an old-time labor foe." The system is constantly being enlarged through contributions from the security departments of member firms, from the transcripts of hearings staged by state and federal "anti-subversive" committees, and from the cullings of a full-time staff reviewing thousands of publications for data on "left-wingers."

Evidently other right-wing groups contribute data also. For example, in 1961 a Minuteman sent in information on putative left-wingers in his area to the Anti-Communism League of America in Park Ridge, Illinois. The League's executive secretary, John K. Crippen, replied in part:

I told Mr. Cyril W. Hooper (a member of the American Security Council, and one of our most important contacts to this fine organization) about your suggestion, and he has agreed to accept the letters furnished to him. These will be Thermofaxed and returned for our files. They will automatically reach the files of the Chicago FBI as well. . . . The ASC is staffed almost exclusively, at the top level, by former FBI men—who, of course, have had the finest training in the country.

What constitutes a left-winger for the ASC? Only the vaguest of guidelines have emerged from the statements of President Fisher. In 1960, in filing for tax-exempt status (it was denied), he explained one purpose of the ASC: "To promote the common business interests of American business organizations in defending themselves against those activities of Communist and other subversive organizations which are directed against the business operations of American business organizations." The idea was more succinctly put in a later pamphlet: "Interest for or against the free enterprise system—that's the thing that starts our interest. If the situation is in line with the current Communist Party line, then it becomes of interest to us." Seemingly this would embrace advocacy of progressive social and labor legislation, and an end to racism and the Vietnam war.

At present the dossier system consists of, in the ASC's words, "seven major files and libraries on communism and statism" as well as "the largest private collection on revolutionary activities in America." The index alone consists of over six million cards. Although the ASC shuns the implication that it is running a blacklist service, and denies it keeps tab on individuals as such, it nonetheless has indexed and collated the names and activities of over a million persons and organizations fitting its standards of dubious loyalty. In 1970 the ASC announced that it had "handled over 195,000 research requests from members, government agencies, congressional committees, and news media." Presiding over the files is research director Lambie, whose office contains a set of transcripts of HUAC hearings—the property of, the flyleaf says, Senator Richard M. Nixon.

The dossier service is available to the ASC's thirty-five hundred member firms and organizations who pay dues that may run well over a thousand dollars a year apiece, depending on the number of employees. Industrial members include General Electric, Lockheed, Motorola, Allstate Insurance, Standard Oil of California, General Dynamics (San Diego), Reynolds Metals, Quaker Oats, Honeywell, U.S. Steel, Kraft Foods, Stewart-Warner, Schick-Eversharp, Illinois Central Railroad, and, of course, Sears, Roebuck. The publishing industry is represented by the *Detroit News,* the *St. Louis Globe-Democrat,* the *Oakland Tribune,* and the Henry Regnery book house in Chicago. The financial, university, and foundation worlds are also represented. All told, the ASC members have "millions of employees," presumably all of them loyal to free enterprise.

It was not until 1960 that the ASC first moved into electoral politics by opening an office in Washington, a move said to have been inspired by General Wood's ties with some of the congressional mossbacks. The first year was nothing to write Chicago about, the most noteworthy accomplishment being the distribution of the HUAC propaganda film *Operation Abolition* to some one hundred member firms for the "education" of their employees. In 1961, however, the ASC looked beyond the domestic communist threat by churning out three position papers on foreign affairs, condemning the proposed nuclear test ban treaty, the admission of Red China to the United Nations, and the Castro government in Cuba.

By 1964 ASC was widely recognized in jingoist circles for its "national security" specialty, so much so that Fisher moved practically full time into the office at 1101 Seventeenth Street N.W. Even Eisenhower, who had taken a parting shot at the military-industrial complex upon leaving the White House, was taken in, supplying a promotional tag for the debut of a new radio program, "ASC Washington Report of the Air." With production costs underwritten by a Schick grant of a quarter of a million dollars a year, the ASC was able to announce that the daily five-minute slot was beamed over "more than nine hundred participating stations coast-to-coast and in Alaska, Hawaii, Guam, and Puerto Rico" as well as the Armed Forces Radio Network and Radio Free Europe. The nature of the fare can be gauged from the fact that the program's co-editor and regular commentator is Dr. Walter Judd, a former congressman noted for his missionary approach to foreign policy. The late Senator Thomas Dodd once served as co-editor at a salary of $6,373.67 per annum, but was dropped when censured by his colleagues for financial irregularities. His replacement is Richard Ichord, chairman of the House Internal Security Subcommittee (formerly

HUAC). Recently, National Liberty Corporation, an insurance firm, picked up where Schick left off (apparently Schick's financial woes have caused it to curtail sponsorship of programs) to the tune of $5,000 per month. The number of stations has dropped to about three hundred fifty.

The program is an extension of the newsletter *ASC Washington Report,* which goes to the membership, members of Congress, and anyone else ponying up the $12 subscription price. Its national editor is William J. Gill, an accomplished right-wing journalist whose *The Ordeal of Otto Otepka* has been zealously promoted by the Liberty Lobby. At one time retired Rear Admiral Chester C. Ward was editor-in-chief, but he is now listed merely as a special editor.* In a 1965 issue, economics editor Lev E. Dobriansky argued that *"any* exports to Communist nations enable the USSR to maintain its campaign to lure underdeveloped countries into its orbit and to subvert the free industrial nations of the West." Both the newsletter and radio program are part of the ASC Press, which spends nearly half a million dollars a year.

With *Oakland Tribune* publisher William F. Knowland, the former "Senator from Formosa," on the National Strategy Committee, it is not surprising that the *Report* has consistently sought the unleashing of Chiang Kai-shek's forces on the mainland. But even Knowland's wildest urgings

* Ward co-authored, with Phyllis Schafly, *Strike from Space* and *The Betrayers,* which advocate increased nuclear and missile capability. He also sits on the ASC National Strategy Board. In 1961 he aroused the ire of Senator Fulbright by giving speeches at "strategy seminars" bitterly criticizing U.S. foreign policy and calling for a doubling of the military budget. Fulbright submitted a memorandum to the Department of Defense citing eleven instances in which high-ranking officers, including Ward, participated in public meetings with exponents of the radical right. "Running through them all," wrote the senator, "is a central theme that the primary, if not exclusive, danger to this country is internal Communist infiltration."

never encompassed what former ambassador to Brazil and Peru William D. Pawley proposed in the December 1960 *Report.* "We can support the beautifully equipped and trained, eager Chinese Nationalist troops in Vietnam for a quarter of what American soldiers cost in that Asian theater," he wrote. "There is no legal, ethical, or moral barrier to our assisting the Chinese Nationalists to regain their homeland and to overthrow on the way home the bloody Communist tyranny which holds much of Vietnam in its grip."

With rubbed-off FBI prestige and corporate respectability going for it, the ASC projects an image of evenhandedness and sophistication. The image has been studiously cultivated, perhaps because so many of the management prepped at J. Edgar Hoover's academy of public relations. The ASC takes pains to point out that it is nonpartisan, meaning that its executive suite Republicans are "balanced" by such Democrats as Richard Ichord. And it scrupulously avoids the more déclassé elements of the ultraright (although a number of its staff and committee members have Birch and Liberty Lobby connections). After Curtis LeMay teamed up with George Wallace in 1968, the general's signature was quietly dropped from ASC reports. By means of this calculated snobbishness, the ASC has become welcome in the corridors of Washington power.

The low profile also enables ASC propaganda to be played straight in the daily press. In June 1970, for instance, the Hearst chain ran an article, "Reds' 'Nuclear Pistol' Aimed at Uncle Sam," by Dr. James D. Atkinson of Georgetown University, a member of the ASC National Strategy Committee. Spiked with alarums about Soviet duplicity, the article promoted a complete Safequard ABM system and sea-based missile defense. Its preface stated simply that the "commentary first appeared in a recent issue of *Washington Report,* published by the American Security Council." Nothing about the ASC's unofficial status or its axe-grinding.

This illusion of objectivity was neatly exploited by the late Chairman L. Mendel Rivers of the House Armed Services Committee in 1967, when the battle between Pentagon militarists on the one hand and Robert S. McNamara and Defense Department civilians on the other was at its height. Rivers commissioned the ASC to conduct a study of the strategic weaponry situation. Its report, issued under the title "The Changing Strategic Military Balance, USA vs. USSR," warned that the Soviets had opened a "megaton gap." It was front-page news across the country with even the *New York Times* reporting it straight. "SOVIETS MAY SEIZE NUCLEAR MASTERY" was one typical headline.

By using the ASC, Rivers had pulled a bit of strategy himself. The report could not have been more overkill in thrust had it been written in the Pentagon, but the apparent impartiality of a civilian research group shielded it from the appearance of military saber-rattling. Badly outflanked, Assistant Secretary of Defense Alain Enthoven issued a rebuttal contending that the ASC report "was prepared for the House Armed Services Committee by a group of retired military officers, but was based on unclassified information. Perhaps for this reason it contains much inaccurate and misleading information." The report's conclusion that the Soviet Union would gain overwhelming mastery over the United States by 1971 was, declared Enthoven, completely wrong. But the rebuttal received little notice in the press.

The success of this ploy encouraged Rivers to commission another ASC study in 1968, this one entitled "The Changing Strategic Naval Balance, USSR vs. USA." Predictably, the report noted a U.S. deficiency and urged that the U.S. proceed "at full speed to augment its naval forces."

The National Strategy Committee that steers ASC policy is a Clausewitzian crowd indeed. The chairman is Robert W. Galvin, chief executive officer of Motorola, a company that held, at last count, $9,495,000 worth of ABM subcontracts (General Electric leads ASC member companies with $45,289,735 worth). Co-chairman is Los Angeles lawyer Loyd Wright, who has advocated preventive war and stated that the Republican Party should have "ten thousand or ten million more members like those I know in the John Birch Society." Prominent among the twenty-one aging military men on the board are General Albert C. Wedemeyer; Admiral Lewis L. Strauss, former Atomic Energy Commission chairman; General Curtis LeMay; General Nathan F. Twining, ex-chairman of the Joint Chiefs of Staff; General Paul B. Adams, once head of the U.S. Strike Command; Admiral Ben Moreell, a Birch Society ally; General Bernard A. Schreiver, former chief of the Air Force Systems Command; and General Thomas S. Power, former commander of the Strategic Air Command. None of this hawk aviary had a wider wingspread than the late General Power, a key ASC figure. In 1968 he told a magazine interviewer: "I think the thing to do is just increase the level of pressure [on Ho Chi Minh]—so that he'll be damned well convinced that those knotheads in the United States who are so loudly protesting for peace are not going to be able to stop our actions." What actions? "I'd destroy the works of man in Vietnam. . . . I mean all targets. All the works of man."

In 1968 the ASC published a cartoon book version of Power's *Design for Survival*, which, naturally, demands a bigger and better military. The book is complete with the ASC symbol, an eagle perched defiantly on top of the world, and was distributed in quantity not only to member firms but to businessmen who happened to visit Strategic Air Command headquarters while Power was in charge there. (When he left, he apparently took along the visitors' register.) One cartoon panel depicts guests at a cocktail party saying that the Russian people don't want war, to which the caption retorts: "The Communist job is made easier by some Americans ranging from subversives to supposedly intelligent patriotic citizens duped by the artful Communist line." A subsequent panel shows Power on a television screen admonishing that "wherever conflicts arise or are provoked the Soviets shrewdly support the side that we are morally or treaty-bound to oppose!" The cartoon strip concludes that the military must be provided with weapons systems sufficient to cope with *any* conceivable Soviet threat.

The civilian membership of the ASC's National Strategy Committee reads like a roster of corporate America. The executives include Patrick Frawley; Bennett Archambault of Stewart-Warner; Clifford F. Hood, past president of U.S. Steel; William H. Kendall of the Louisville & Nashville Railroad; James S. Kemper Jr., president of Lumberman's Mutual Casualty Company; and retired Vice Admiral Robert L. Dennison, now a vice president of Copley Press. Academia is represented by Dr. Robert Morris of the University of Plano, near Dallas, who is one of the most ubiquitous figures on the far right; Dr. Eugene P. Wigner, a Princeton physicist; and Dr. James D. Atkinson of Georgetown University's department of government. The theoretician seems to be Dr. Stefan T. Possony of Stanford's Hoover Institution on War, Revolution and Peace, while the scientific heavy is Dr. Edward Teller, known as the "father of the H-bomb." Henry Duque, Richard Nixon's former law partner, is also a member.

Although the ASC denies being a lobby as such, it behaves exactly like one. The struggle over the ABM system provides a good look at it in action. In the first place, the ASC maintains a "Congressional-Pentagon liaison office," which is a de facto lobbying effort. As the battle lines were drawn, this office acted as a channel between key members of Congress and the ASC. First, the ASC National Strategy Committee cranked out a report called "The ABM and the Changed Strategic Military Balance, USA vs USSR," which was not commissioned by Rivers but was patterned after the earlier reports that were. The report was released in May

1969, three months before the showdown vote and just in time to be incorporated into the mail-outs of, for one, Senator Robert Dole of Kansas, a leader of the pro-ABM forces. Then the ASC helped rally public support by taking out full-page ads that reproduced parts of the official-looking report in one hundred twenty newspapers around the country, and by mailing out over a million letters to voters in key sections. As a result, ASC boasted, a hundred thousand letters poured into Capitol Hill urging passage of the bill.

It was in recognition of this yeoman effort that Richard Nixon wrote his letter of thanks. "In surveying the events of the past year," he told Fisher on February 4, 1970, "it is clear that the passage of the legislation authorizing a Safeguard ABM system was of monumental importance in maintaining our vital national security posture. The American Security Council played a major role in achieving that victory.... I want you to know that your group's understanding, commitment to the national security, and its active support are sources of great strength to me as Commander-in-Chief."

In 1970 the ASC trained its sights on senators up for re-election whom it deemed soft on national security. In a letter to members and "special friends" early in the year, Fisher announced a "National Security Issues Poll" that would produce a "voting index" on members of Congress. To rate high, a member had to be on record against the admission of Red China to the United Nations, and in favor of the ABM, a markedly superior military and nuclear capability, a "national objective of victory in the Cold War [and] Vietnam," and a Freedom Academy "to train leaders for new forms of nonmilitary conflict."

The ASC seeded the project with $68,000, part of which was earmarked for a publicity campaign against Senate doves up for re-election in November. "Many voters are not aware," Fisher declared, "of how some senators such as

Kennedy, Gore, Muskie, Fulbright, Goodell, McGovern, Yarborough, and others have taken positions on national security matters which weaken America in its fight against communism." In order to vote in the poll, the recipient of the letter was required to "validate" his ballot with a ten-dollar check, and contributions of up to fifteen hundred dollars were urged to help "compile and publicize" the results. According to its later statements, the ASC received 42,964 responses that included the ten-dollar fee or more, with an additional 45,456 responding to the poll, presumably with lesser amounts. Indications were that more than half a million dollars went into the war chest.

On September 28, 1970, Fisher sent a letter to his mailing list reporting that the poll showed: "There are eighteen senators who have a National Security Index of zero! Among the zero-rating senators are these six running for re-election: Goodell, Hart, Kennedy, Proxmire, Tydings, and Williams (N.J.). . . . In several elections, the voter has a clear choice. . . . For California Senator, it is Murphy with an Index of '100' against Tunney with '0.' In New York State both Goodell (R), and Ottinger (D), who score '0,' are opposed by Buckley, the security-minded Conservative candidate."

This letter announced "Operation Alert," a "voter education program." Fisher disclosed that the ASC planned "two hundred full-page newspaper ads, prime-time TV spots, distributing millions of Operation Alert folders through cooperating organizations, and other major public information efforts." Noting that this would cost at least $238,000 "beyond our present budget," Fisher asked, "What is a strategically secure America worth to you?" By contributing, the recipient could "help make America Number 1 again." The full-page ad, which appeared in the *Los Angeles Times,* among other newspapers, on October 30, 1970, depicted a huge Russian missile overshadowing an American one, with the caption: "Comparative Missile Megatonnage. Did *you* vote for . . . a real missile gap? A new Cuban missile crisis? Unilateral disarmament? No? Well, that's what you got! And a powerful coalition of members of Congress is trying to further reduce our defenses." The ad solicited readers to join Operation Alert, warning that "the 1970 elections may be [your] *last chance* to vote for Peace through Strength."

Whether the ASC was a decisive factor in the defeats of Goodell, Tydings, and Gore is hard to assess. After the election Fisher generalized: "Key Republicans and Democrats have told me that Operation Alert was an important factor in electing a working majority in Congress for sound decisions on national security and foreign policy issues." If one accepts the ASC's statistics at face value, it is a formidable molder of public opinion. It reports it distributed twenty-five million copies of the brochure "Operation Alert," took out more than a hundred full-page newspaper ads, and secured 42,952 members for the Voters Action Board, which at ten dollars a head would mean revenues of $429,520.

But at the same time its cherished image of evenhandedness took a thrashing. Terming the ASC a "right-wing outfit," Congressman Jonathan V. Bingham of New York labeled the poll "right-wing propaganda" and the security ratings "a fraud upon the public." When presidential aide Charles Colson, who was responsible for smear ads against Tunney, Goodell, and Tydings, mailed out Operation Alert material under cover of White House stationery, the ASC came in for more fire. Senator William Proxmire chipped in with a blast at the ASC's injection of the Subversive Activities Control Board as a crucial defense issue. "The fact is that a vote to support my amendment [for abolition] was simply a vote to save more than $400,000 of the taxpayers' money which was utterly wasted on a do-nothing board" (*Congressional Record*, October 2, 1970).

Still another facet of the ASC operation is the Freedom Studies Conference Center, situated near South Boston,

Virginia, in a Tudor-style country estate. Functioning under the tax-deductible umbrella of the affiliated Institute for American Strategy,* the Center is a kind of Camp David for militarists and their hardware suppliers. As one ASC brochure modestly puts it, "over one thousand opinion makers have gathered and participated in national security seminars" at the retreat. For a registration fee of two hundred dollars, the elite listen to lectures by such regulars as Fisher, Walter Judd, and research director William Lambie, who is advertised as "one of the nation's most informed men on communist and other revolutionary activity on campuses and on the streets." The regulars are joined by a "distinguished guest lecturer." In February 1969 the latter role was filled by General William C. Westmoreland, who delivered an "off-the-record briefing." Plans for expansion of the Center are in the works. On the drawing board is a "Cold War College," to be built at a cost of $460,000. Clare Booth Luce has signed a fund appeal letter.

In addition to its continuing programs, the ASC has become involved in a number of ad hoc ventures. In 1965, on the occasion of its tenth anniversary, it bestowed a series of awards, naming Patrick Frawley "Business Citizen of the Year" and also honoring Motorola's Robert Galvin. Frawley earned his encomium, for his companies had underwritten a $100,000 essay contest on the cold war. First prize winner was young James P. Lucier, who had written for *American Opinion* before joining Senator Strom Thurmond's staff. Also a prize winner was Richard V. Allen, then of the Hoover Institution and now an aide to Nixon's national security advisor, Henry Kissinger.

* The Institute is the outgrowth of conferences held by the Chicago chapter of the Society for American Military Engineers. It was formed in 1958 as a more structured approach to cold war strategy-making. Fisher is president.

THE AMERICAN SECURITY COUNCIL

Lately the ASC has become more and more engaged in domestic issues through front organizations. When Spiro Agnew first waded into the news media, a "Press Ethics Committee" sprang up, with Fisher, retired Vice Admiral Fitzhugh Lee of the ASC National Strategy Committee, and Walter Trohan of the *Chicago Tribune* as officers. As announced by veteran publicity man Frank Kluckhohn, who has written a glowing portrait of George Wallace and who appeared in the Liberty Lobby film espousing the Otto Otepka cause, the purpose was to monitor news programs and lodge protests about, among other derelictions, news coverage that makes the police "appear as vicious bullies, while lawless mobs receive sympathetic treatment." In 1970 another front materialized, this one the American Council for World Freedom, with Fisher as president and General Power, Dr. Possony, and Judd as officers. Its main public relations man is Lee Edwards, who promoted the Committee of One Million Against the Admission of Communist China to the United Nations. With Edwards and Judd aboard, the council seemed to be another incarnation of the old China Lobby.

Among new projects in the works are another in the line of studies, "Meeting the Revolutionary Challenge to America," and the laying down of taproots throughout the land by means of local chapters. A pilot chapter, the Missouri Council on National Security, has been set up with Governor Warren Hearnes as honorary chairman. Co-chairman is Ollie Langhorst of the Greater St. Louis Labor Council, an appointment that may signal an ASC bid for "hard-hat" support. In August 1970 the chapter held a meeting in a St. Louis carpenters' union hall attended by some three hundred labor leaders and businessmen. General Westmoreland was there in uniform, and was presented with a hard hat as "a symbol of the millions of red-blooded American men who have done so much to make our nation the greatest in the world."

In the spring of 1971 an experimental seminar on the

213

course of the cold war was held in Anaheim, in the heart of Orange County; the speakers included Richard Ichord, chairman of the House Internal Security Subcommittee, and Herbert Klein, Richard Nixon's communications director.

Clearly, the American Security Council has become a force to be reckoned with. As the embodiment of the military-industrial complex and a "respectable" voice of neo-nationalism, it has moved to the vanguard of the fight to thrust Pax Americana upon the world.

11
THE POLICE
blue power

You don't often find a liberal in policing. And if you do, by the time he's been in a while longer, he's going to be voting for Governor Wallace.

—Gordon Misner, associate professor of criminology,
University of California

We will throw our weight behind the candidates who stand for law and order at all times, not just when voting time approaches.

—Carl Parsell, president of the
International Conference of Police Associations

As originally conceived, police power in the United States was dispersed through local control. In the past few years, however, the nation's police have emerged as a cohesive political force employing the tactics of propaganda and pressure. The "Thin Blue Line" has been transformed into a potent brand of "Blue Power" oriented well to the right of center.

Once self-conscious and politically passive, the police are flexing their newfound muscle in ways sometimes as blunt as the tip of a nightstick. Perhaps the epitome was in October 1970, when some thirty-five hundred policemen from forty-four states massed on the steps of the Capitol in Washington demanding federal legislation against attacks on law officers. Beefy John J. Harrington, president of the Fraternal Order of Police, exhorted them to "show the people of this country we are fed up." Said Harrington: "The thin line between civilization and the jungle—which is us policemen—is being shot to hell, and something has to be done about it." Senator Richard S. Schweiker of Pennsylvania, who has introduced police-sought legislation over the years, led a congressional covey assuring the demonstrators that the legislation would be passed.

One of the most dominant traits of this growing police militancy is its absolutism. In September of 1969 I spoke before the venerable City Club of Cleveland on the subject of Blue Power. The issue was sharply drawn in the city at the time. Carl Stokes, the first black mayor of a major American city, was up for re-election at the time (he would win narrowly in November), and the local chapter of the Fraternal Order of Police was trying in every way possible to defeat him. During the post-speech question-and-answer period, the chief of police of a suburban community arose and coldly declared, "I can refute *everything* you said."

This black-and-white rigidity and hypersensitivity to criticism is rooted deep in the police psyche. In fact, the evolution—or revolution—of police power in America strikingly parallels that of other aggrieved minorities. For many years the police have considered themselves a "voiceless minority" misunderstood by the public, exploited by the politicians, and overruled by a judicial system dealing out "turnstile justice" and freeing felons. To a degree, there was a basis for this smoldering resentment. But in one sense the police have been their own worst enemies. Beset by frequent accusations of malpractice, venality, criminality, and connivance with organized crime, they have withdrawn into their shell rather than cope with the problems openly. They are a brotherhood, and their code has been similar to the Mafia's *omerta*. As Albert Deutsch observed in *The Trouble with Cops,* a generally sympathetic treatment, "A perverse sense of loyalty tends to brand as a traitor to his group any police officer who publicly exposes dishonest colleagues."

This clannishness is intensified by the homogeneous nature of the police. Most recruits come from a lower-middle-class background that stresses such virtues as cleanliness, frugality, punctuality, membership in conventional fraternal and ethnic organizations, and participation, if only token, in organized religion. The overwhelming majority of policemen are of European derivation, and the tradition of police service in many families is as strong as the tradition in some Irish-American families of one son entering the priesthood. As a class, they resemble the blue-collar workers, and they exhibit a flag-draped type of patriotism. Former New York City policeman Arthur Niederhoffer in his *Behind the Shield: The Police in Urban Society* (1967) reports that "for the past fifteen years, during a cycle of prosperity, the bulk of police candidates has been upper lower class with a sprinkling of lower middle class; about ninety-five percent has had no college training." His survey found that more than three-quarters of the recruits' fathers were manual or service workers.

The inevitable result of police separatism is hostility toward and suspicion of society as a whole, with particular suspicion of other subgroups that diverge significantly from society's norms. This has had a synergistic political effect. Not only is the "straight" policeman intolerant of differing lifestyles, he is acutely aware that it is "they" who clamor for community control of the police, for abolition of the paramilitary tactical squads, for abolition of the marijuana laws, for an end to war in the name of patriotism, and for many other causes that are anathema to the police mind.* As the

---

* In his column of December 11, 1968, Charles McCabe of the *San Francisco Chronicle* told of returning to his old neighborhood in New York and encountering a childhood friend, now a policeman, and a couple of his fellow cops. "It was really terrifying," said McCabe of their saloon conversation. "These guys, all about my age, had been to Manhattan and Fordham and St. John's. They had brought up decent families. But they had become really quite mad in their work. On the subject of hippies and black militants, they were not really human. Their language was violent. 'If I had my way,' said one, 'I'd like to take a few days off, and go off somewhere in the country where these bastards might be hanging out, and I'd like to hunt a couple of them down with a rifle.' The other cop nodded concurrence. I could only listen."

late Chief William H. Parker of Los Angeles once put it, the police are "conservative, ultraconservative, and very right-wing." It was, said Parker, "a very human reaction to the treatment police are afforded by liberal groups. They are driven together as fellow sufferers."

Until the recent past the police bias was able to manifest itself only in a fragmented and mostly individual way. Given a unique grant of power from the state to deprive a citizen of his liberty and use force up to and including deadly force, many policemen unwilling or unable to submerge their personal prejudices exercised this power in a discriminatory manner. One reason the "crime rate" in the ghettoes has been so high is that the police are more apt to make dragnet arrests on catch-all charges there. Yet one of the most common complaints heard by federal task forces looking into crime and violence is that ghetto people who are themselves the victims of crime cannot get fast police service and sometimes cannot even get it at all. The most dramatic evidence of police sociopolitical hangups has come in the drastic way they have dealt with demonstrations against the established order. The Chicago police conduct at the 1968 Democratic convention was unusual only in that it was thoroughly covered by national television. Similar overkill was displayed by the San Francisco police in beating down a protest over the appearance of Dean Rusk on Nob Hill in January 1968; the Los Angeles police in working over demonstrators against Lyndon Johnson at the Century Plaza Hotel in June 1967; the Alameda County Sheriff's elite squad in their rampage against the People's Park protesters in Berkeley in May 1969; and the New York police in their assault against Yippies in Grand Central Station in March 1968. Some who have witnessed several departments in action contend that if the Democratic convention had been held in New York instead of Chicago there most likely would have been a number of demonstrator fatalities. This speculation is lent credibility by the report of Albert J. Reiss on his study of police in Chicago, Boston, and Washington in which he observes that Chicago police were much less likely than those in the other two cities to blame "civil rights groups" for arousing the public against the police.

Perhaps no single issue has more aroused the police than that of civilian review boards and community control of police. Like most components of the right, they tend to look upon outside review as one more piece in a conspiratorial mosaic. Examples abound. In 1962, Inspector Edward M. Davis, now chief of the Los Angeles department, admonished a civic group, "If you cooperate with the executive director of your review board, you will probably get the full support of at least one vocal element of our press—*People's World* [the West Coast Communist Party organ]. . . . Why are we such prime targets of the darlings of *People's World*?" Chief Daniel S. C. Liu of the Honolulu department has archly described review boards as "a secret weapon of a foreign ideology," and the November 1960 edition of the *California Police Officer* hysterically denounced the boards as "a page out of the communist manual." Despite their hysterical arguments, police have prevailed in quashing civilian review boards around the country.

Afflicted with this high-strung anti-communism, many police have gravitated into the orbit of the John Birch Society and other radical groups. When Louisiana State University political scientist Fred Grupp sent out a questionnaire to a random sampling of Birch members, more than three percent of those responding listed their occupation as policeman, a percentage four times that of policemen in the national labor force. A Birch Society regional spokesman has placed the membership in the New York force at five hundred, which tallies with the observation of a reporter at a Birch-sponsored rally in July 1965 at New York's Town Hall that a majority of the audience wore Patrolmen's Benevolent

Association badges. In 1963 in Philadelphia it was discovered that fifteen officers were Birchers, probably only a fraction of the total, prompting Mayor James H. J. Tate to institute disciplinary proceedings on the grounds that the society's philosophy "is against certain groups in the big cities." Other incidents involving Birch activity have cropped up in Santa Ana, California; Trenton, New Jersey; Independence, Missouri; and Boston. And of course many Deep South law enforcement officers are either Klan members or sympathizers.*

However, the police seem to be going more and more in the direction of forming their own rightist groups. Young militants in the New York department have formed the Law Enforcement Group (LEG), which evidently reflects a discontent with the traditional Patrolmen's Benevolent Association, even though the PBA is not exactly inert. Former president John J. Cassese of the PBA saw the revolt coming and tried to head it off by challenging civilian control of the department. On August 12, 1968, he instructed his membership, which includes about ninety-nine percent of the sworn

* Police affiliation with radical right groups is not new. In the 1920s and 1930s Klan leaders, according to one account, "took particular pride in emphasizing the large number of law enforcement officers . . . that had joined their order." The Chicago Klan included in its program "Supporting Officials in All Phases of Law Enforcement," a slogan reminiscent of the current Birch appeal, "Support Your Local Police." Klan membership lists seized in California indicated that about ten percent of the policemen in practically every California city belonged, including the chiefs of the Bakersfield and Los Angeles departments. The fascistic Christian Front of the 1930s, headed by Father Charles Coughlin, attracted 407 members from the ranks of the New York PD. The Black Legion, another fascist-type organization that flourished at the time in the industrial Midwest and specialized in terrorism, attracted many policemen, including top officials in Pontiac, Michigan. The nativist and anti-Catholic American Protective Association also attracted large numbers of policemen.

officers, "to uphold the law and disregard any unlawful order not to do so." New York's finest had been particularly rankled by directives from higher up to "cool it" during demonstrations following the assassination of Dr. Martin Luther King and during outbreaks in the summer of 1968. Raising the shopworn canard that the police were "handcuffed," Cassese warned that a "direct conflict" with City Hall was in the offing if the interference continued.

City Hall did not capitulate. Police Commissioner Howard R. Leary and Mayor John V. Lindsay reasserted their authority by warning that any officer disobeying orders would be subject to disciplinary action, and a mutiny never materialized. But in the opinion of Sylvan Fox, the *New York Times* reporter who was formerly deputy police commissioner in charge of press relations, Cassese was merely trying to defuse LEG by putting on a show of radicalism of his own. "He responded just like the black militants to guys coming up from below," Fox wrote in the *Times* of August 16, 1968. "This was an attempt by a union leader to get out in front of his membership."

LEG was far from finished, however. On September 5, 1968, it broke into print when some members were among the one hundred and fifty off-duty policemen and civilians who attacked Black Panthers in a Brooklyn courthouse. In a *San Francisco Chronicle* interview printed on December 16, 1968, LEG's Michael Churns explained that his group differed from the union-like Patrolmen's Benevolent Association in being more concerned with "Constitutional and moral" issues than with "purely monetary considerations. We're for better conditions in the country." In line with this thinking, LEG has taken aim at the lower courts, long a source of police gripes. LEG assigned off-duty members to attend court sessions and record "misbehavior" by judges, prosecutors, and other officials, thereafter singling out those deemed "coddlers" and demanding a grand jury investigation.

Said Lieutenant Leon Laino, a LEG co-founder: "Nowadays the courts let people get away with anything. Even disrespectful conduct while in court. But since we have instituted a policy of court watchers . . . we have noticed a change in the behavior of these judges." LEG has also supported the re-election efforts of U.S. senators who stood against "another Warren court" by voting against the confirmation of Abe Fortas as chief justice and for the confirmations of Haynsworth and Carswell as associate justices.

The LEG court surveillance was emulated by the San Diego Police Officer's Association, which announced plans to keep a "tally sheet" on several judges considered "too soft" on suspects and take the results to the citizenry. "Judges have abused their discretion in releasing people who have been involved in violent crimes," Sergeant Robert Augustine of the association asserted. Even in conservative San Diego the move provoked an outcry over police interference in the judicial role.

The most powerful police megaphone on the West Coast is that of the Los Angeles Fire and Police Protective League and its twin Fire and Police Research Association (Fi-Po).* Composed mostly of policemen, it states: "Our objective is to inform the membership and the general public of the subversive activities which threaten our American way of life." Fi-Po's notions of the American way are virtually identical with the Birch Society's. The moving force in Fi-Po is Sergeant Norman Moore, who doubles as state chairman of the American Legion Subversive Committee and lobbyist in Sacramento. Moore, who took a leave of absence to serve as a Goldwater bodyguard in 1964, is credited with the *Fi-Po News* "scoop" that folk music is a communist plot; the wire

---

* Whereas all members of Fi-Po belong to the League, not all members of the League belong to Fi-Po. The League has "officially" taken a position against Fi-Po's extremism.

services picked up the revelation and Fi-Po became something of a nationwide laughing stock.

There is nothing funny about Fi-Po's activities, however. It books prominent right-wing figures such as Dr. Fred Schwarz and W. Cleon Skousen to speak before police audiences, often at the police academy, and sends its own speakers before local right-wing and civic groups. On March 5, 1965, for example, officer Gordon M. Browning gave a talk before the North Hollywood chapter of the Birch Society that was billed as an exposé of "the subtle, well-planned attacks on our police organizations by the Communists, the Fabian Socialists, and their fellow travelers on the Extreme Liberal Left." Former Fi-Po director Sergeant Jack Clemmons was one of the four men indicted for conspiracy to commit criminal libel against Senator Thomas Kuchel. For a nominal charge of ten dollars, Fi-Po will supply a name check to industry and commerce purportedly compiled from "open sources" (the John Birch Society at nearby San Marino has occasionally utilized the service). And Fi-Po reputedly has its cwn paramilitary arm, but no one is talking about that.

The Goldwater campaign of 1964 first brought out widespread and undisguised police partisanship. In New York City some officers openly peddled copies of the pro-Goldwater tract *None Dare Call It Treason* in precinct stations, while "Support Your Local Police" circulars blossomed on bulletin boards. Then, on election eve, someone broadcast Goldwater slogans over the police radio, evoking enthusiastic responses from men in the cars. In Los Angeles politicking became so brazen that Chief Parker issued a departmental order forbidding officers to become "identified with any political controversy while engaged in the official performance of duty."

The Wallace campaign of 1968 brought more reports of police in politics while on duty. In Washington, D.C., and several other cities there were instances of police handing out Wallace-for-President literature while in uniform. In Dayton, Ohio, a police lieutenant who publicly endorsed Wallace was reprimanded. And Fraternal Order of Police President John Harrington went from city to city on behalf of Wallace, spreading the inflated claim that "ninety-nine percent of the police" were behind the Alabaman.

The police are active on the local level also. In Boston they rallied behind Louise Day Hicks, the vocal opponent of school busing, in her unsuccessful campaign for mayor in 1967 and again in her successful quest for a congressional seat in 1970. In San Francisco in 1969 they were visible in the campaign of James Rourke, a Teamster official who ran unsuccessfully for the Board of Supervisors on a strict law-and-order plank. Across the bay in Alameda County, off-duty policemen sold ten-dollar tickets to a testimonial dinner for Robert Hannon, a Republican candidate for state senator noted for his hard line on law and order. Detective Sergeant Jack Baugh of the Alameda County Sheriff's Department, co-chairman of the dinner, commented that the record of Hannon's opponent, liberal Democrat Nicholas Petris, was "repulsive to a police officer." In Cleveland in 1969 when Mayor Carl Stokes ran for a second term, police factions bitterly opposed him. The police animus against the black Stokes had been heightened the previous summer when he had ordered police withdrawn for one night during disturbances in the black ghetto in order to allow neighborhood leaders to quiet the situation. Patrol car radios erupted with racist abuse against the mayor, and some officers refused to ride with black partners in the troubled area. In the station houses, placards with Stokes's picture and the legend "Wanted for Murder" appeared, and the local chapter of the Fraternal Order of Police demanded the scalp of Safety Director Joseph F. McNanamon, who had carried out Stokes's directives. During the re-election campaign a policemen's wives' auxiliary pushed hard against the mayor and took full-page ads decrying him in the local dailies. Stokes was almost beaten.

Policemen, of course, are entitled to free political expression as long as it is not tied to their work. But what has been happening in the recent past is a politicization of the police as a group. In my book *The Police Establishment,* published in 1968, I called attention to the growing solidarity and intercommunication of the nation's urban police and the surging potency of their national lobby groups. "Despite the intramural bickering," I concluded, "the police establishment presents a unified front in lobbying for more power and less outside control. Its principal objectives are to nullify Supreme Court decisions by legislation, legalize Big Brother devices in the interests of the 'crime war,' obtain more repressive laws, perpetuate the punitive theory over rehabilitation, and become a national thought-police system."

In a few short years these objectives have largely been realized. Tucked in the Omnibus Crime Act of 1968 were authorization for court-supervised electronic surveillance by local police, and the anti-riot law, which amounts to a thought-police device. In the 1970 crime act passed for the District of Columbia, intended by its authors to be a model for state legislatures across the country, there are provisions for no-knock entrance to suspects' homes, for stopping and frisking without evidence of a crime, and for preventive detention.

The trend has become so firmly established that the Skolnick report to the National Commission on the Causes and Prevention of Violence, released in mid-1969, took note of "the emergence of the police as a self-conscious, independent political power. In many cities and states the police lobby rivals even duly elected officials in influence." By way of illustration the report related:

Aides to New York Mayor John Lindsay are reported to feel that the mayor's office has lost the initiative to the police, who now dominate public dialogue. And some observers feel that ultimate political power in Philadelphia resides in Police Commissioner Frank L. Rizzo,* not the mayor. The implications of this situation are pointed to by Boston Mayor Kevin White: "Are the police governable? Yes. Do I control the police, right now? No."

White happens to be at odds with the militant Boston Patrolmen's Association, headed by blond, crew-cut Richard MacEachern. But Blue Power is on the rise everywhere. Henry Wise, a labor lawyer retained by the Patrolmen's Association, was quoted by the *Washington Post* of December 15, 1968, as saying: "We could elect governors, or at least knock 'em off. I've told [the police] if you get out and organize, you could become one of the strongest political units in the commonwealth."

Not only have the police opposed some candidates and

---

* The blunt, burly Rizzo is a throwback to an earlier era. In his days "on the bricks" he earned the nickname "Cisco Kid" for his penchant for raiding homosexual hangouts and wearing twin revolvers. After a series of police battles with blacks in the summer of 1970, he labeled the Black Panthers "yellow dogs" and "imbeciles" even though their connection with the incidents had not been established, and cried, "This is revolution!" He has been under fire from civil libertarians for his dragnet tactics and his huge dossier system on "potential" troublemakers. "Rizzo sees the world divided between goodies and baddies," explained the ACLU's Spencer Coxe. "He is a highly moral man, almost straightlaced, but he's very emotional. That, together with his authoritarianism, is what makes him dangerous." But to "law and order" exponents, Rizzo is a hero. When he resigned to run for mayor in 1971, he was endorsed by outgoing Mayor James H. J. Tate and funded by white ethnic and Democratic machine groups. Rizzo won the Democratic primary over three opponents by forty-nine thousand votes.

aided others, they have stepped out of uniform to run themselves. In New York, Chief Inspector Sanford Garelik was elected president of the City Council on the Republican-Liberal ticket; in Minneapolis former burglary detective Charles Stenvig is mayor; in Detroit ex-sheriff Roman Gribbs is mayor, having been backed financially and otherwise by the Detroit Police Officers Association. The police also campaign for ballot referendums and propositions. In 1970 the San Francisco Police Officers Association poured money into an advertising push on behalf of a proposition that would have expanded police benefits. A classic example is the great battle over the New York City civilian review board.

The Patrolmen's Benevolent Association of New York, twenty-nine thousand strong, ranks as one of the most influential components of the city's political scene. Until recently, it was presided over by rough-hewn, balding John Cassese. The PBA's impact began to be felt following the election of John Lindsay in 1965. The mayor's philosophy was hardly palatable to the police, and they began to oppose him at every turn. When he tried to have police cadets take over traffic duties, the PBA successfully lobbied against him in the state legislature. The PBA has forced the mayor to retreat on such issues as one-man patrol cars and consolidation of precincts, and was again a winner in Albany in getting a freer hand in the use of deadly force. In March 1968 the well-heeled PBA threw a party for members of the state legislature at the DeWitt Clinton Hotel in Albany that was attended by more than five hundred persons; Lindsay must have winced.

By far the PBA's most impressive accomplishment was the abolition of the despised civilian review board that Lindsay had installed in fulfillment of a campaign promise. Actually, the mayor merely appointed a majority of civilians to the already existing board previously dominated by police representatives, and brought in as commissioner Howard

Leary, who said he had "learned to live with civilian review" in Philadelphia. But the police were affronted, which was predictable after the display they had put on at a hearing on review boards on June 29, 1965. Thousands of off-duty policemen in uniform and wearing PBA buttons tightly ringed City Hall carrying such signs as "WHAT ABOUT CIVIL RIGHTS FOR COPS," and "DON'T LET THE REDS FRAME THE POLICE." Inside the City Council chambers, Cassese was declaiming that a "black book" at headquarters contained the names of many proponents of civilian review who were Communists or sympathizers. Pressed for names, he lamely came up with old ACLU warhorse Roger Baldwin—hardly a radical.

Rather than giving the Lindsay-style board a chance, the PBA sued successfully for the issue to go on the ballot in November 1966. The PBA campaign was managed by Norman Frank & Associates, a classy Madison Avenue publicity outfit that for nine years had served as the policemen's "public relations counsel." The Frank strategy was to put the outspoken Cassese under wraps for the duration and stage a smooth media project to unsell the review board. The effort was initially budgeted at half a million dollars, with another million in reserve, pledged from the PBA treasury. The referendum quickly became a national cause for ultraconservatives. Contributions came in from out-of-town, including $10,000 from H. L. Hunt, and the Conservative Party of New York, itself a significant force, rallied to the flag.

Not all was solidarity in the police ranks, however. The Guardians Association, representing 1,360 black policemen and on record in favor of civilian review, brought suit against the PBA for illegally spending members' dues for political purposes. But the suit wasn't filed until four days before the elections and became moot. At the same time Harlem's *Amsterdam News* was reporting "a growing fear by Negro policemen over the rise of John Birch Society attitudes on the part of many white policemen while on duty."

The bluecoats put on an unprecedented street campaign to win their point. They buttonholed pedestrians on the sidewalks of Manhattan, giving them the message. They converted patrol cars into rolling billboards. They issued citations to review-board supporters on the slightest pretext and ignored violations by vehicles bearing anti-board bumper strips and signs.

The PBA won a resounding victory. When the outcome was decided, John Cassese emerged to go on television and exclaim, "Thank God we saved this city."

In 1969, after his closest advisor was accused of misusing PBA funds, Cassese resigned the presidency and retired from the force. He was not out of the spotlight long. In May 1970 he popped up in Denver at the organizing convention of the International Brotherhood of Police officers, a Boston-based fledgling union, which said it represented ten thousand policemen. The seventy-five delegates from twenty-six cities drew up a constitution and elected Cassese president pro tem. Perhaps because there had been considerable public apprehension about threatened police strikes across the nation, the constitution contained a no-strike clause. But there was no prohibition of other forms of emphasizing a demand, such as slowdowns in writing traffic tickets and outbreaks of "blue flu." The union is seeking AFL-CIO recognition and has affiliated with the National Association of Government Employees. In recruiting ads in major newspapers the union promised "improved pay and working conditions" and the counsel of civil service experts, among other benefits, all for dues of ninety cents a week. Lest anyone fear that this was just a labor union, Cassese declared that the IBPO would work against civilian review wherever it raised its head, would speak out against public officials on the wrong side of the fence, and would campaign to defeat them in elections.

Rivaling Cassese as top man among the rank and file is Patrolman Carl Parsell, president of both the Detroit Police

Officers Association and the International Conference of Police Associations. As the result of a chronically strained city budget, the Detroit police are undertrained and ill-equipped, with a severe morale problem. They are also racist. Former police commissioner and federal judge George Edwards has estimated that ninety percent of the forty-eight hundred-man force are bigoted, noting that their dislike of blacks is manifested in frequent verbal and physical abuse. Yet as militants the Detroit police are unexcelled. In the early 1960s the DPOA first began to assert itself. "They began running with the ball in Edwards's time," recounted Marvin Brown, a community relations aide, in the March 1969 *Atlantic*. "In Girardin's time, they really began running downfield," Brown continued. "They didn't even need interference." Ray Girardin was the elfin ex-newspaperman who succeeded Edwards as police commissioner; it was during his reign, in 1967, that the DPOA authorized the first police strike since the Boston strike of 1919 that catapulted Calvin Coolidge into the national limelight. The DPOA won a pay hike to $7,500 for beginners and $10,300 for four-year veterans, giving the police a higher scale than Detroit teachers and social workers.

With this victory, the DPOA became more brazen. It clashed openly with the progressive mayor, Jerome P. Cavanagh. In November 1968, off-duty policemen attending a dance given by the Detroit Police Officers Wives Association beat up a group of black youths who allegedly had made obscene gestures. The investigation was getting nowhere fast when Cavanagh charged that a "blue curtain" of police secrecy in the form of the DPOA was hindering it. In the end, nine officers were suspended and two charged with criminal assault. Complaints had also stemmed from a mounted police assault on demonstrators from the Poor People's Campaign at Cobo Hall and protesters against an appearance of George Wallace, as well as a series of lesser incidents.

As a result, a blue-ribbon panel of community leaders calling itself New Detroit Inc. announced plans to undertake an expensive study of police practices and management policies. DPOA President Parsell equated the study to an investigation and sarcastically proposed that the money be used instead for a new helicopter and other hardware. In an editorial in the DPOA weekly, *Tuebor,* he fumed:

> The DPOA believes . . . the charges of police brutality are part of a nefarious plot by those who would like our form of government overthrown. The blueprint for anarchy calls for the destruction of the effectiveness of the police. Certainly it must be obvious that every incident is magnified and exploited with only one purpose. A lot of well-meaning people, without realizing their real role, are doing the job for the anarchists.

The notion of the city's starchiest elite as pawns in an anarchist conspiracy was a fantasy only the police could entertain, but there was little doubt that the inmates were running the institution. "There's always been a saying among cops in Detroit: 'We don't give a damn who's commissioner. He'll do things our way, or we'll break him,' " discloses Richard Marks of the Commission on Community Relations. To which Tom Johnson of the Michigan Civil Rights Commission adds: "When you get right down to who runs the department, I'd say the DPOA runs it. They may not be in the commissioner's chair, but the decisions that the commissioner makes are influenced by what the DPOA will do."

When he took over from Girardin in 1968, Johannes F. Spreen tried to court the DPOA— without noticeable success. Not only were many police uninhibited in their support of George Wallace, but the DPOA spent more than a quarter of a million dollars on an ad-and-billboard blitz against a referendum endorsed by Mayor Cavanagh that would weaken police pension benefits (the referendum narrowly passed). Spreen merely asked his men not to affix bumper strips on city cars or campaign in uniform. The request was ignored. Spreen didn't last long, and was replaced by Patrick V. Murphy, who didn't last long either. In September 1970, Murphy—who as head of the Washington Police Department had been accused of "kid-glove handling" of rioters after the King assassination—accepted the post of New York commissioner. Parsell fired a parting shot by saying Murphy took the New York job in order to be appointed FBI director should John Lindsay gain the White House.

The International Conference of Police Associations, of which Parsell was elected president in 1970, describes itself as "a national organization composed of police organizations that have banded together for a common goal—the professionalization of the police officer." Headquartered in Washington, the ICPA says it represents one hundred twenty-five thousand police officers in one hundred thirty-three associations in the United States and Canada. "We do not engage in lobbying as such," states Royce L. Givens, executive director and "legislative advocate." "However, I do make contact with members of Congress when requested to do so by officers of our member associations for information and so forth." The ICPA was formed in 1953 on the initiative of the Detroit Police Officers Association, which had noted with satisfaction the success of a lobbying effort the year before to persuade Congress to exclude police pension programs from Social Security.

The ICPA operates a ponderously titled Committee on Subversive Intervention into Law Enforcement, chaired by Inspector Henry W. Kerr of the Los Angeles police (Kerr is also on the board of the Fi-Po Research Association). The committee functions as a kind of unofficial clearinghouse for the exchange of Red Squad intelligence between cities. At the 1966 ICPA convention in San Francisco, Los Angeles officer Ted Coombs complained that war-on-poverty funds were being diverted to political purposes by persons with "known subversive backgrounds" and called for an exposé. At the 1968 meeting in Dallas a resolution was passed condemning the Walker report on the Chicago "police riot" because it "cast a stigma on professional law enforcement throughout the length and breadth of North America." The 1970 convention in Montreal turned into a newsmaker. Along with the usual cant about lenient judges and easy bail provisions, it passed a resolution in the wake of the sniper-slaying of two Chicago policemen, calling for "all-out retaliation for these senseless killings even if it is in the form of on-the-street justice."* Overshadowed by this controversial move was Carl Parsell's affirmation that the police would actively campaign to remove "incompetent and incapable" judges from the bench and support candidates in elections at every level. "We will throw our weight behind candidates who stand for law and order at all times, not just when voting time approaches."

One of the oldest and largest of the rank and file groups is the Fraternal Order of Police, based in Cincinnati. The FOP boasts a membership of more than one hundred thirty thousand, distributed through thirty-seven states, and the national lodge in Washington maintains a legislative committee that lobbies members of Congress on legislation the police desire. The president of the FOP, John J. Harrington, is a former sergeant on the Philadelphia force. A bulky, crew-cut man of fifty-eight, Harrington fires verbal shots straight from the shoulder. When I talked to him in his FOP Lodge 4 in Philadelphia several years ago, he expressed admiration for the Birch Society ("A lot of Catholic priests are members and I

* The resolution passed despite a telegram from the Chicago Police Association that said, "We cannot concur with your resolution and plead with you to reconsider."

figure they know what they're doing") and exhibited a total lack of diplomacy ("Sunday morning is the quietest part of the police week because the drunks are sleeping it off, the good people are in church, and the niggers are out in the suburbs looking for houses").

Harrington was first elected in 1965 in Philadelphia, the site of the first full-fledged civilian review board, set up in 1958. His mission was to get rid of that despised symbol of outside scrutiny, and he succeeded. Through a series of lawsuits reinforced by incessant propaganda, the FOP in 1969 finally rendered the review board impotent. The energetic FOP president frequently takes his rhetoric on the road. In 1966, in Providence, Rhode Island, he termed recent court decisions "idiotic," and in 1968 he toured the East and Midwest decked out with a Wallace button and putting in a word or two for the Alabama white hope. In a 1970 speech before the Louisiana FOP convention, he soared to new heights. After labeling pop music festivals a "communistic plot to destroy our youth," he threatened that unless the courts halted their permissiveness and the public got behind the police, "the feeling of the policemen is maybe we better resort to the old Mexican *deguello*—a shootout in which we take no prisoners."

There appears to be no room in the FOP for more moderate viewpoints. On June 25, 1969, for example, the Cincinnati lodge terminated the honorary lifetime membership of the city's safety director, twenty-five year police veteran Henry Sandman. His offense: "giving in too much to minority groups." The lodge was incensed because Sandman had requested that a civil rights leader jailed after an altercation with a policeman be released on his own recognizance.

The nation's police executives have their own voice and lobbying agent in the International Association of Chiefs of Police. Although not registered as a lobby and hence tax-exempt, the IACP nonetheless has maintained close contact with Capitol Hill, and in 1967 appointed a full-time non-lobbyist with the explanation: "A number of conscientious federal lawmakers have contacted IACP headquarters seeking guidance concerning legislation which they would like to introduce, and we have responded. The tempo of this interest has increased to the point where we have designated a staff member to make himself available at all times to answer congressional inquiries for advice and assistance."

One technique of the IACP nonlobby is to get itself "invited" before congressional committees. The 1964 Free Speech Movement on the University of California Berkeley campus provides a look at how it works. Following the disturbances, in which police were accused of overzealousness in making arrests, IACP publicity director Charles E. Moore Jr. was invited to Berkeley by its police chief to size up the situation. The glib, personable Moore, a former FBI publicity man, disclosed his findings in a feature article in *Police Chief,* the IACP monthly, for April 1965. Entitled "Anarchy on the Campus: "The Rebels and the Law," the piece was pure demonology. It quoted without reservation *Tocsin*, the organ of the ultraright Students Association Against Totalitarianism, and the American Security Council's *Washington Report,* as well as the red-baiting of Ed Montgomery of the *San Francisco Examiner,* the FBI's journalist-pipeline in the Bay Area. "One of the more alarming aspects of these student demonstrations," the article stated, "is the ever-present evidence that the guiding hand of Communists and extreme leftists was involved." Moore printed the words of his police host: "According to those experts who are best informed regarding Communist plans for world domination, a basic objective is to capture the minds of students and whenever possible to take over institutions of higher learning."

A more balanced evaluation was later delivered by an investigating committee appointed by the university regents. "We found no evidence that the FSM was organized by the

Communist Party, the Progressive Labor Movement, or any other outside group," its report asserted. Despite "a number of suggestive coincidences," the committee found that the FSM was a spontaneous response to a rule limiting political activity on campus.

Nevertheless, Moore's version received wide currency. He was invited to testify before the Senate Internal Security Subcommittee "with respect to student demonstrations and the influence of subversive elements." His testimony was carried by the wire services, and received, said the IACP, "wide publicity in the nation's news media." The original article was reprinted and distributed by the IACP.

Although founded in 1893, the IACP remained a loosely run, rather static, organization until the advent of Executive Director Quinn Tamm in 1961. A stern-faced man with close-cropped white hair, Tamm had been an FBI assistant director until retiring prematurely after a falling out with J. Edgar Hoover. Under Tamm's steady hand the IACP has grown to nearly sixty-five hundred members and employs a paid staff of more than fifty operating on an annual budget of $2.3 million. It is funded by dues, grants, and contributions from corporations whose interests coincide with law enforcement's, among them American District Telegraph Co. (ADT burglar alarm systems), the Mosler Foundation (Mosler safes), General Telephone and Electronics, and the Wackenhut Corp., a large personnel screening and private detective firm once retained by former governor Claude Kirk of Florida as an extra-official spying agency.

Along with studying police management problems and trying to upgrade police status, the IACP dispenses police propaganda through *Police Chief* and the lectures of its spokesmen. Tamm is especially busy on the speechmaking circuit. At a testimonial dinner for a Louisiana sheriff on April 20, 1966, he proclaimed: "Mobs stage insurrections in our streets, on our campuses, even in our nation's capital, the citadel of the world's hopes for freedom. And when those who are sworn to maintain law and order perform their duty with a calmness and fortitude that never ceases to fill me with pride, they are reviled by cries of 'police brutality.' " His philippics on campus unrest compare with the best of Spiro Agnew. "Today, we too often see and read of the young people on campuses and in our streets flaunting the law because they say they had no part in making the law," he told the Beaumont, Texas, Lions Club on September 1, 1966. "We see them, as evidenced on the Berkeley campus, in a state of open rebellion, cleverly egged on by known subversives, and cheered on by some of the maudlin, oversentimental, self-claimed idealists from the faculty. We read of some of them performing near-treason by burning their draft cards and joining with the Communist sympathizers in tirades of denunciation against our nation's effort in Vietnam to contain communism."

The IACP annual conventions feature manufacturers' exhibits of the latest in police hardware, from improved Pepperfog machines to armored personnel carriers. The gatherings usually generate news copy. At the 1970 convention in Atlantic City, the featured speaker was Attorney General John Mitchell, who disclosed that the federal government was rapidly expanding its use of wiretapping against suspected criminals as authorized by the 1968 Omnibus Crime Control Act. Calling fears of ominpresent surveillance "bogeys," he contended that the "only repression that has resulted is the repression of crime."

Any treatment of police political power must necessarily include the top cop, J. Edgar Hoover, and his FBI. So deeply rooted is Hoover's personal power that he has survived eight administrations, of which at least one, Kennedy's, devoutly wished to be rid of him. It is an article of common belief that Hoover keeps his stranglehold on the office through the power of intimidation of a massive dossier system that harbors the secrets of practically every important figure in public life. "He doesn't threaten," *Newsweek* quoted a congressional source on May 10, 1971. "All he does is call up someone on the Hill and say, 'Senator, you don't have to worry about a thing. I've taken your file out of the main record section and I'm keeping it right here where I can keep my eye on it.' "

Intimidation is only part of the reason for Hoover's success, overlooking as it does his formidable if unrecognized talents as a politician. The myth that Hoover is above politics derives, I believe, from the fact that his alliances do not divide along party lines. His relationship to the Nixon administration is a close philosophical one, reinforced by the FBI's coziness with Nixon during the red-hunting days. But Hoover had also cultivated strong personal ties to Lyndon Johnson that enabled him to weather the storms erupting over his outrageous remark about Dr. Martin Luther King Jr.—that King was the "most notorious liar in the country"—and the wiretapping furor of 1967. The Hoover-Johnson rapport went far deeper than the fact they once were neighbors in Rock Creek Park. Very simply, one of Johnson's early political benefactors, the late Clint Murchison Sr. of Dallas, happened to be one of the director's closest friends.

In addition, Hoover has acquired a coterie in Congress that is highly ideological in nature. It numbers such conservative heavyweights as Senators Mundt, Eastland, and McClellan, and Congressmen H. R. Gross of Iowa, a conduit for FBI viewpoints, John Rooney of Brooklyn, who allots the FBI its full budget requests, and H. Allen Smith of Los Angeles, himself a former agent. When the chief sneezes, a number of congressional hankies are pulled out. In April 1971, when Democratic majority leader Hale Boggs likened the FBI to the Gestapo on the floor of the House, two of the first on their feet in outrage were Bircher John Schmitz of California and John Rarick of Louisiana.

The controversy over Hoover, sparked by his reference to Ramsey Clark as a "jellyfish," quickly took on a political coloring outside of Congress. The conservative press, from the *Chicago Tribune* to *American Opinion*, rose unanimously to Hoover's defense, portraying his attackers as dupes of the leftist conspiracy. An attack on Hoover, the theme went, was an attack on all law enforcement and indeed, on the national security. The conservative tone of Hoover's supporters was exemplified by a group that sprang up calling itself "Friends of the FBI." At its head were none other than Lee Edwards, the longtime right-wing publicist, and Luis Kutner, the Chicago attorney who showed up at the meeting of the Information Council of the Americas to take on William Kunstler. As honorary chairmen, Kutner and Edwards co-opted actor Efrem Zimbalist Jr., star of the television series "The FBI." In a letter soliciting funds, Zimbalist wrote that "the FBI and J. Edgar Hoover are now being subjected to a vicious partisan attack by self-serving politicians, their supporting media and certain radical elements that ultimately seek the destruction of all law and order in the United States."

The Nixon administration appears to have ambivalent feelings about Hoover. Despite Nixon's longstanding friendship with Hoover, and the aging chief's eminence as a law-and-order status symbol, Nixon aides are said to consider Hoover's preoccupation with image cultivation as a liability in the push on organized crime. Yet Hoover stays on, picking out every stick of furniture for the rising new FBI building, due for completion in 1975. The space allotments for the building, whose cost of $105 million will make it the most costly government building to date, give some idea of how far the Bureau has advanced Big Brotherism: there will be 550,000 square feet for files and only 23,000 for criminal investigation. The Times-Post Service reported on June 6, 1970, "No less an authority than Attorney General John N. Mitchell believes that the choice of the next FBI director will be, because of the power of the job, the most important presidential appointment of this century."* A sad commentary—that the head of our national secret police should wield such power.

As the titular head of American law enforcement, Hoover's pronouncements carry wide authority. For many years now the Bureau chief has been waging a neurotic war on domestic communism, to the point of becoming one of the most divisive influences in the country. The 1969 Skolnick report to the National Commission on the Causes and Prevention of Violence concluded: "From a systematic sampling of police literature and statements by law enforcement authorities—ranging from the director of the Federal Bureau of Investigation to the patrolman on the beat—a common theme emerges in police analyses of mass protest: the search for [Communist] leaders." And it added that Hoover's utterances in this vein were "significant not only because he is our nation's highest and most renowned law enforcement official but also because his views are reflected and disseminated throughout the nation—by publicity in the news media and by FBI seminars, briefings, and training for local policemen."

The case of the Black Panthers may well be an example of Hoover's powers to incite. On June 4, 1969, heavily armed FBI agents staged a pre-dawn raid on Black Panther Party

* If the choice falls to Nixon, the appointee may well be Cartha "Deke" DeLoach, former assistant to the director in charge of public relations. When DeLoach retired at the minimum age of fifty in 1970, he was written off as a candidate by the press. In their syndicated column of June 14, 1970, Rowland Evans and Robert Novak said that had "DeLoach ever succeeded Hoover (as seemed quite probable a few years ago), the charges against him of right-wing bias and blatant opportunism would have racked and possibly wrecked the FBI." However, DeLoach moved over to Pepsico, headed by old Nixon funder Donald Kendall, and now can be appointed by Nixon as an "outsider."

headquarters in Chicago on the pretext of looking for a fugitive (who wasn't there). Shortly thereafter, on July 15, Hoover charged that among black militant groups "the Black Panther Party, without question, represents the greatest threat to the internal security of the country." In December, only days apart, Chicago and Los Angeles police conducted pre-dawn raids on Panther headquarters, with bloody results. In Chicago, two Panthers were killed, including leader Fred Hampton, who was shot while lying in bed. No matter that Charles Gain, the police chief of Oakland, California, where the Panthers first started in 1966, told CBS television that he did not agree with the FBI chief that the Panthers represented a national threat. Gain does not have a loudspeaker in Hoover's class.

Such is the overpowering ambition of Hoover that perhaps unwittingly he has brought his Bureau to the status of a de facto national police. Already the FBI has control of important "cooperative services" to local law enforcement: the central fingerprint file; the National Crime Information Center, a computerized data storage and retrieval bank hooked into by some twelve hundred local agencies and the Royal Canadian Mounted Police (who have raised a controversy in Canada by kicking U.S. deserters back over the border into the arms of the FBI); and the FBI National Academy, which has recently been expanded to accommodate two thousand policemen at a time, a tenfold increase.* In the last several years Hoover has moved to take over all training of local police, over the resistance of the IACP. For years the IACP was dominated by the Bureau, but in 1959 a liberation movement developed with the nomination of Chief Parker of Los Angeles for the presidency. The blunt Parker

* President Nixon attended the June 1971 graduation ceremonies of the Academy. As far as I know this is the first time a president has ever done so.

had been feuding with Hoover and would have declared IACP independence, but he was outflanked by FBI lobbyists, who managed to put up and elect their own candidate. When Tamm took over as executive director in 1961, he announced that he would reinstate the IACP as "the dominant voice in law enforcement"—a none-too-delicate allusion to the FBI. The showdown came when money became available in 1967 for training under the Law Enforcement Assistance Act. The FBI chief tried to have inserted in the act a clause that federal funds would go only to those cities which acquiesced to FBI training. And at the 1968 convention in Honolulu, FBI agents again buttonholed delegates, this time to try to strip Tamm of much of his authority. In his turn, Tamm put the IACP on record that to "centralize police training in the hands of the director of the FBI could become the first step toward a national police."

The internal struggle goes on, with the only certainty that whoever wins, Blue Power is here to stay. Police red squads are being beefed up, laws enacted to expand their powers to snoop and pry, and license granted to plant undercover agents, informers, and provocateurs on campus. All of this poses the dilemma that our enforcers of the law are now in the position of influencing the making of the law. The police are able now to deliver blocs of votes, to pressure lawmakers, to propagandize, and to use police power to further their political aims.

States Harold B. Foner, a New York lawyer who defends police clients: "Unless there is direction and control, law enforcement is as great a threat to America right now as criminal behavior."

12
POWER ON
THE RIGHT

Fascism in general has been negative reaction against socialism and democratic equalitarianism, its roots reaching back to reaction of ruling classes against French Revolution.

—The Columbia-Viking Desk Encyclopedia

Shortly after some thirty-five hundred demonstrators blocked the Oakland Army Induction Center in October 1967 and were violently dispersed by hundreds of police in riot gear, California Governor Ronald Reagan complained that such protests were "lending aid and comfort to the enemy" and proposed that wartime rules be invoked against violent antiwar demonstrators even though the United States was technically at peace. The proposal was thoroughly in character for the chief executive of what writer Kenneth Lamott* calls "our first parafascist state." During the 1966 campaign Reagan had urged that Congress investigate the possibility of declaring war on North Vietnam—one advantage of which would be to enable prosecution of antiwar demonstrators for treason.

The governor was able to commit at least California to a state of war against demonstrators. Under his emergency plans, the Berkeley "People's Park" protest of May 1969 quickly grew into a Vietnam-like action. When police blocked the line of march, they were briefly pelted with debris, providing them with a convenient pretext for escalation. A tactical squad of sheriff's deputies rampaged through the streets of Berkeley, leaving one man dead, another blinded, and

---

* Kenneth Lamott, *California: Our First Parafascist State* (Little, Brown & Co., 1971).

scores of bystanders injured. The National Guard moved in with fixed bayonets, and a Guard helicopter laid down clouds of tear gas. It was massive retaliation, not flexible response. But Reagan rode even higher in the electorate's esteem. In 1970, despite the state's economic woes and his well-documented ties to big money, Reagan whipped challenger Jesse Unruh by half a million votes. The election confirmed, with a different politician, Hans J. Morgenthau's observation that "the American people were no more victimized by McCarthy than were the German people by Hitler; both followed their tempters with abandon."

Richard Nixon, who likes to style himself a centrist, illustrates just how far to the right the political center has moved. Nixon's fist-pounding, cliché-ridden fulminations against "violence" during the 1970 campaign—an attempt to promote the fortunes of conservative Republicans—were as demagogic as anything Reagan has produced.* Nixon dispatched his stalking horse, Spiro Agnew, the length and breadth of the land, and named William Buckley to the U.S. Information Agency while dumping Secretary of the Interior Walter Hickel for sounding off in behalf of youth and against big-corporation greed. And he shafted Senator Charles Goodell, the liberal Republican in New York, in order to pull

* In an Arizona speech telecast on election eve by the Republicans, Nixon played the law-and-order theme to the hilt. He attempted to capitalize on an alleged rock-throwing incident a few days earlier, on October 30, at a San Jose, California, appearance on behalf of Senator George Murphy. Nixon cast himself in the role of the dauntless leader who would not be intimidated by such "violence," all the while portraying the Democrats as johnnies-come-lately to the law-and-order cause. The president's histrionics overshadowed a statement by San Jose Police Chief Ray Blackmore that the incident was vastly overplayed. In January 1970 a San Jose grand jury that investigated the incident found no evidence of a crime, moving Judge Vincent Bruno to comment that it was "magnified all out of proportion" and that "certain people know why that was done."

the chestnuts out of the fire for Conservative Party candidate
James Buckley.*

As Justice Louis Brandeis once said, "The greatest dangers to liberty lurk in the insidious encroachment by men of
zeal, well-meaning but without understanding."

The encroachments by men of zeal which began inter-
mittently during the Johnson years have increased in fre-
quency during the Nixon years. The wiretapping provisions
and thought-police authority of the Omnibus Crime Control
and Safe Streets Act of 1968 have been extended in the form
of a model preventive detention statute for the District of
Columbia, engineered by John Mitchell, and a staggering
proposal for uncontrolled electronic eavesdropping in
"national security" cases. With little fanfare, Mitchell's
Justice Department has reactivated the Internal Security Division, dormant since the Eisenhower days. Led by Assistant
Attorney General Robert C. Mardian, a tough conservative,
the division correlates intelligence raw material and ramrods
the investigation and prosecution of radicals for anything
that can be hung on them—the Berrigan "conspiracy" case
and the Leslie Bacon grilling in Seattle are two examples. As
Newsweek commented on May 31, 1971:

The expensive bail bonds and lengthy proceedings are
undeniably effective in tying up radical leadership while
drying up its sources of support. "It makes people think

* In addition to unleashing Agnew, Nixon green-lighted Wall Street
Republicans, who dropped some $400,000 into the Buckley war chest.
In order to shield the fact that they had abandoned Goodell, the GOP
standard bearer, the donors anonymously contributed to Buckley
fronts permissible under loopholes in the campaign laws. Among the
fronts: Citizens for a Citizen's Government, Students for a Stable
Society, Committee to Keep a Cop on the Beat, the League of Middle
American Women, the Town Meeting Preservation Society, and
Scientists for Sensible Solution of Pollution.

twice about organizing any type of demonstration," one May Day leader ruefully admits. "Now a businessman asked to donate money or time to the movement thinks to himself: 'My God, I may get indicted if anything goes wrong.' People are getting increasingly reluctant to get involved."

Not since the heyday of McCarthy has the "security" apparatus been so bloated. Nixon recently approved a thousand extra FBI agents, and a supplemental appropriation to pay for them, largely in order to step up campus surveillance. And as the documents stolen from the FBI's Media, Pennsylvania, agency reveal, no individual or group actively seeking social justice or an end to the war is beyond scrutiny and harassment. (One FBI memorandum exhorts agents to step up the quizzing of radicals "for plenty of reasons, chief of which are it will enhance the paranoia endemic in these circles and will further serve to get the point across there is an FBI agent behind every mailbox.") The long-moribund Subversive Activities Control Board, saved from extinction in the waning days of the Johnson administration, has been revived by Nixon. Appointed executive director was a man whose name conjures up ghosts of the past: Francis J. McNamara, former staff director of HUAC and editor of *Counterattack* and *Red Channels,* both journals involved in the blacklisting scandals of the 1950s. And nominated by Nixon for a five-year term was none other than Otto Otepka.

That Otepka's nomination was a victory for the new right was immediately obvious. Retired senator Stephen Young testified at a Judiciary Subcommittee hearing in May 1971: "The SACB is concerned out of all proportion with the diminished threat of native communism, but this nomination reflects a glaring insensitivity to the opposite and perhaps even more dangerous subversion of democracy by the hard-core right-wing extremists." Stephen I. Schlossberg, general counsel of the United Auto Workers International Union, added: "A Subversive Activities Control Board helping the Birch Society achieve the objectives of combatting the 'communist influences which surround President Nixon,'* advancing the American Security Council's objectives of casting doubts about the 'patriotism' of senators and congressmen who do not share their view of military priorities, is a step down the road toward authoritarianism." Sharing the credit for the Otepka nomination was the Liberty Lobby, which, along with other right-wing groups, promoted Otepka assiduously.

Perhaps more significant in the long run than visible successes like the Otepka nomination are the more invisible effects of right-wing pressure. Witness the case of Walt Whitman Rostow, once a liberal professor at MIT, who became a top security analyst to both Kennedy and Johnson. As the Pentagon Papers now confirm, Rostow turned into a most influential hawk. Like Abe Fortas and others with a liberal reputation, Rostow had been the target of a sustained Liberty Lobby attack that alleged he was pro-communist. Drew Pearson and Jack Anderson in their column of April 22, 1969, quoted Rostow's friends and associates as being convinced his hawkish stance had been assumed to "counteract the unfair accusations of the Liberty Lobby and other right-wingers who kept up a steady barrage against him because of his Jewish, socialist background."

Ironically, the espousal of sweeping government political surveillance by the right wing represents a glaring departure from its own traditional credo of decentralization, dispersal of police power, and individualism—a tradition perhaps best exemplified by the late R. C. Hoiles of the Freedom Newspapers chain, who went so far as to urge the

---

* Apparently an allusion to a commentary by Robert Welch in the *Birch Bulletin* for November 1968.

abolition of public police forces. Lately there has been an almost complete eclipse of the libertarian ethic that was once an integral part of conservatism in the United States.* Replacing it is the pseudo-traditionalism epitomized by Nixon and Reagan, both of whom are passionate believers in stability, law and order, and the preservation of "natural law" and Western culture. For such true believers, "national security" has become a shibboleth, a theme central to governmental planning, and consequently, it has also become a convenient area of operation for the organized right—as the American Security Council's role in the ABM fight demonstrates. President Nixon himself acknowledged the ASC's "major role in achieving that victory."

Complementing the right's success in Washington is the new and unprecedented success it has achieved among the young, particularly on college campuses. In September 1970 Ronald R. Docksai, national secretary of Young Americans for Freedom, an organization godfathered by Ronald Reagan and Barry Goldwater, placed his organization's numerical strength at fifty-five thousand, distributed over five hundred chapters. In California the aging and not overly gifted Senator George Murphy attracted some six thousand youthful workers to his unsuccessful 1970 re-election campaign. In Michigan a virtually unknown conservative named Robert Huber nearly toppled Lenore Romney in the GOP primary on the strength of a sizable student effort. In New York the Youth for Buckley drew five thousand volunteers. "This is the first time that we've had a conservative youth movement en masse," Buckley enthused. His enthusiasm is shared by Willis Carto, who was quick to move in on the Youth for Wallace movement and its successor, the National Youth

---

* Among the survivors: Murray Rothbard, publisher of the *Libertarian Forum;* Jarret B. Wollstein of the Society for Rational Individualism; and Donald Ernsberger, who puts out *The Individualist.*

Alliance, and by Patrick J. Frawley Jr., whose protégé Edward Butler is working to build a campus counterforce to the New Left.

This emergent youth movement suggests that continuity in the access to administrative power has now been achieved by the right. The youth movement promises to infuse new energy into such established organizations as the American Security Council and the Liberty Lobby—and even into God-and-flag fundamentalism, as the Jesus freaks demonstrate. No doubt new groups and institutions will emerge from it, led by the alumni of Young Americans for Freedom, Youth for Goldwater, and the National Youth Alliance.

The appearance of a right-wing youth movement is one index of the overall success of the individuals and organizations who make up the new American right. Some of these organizations are negligible—stagnant, like the John Birch Society, or marginal, like the Minutemen—but their collective impact has clearly realigned the American political scene. For years now the airwaves of Middle America have been saturated with the rhetoric of the Carl McIntires, mailboxes have been stuffed with the ultranationalistic tracts of the Liberty Lobby and its competitors, and the media have been fed with the not always subtle messages of military superiority sponsored by the companies of men like Patrick Frawley. Meanwhile members of Congress live with the knowledge that to vote against ever-larger defense and security appropriations is to invite the well-publicized wrath of the American Security Council, and advocates of progressive law enforcement and a reformed judicial system must contend with the coalescing political power of the police. While the efforts of the right have not been fully orchestrated—there is too much intramural feuding, backbiting, and status-seeking for that—the cumulative effect is unmistakable. There is nothing to indicate that the pressure will abate in the near future.

The excesses of the Nixon administration led William L.

Shirer, who observed the rise of Nazi Germany at first hand and wrote *The Rise and Fall of the Third Reich*, to draw an interesting parallel between then and now. In a *San Francisco Chronicle* interview in March 1970, Shirer said he had observed a pervasive fear of speaking out on the part of citizens coupled with a public "mood" to sanction the outlawing of dissent. He said he thought the administration was trying to turn the middle and lower classes "against the blacks, against youth, against the students who demonstrate," and that "Agnew—certainly in league with Nixon—is now appealing to the very worst in our people, the knownothingism." In a phrase that could someday be the obituary of American democracy, Shirer concluded: "We may be the first country to go fascist by free elections."

INDEX

252; Operation Alert, 210–11; purpose, 199, 201–03; relationship to other right-wing groups, 201, 205; subscribers to services of, 201–04 passim; on USSR, 204–08; on Vietnam war, 205, 207, 209
American–South African Council, 162, 164
American Vigilante, 201
"American Voluntary Guerrillas," 110
American Volunteer Groups (AVG), 110–11
Americanism Educational League, 43, 184
Americans for Constitutional Action, 184
Americans for Democratic Action (ADA), 107
Americans for National Security, 157, 165–66
Americans for Peace Not Surrender, 188
Amsterdam News, 230
Amyx, Hurst, 166
Anaheim Bulletin, 41, 165
Anderson, Jack, 152 n, 251
Anderson, Tom, 33, 133
Andrews, Rev. Stanley M., 165
Anti-communism, 23, 41, 43–44, 56, 83, 88, 101, 159, 172, 183–85, 188, 192–93, 240; of Patrick Frawley, 176, 178–80, 189; of John Birch Society, 22, 31; of paramilitary factions, 70, 75, 77, 88–90, 95, 103, 111; of police, 221, 239; of religious groups, 122, 127, 130–32, 137–38, 183
Anti-Communism League of America, 95, 201
Anti-Communist League of the Caribbean, 95
Anti-Communist Voters League, 192
Anti-Defamation League, 31, 53, 101, 114, 164–65
Anti-Semitism, 82, 87, 94 n, 101, 108, 132, 140–41, 183, 201; of Ku Klux Klans, 52, 54. *See also* "International Zionist Conspiracy"

Anti-War Movement, 16, 76, 119, 120 n, 123, 219, 247; May Day, 250; Moratorium, 188; New Mobilization Committee, 75
Apostles of Deceit, 135
Apostolic Orthodox Old Roman Church, 96
App, Austin J., 163
Aptheker, Herbert, 73
Archambault, Bennett, 208
Arms Race. *See* "Hawks"
Arnett, George, 83
Assassination, 72–73, 96, 107–09, 115–16; Robert DePugh, intervention by, in, 71–72, 77, 98; of J. William Fulbright, plans for, 71, 77, 109; investigations of, 60 n, 96–97, 105–07 n; of John F. Kennedy, 58–59, 94, 96–97, 105–09, 186–87; of Robert F. Kennedy, 109, 194 n; of Martin Luther King, 60–61, 104, 223, 234; by Ku Klux Klans, 58–59; Minutemen, plans for, 71–73, 76–77, 93–94; by Lee Harvey Oswald, 96–97, 105–06, 186–87; of George Lincoln Rockwell, 76, 94; Warren Commission Report on, 105–06
Associated Press, 115, 120 n
Atkinson, Dr. James D., 205, 208
Atlantic, 232
Augustine, Sgt. Robert, 224
Author of Liberty, 119

Badham, Robert, 37, 45
Bagwell, Robert, 80–81, 87
Bancroft, Clayton, 127–28
Banister, W. Guy, 72, 95–97
Barnett, Ross R., 57 n
Baugh, Sgt. Jack, 226
Bay of Pigs, 96, 97 n, 105, 155–56. *See also* Cuba
Bealle, Morris A., 146
Beckwith, Byron de la, 27
Behind the News, 165
Behind the Shield: The Police in Urban Society, 219
Belin University, 132

Catholic World, 180
Catholics Concerned, 182
Cavanagh, Jerome P., 232–33
C.E.D. Associates, Inc., 112
"Chandler, Capt. Alexander," 115
Chandler, Norman, 166
Chaney, James, 51, 55
Chavez, Cesar, 42, 182. *See also* United Farm Workers
Chennault, Maj. Gen. Claire, 110, 135
Chicago, Ill., 38, 61, 101; *Daily News*, 119; Police Association, 235 n; Police Department, 15, 140, 220–21, 235, 243; *Sun-Times*, 140, 201; *Tribune*, 213, 241; *Tribune-New York Daily News* Service, 42
China Lobby, 213
Choice Not an Echo, A, 191
Christian Admiral Hotel, 126–27, 129
Christian Anti-Communism Crusade, 23, 43, 76, 130, 171, 172, 178–79, 191. *See also* Schwarz, Dr. Fred
Christian Beacon, 125, 136
Christian Crusade, 21, 43, 76, 121, 131–33, 165; *Christian Crusade* magazine, 133; *Weekly Crusader*, 133. *See also* Hargis, Billy James
Christian Defense League, 101–04, 109; *Christian Defense News*, 101
Christian Echoes National Ministry, Inc., 131
Christian Economics, 142
Christian Freedom Foundation, 141
Christian Front, 222 n
Christian Liberty Academy, 33
Christian Nationalist Alliance, 109
Christian Nationalist Crusade, 78, 100, 140–41, 151
Christopher, George, 192
Church, Frank, 79, 160
Church of the Christian Crusade. *See* Christian Crusade
Church of Christian Liberty, 33
Church of Jesus Christ–Christian, 100
Church League of America (National Laymen's Council), 130, 134–40, 183, 193
Churns, Michael, 223

CIA (Central Intelligence Agency), 17, 90, 97 n, 155, 156 n
Circuit Riders, Inc., 131
Citizens for a Citizen's Government, 249 n
Citizens Congressional Committee, 140
Citizens Councils of America, 57 n
Clark, James, 82
Clark, Gen. Mark, 32
Cleland, Robert Glass, 39
Clemmons, Sgt. Jack, 225
Coast and Southern Federal Savings and Loan Association, 23
Coberly, William, 193
Cohn, Roy, 137 n, 179
Cold War, 199, 209, 212–14. *See also* USSR
Collectivism in the Churches, 135
Collingswood (N.J.) Presbyterian Church, 122, 124–25
Collison, Judge William R., 98
Colson, Charles, 211
Committee Against Socialized Housing, 32
Committee to Investigate Communist Influence at Vassar College, 32
Committee to Keep a Cop on the Beat, 249 n
Committee of One Million Against the Admission of Communist China to the United Nations, 213
Communism on the Map, 44, 184
Communist Attack on U.S. Police, The, 200
Communist China. *See* People's Republic of China
Communist Party, 32, 73, 75. *See also* Anti-communism
Community Crusades for Americanism, 23
Comparet, Bertrand, 101
Congress, U.S.: investigations by, 27, 54, 107, 135, 166, 182, 185, 190, 217, 240; relationship with: American Security Council, 208–11; John Birch Society, 31–32, 132; Liberty Lobby, 147, 158–61
Congress of Freedom, 59, 79, 150–51

Hargis, Billy James, 27, 43, 76, 128 n, 130–34, 142; and John Birch Society, 21, 33. *See also* Christian Crusade
Harrington, John J., 217, 226, 235–36
Harris, Roy V., 57 n
Hart, E. Edgerton, 140
Hart, Merwin K., 165
Hart, Philip A., 161, 210
Hartke, Vance, 16
Harvey, Paul, 175
Harwick, E. S., 193
Hatch, Rev. Robert I., 89
Hatfield, Mark O., 134
"Hawks," 119, 182, 204 n, 206–11, 251. *See also* Vietnam war
Haynsworth, Clement F., 159, 224
Hearnes, Warren, 213
Hearst syndicate, 181, 205
Herald of Freedom, 189
Hickel, Walter J., 248
Hicks, Louise Day, 226
Hicks, W. B. Jr., 153–54
Highland College, 125
"Hitler in Havana," 176, 186
Hoiles, Raymond C., 41, 251–52
Holiday Magic cosmetics, 124 n
Holstine, Willard Noble, 103
Holt, Norris B., 152
Hood, Clifford F., 208
Hooper, Cyril W., 201
Hoover, J. Edgar, 28, 33, 44, 53, 94 n, 129, 183–84, 238; and FBI, 239–44; and Minutemen, 66, 70 n, 88–90; publications by, 24, 125, 141. *See also* FBI
Hope, Bob, 177
Hoppe, Arthur, 193
Horsfall, Mary Ruth, 86–87
Horsfall, Victor, 77, 86–87
Houghton, Troy, 81–82, 99, 107, 110–11
House Internal Security Subcommittee, 31 n, 203, 214
House of Representatives, U.S. *See* Congress, U.S.
HUAC (House Un-American Activities Committee) (currently House Internal Security Subcommittee), 71, 193, 202–03; on Ku Klux Klans, 51–54 passim

Howard, Lawrence, 105–06
Hubert, Robert, 252
Human Events, 136, 153, 193
Hunt, H. L., 14, 42, 124 n, 172–73, 230
Husted, Raithby Roosevelt, 82–83

Ichord, Richard, 203, 205, 214
"Illuminati," 79, 112
Illuminator, 112
Imperium, 145, 147–50, 163
Independence, Mo., 81, 86, 99
Independent Board of Presbyterian Foreign Missions, 122
Individualism, 21, 40–42, 153, 251, 252 n
Individualist, The, 252 n
Industrial Enterprise Foundation, 112
Information Council of the Americas (INCA), 171–72, 185–88, 241
Information Digest, 139–40
Institute for American Democracy, 21, 31, 129, 171
Institute for American Strategy, 212
Institute for Defense Analysis, 17
Institute for Special Research, 134
Intelligence (data), 95, 97 n, 102, 115, 137, 228 n, 249; American Security Council, 199–202; FBI, 239–40, 243
Intelligence Digest, 194 n
Intercontinental Penetration Group, 106
Internal Security Division. *See* Justice, Department of
Internal Security Force of Illinois, 68 n
International Association of Chiefs of Police (IACP), 236–39, 243–44
International Brotherhood of Police Officers (IBPO), 231
International Christian Relief (ICR), 128
International Conference of Police

183. *See also* John Birch Society, "God, Family & Country" rally; "March for Victory"

Ramparts, 67

Rarick, John R., 240; and John Birch Society, 21, 32–33; and Liberty Lobby, 159, 161, 165–66; and "March for Victory," 119, 121

Reader's Digest, 120 n

Reagan, Ronald, 28, 37, 43, 79, 106, 135, 178, 247–48; and Patrick Frawley, 171, 175, 191–94; *Ronald Reagan on the Welfare State,* 135

Real Minutemen, 99

Red Channels, 138, 250

Redmond, Wash., 66, 84–85

Reeb, Rev. James, 57

Reeves, Adm. J. W., 165–66

Reiss, Albert J., 221

Repression (of dissent), 227, 239, 250, 254

Republican Party, 16–17, 43, 46, 78, 207, 248; Anaheim (Calif.) Republican Assembly, 45; and Willis Carto, 153, 158; election campaigns, 249 n, 252; and Patrick Frawley, 177, 189–92

Review of the News, 32

Revolution Is My Business, 187 n

Richardson, Warren S., 159

Richfield Oil, 179

Richter, Rev. Charles E., 124

Right, 150–52

Right-to-work laws, 14, 46, 178, 180

Rise and Fall of the Third Reich, The, 254

Rivers, L. Mendel, 159, 206, 208

Rizzo, Frank L., 228 n

Roberts, A. Lee, 156

Roberts, Oral, 131

Robertson, Charles F., 140–41

Robnett, George Washington, 134

Rockwell, George Lincoln, 76, 88 n, 93–94, 102, 113. *See also* American Nazi Party

Roman Catholic Church, 235; and Patrick Frawley, 171, 173, 179–82, 191; as object of right-wing hostility, 52–53, 123, 125–26, 222 n

Romero, Robert R., 103–04

Rooney, John J., 240

Root, E. Merrill, 32

Rostow, Walt Whitman, 251

Rothbard, Murray, 252 n

Rourke, James, 226

Rousselot, John H., 24–26, 28, 31–32, 193

Rowe, H. Edward, 141

Royko, Mike, 119

Rubel, A. C., 192

St. Bernard Parish, La., 58, 61

St. Louis Post-Dispatch, 120, 191

Saltzman, Harry, 175

Salvatori, Henry, 191–92, 194

Sambo Amusement Co., 55

San Diego Police Officers' Association, 224

San Francisco Chronicle, 27, 219 n, 223, 254

San Francisco Police Officers Association, 229

Sandman, Henry, 236

Santa Ana Register, 41–42, 45, 151

Santa Monica Evening Outlook, 195

Sapp, Charlie, 60 n

Saturday Evening Post, 133

Save Our Servicemen Committee (SOS), 32

Scherle, William, 164

Schick Electric, Inc., 174–75

Schick-Eversharp, 176–79, 202

Schick Investment Co., 175, 181

Schick Safety Razor Co., 171–72, 174–77, 179, 181, 184, 186–91, 203–04

Schlafly, J. Fred Jr., 172, 179

Schlafly, Phyllis, 179, 181, 191, 204 n

Schlamm, William S., 28

Schlapia, Adelbert Harold, 103–04

Schlossberg, Stephen I., 250–51

Schmitz, John G., 31–32, 46, 240

Schreiver, Gen. Bernard A., 207

Schuyler, George, 183

Schwarz, Dr. Fred, 23, 130, 225; and Patrick Frawley, 173, 176, 178–79, 188, 191. *See also* Christian Anti-Communism Crusade

Schweiker, Richard S., 217

Schwerner, Michael, 51, 55

Scientists for Sensible Solution of
Pollution, 249 n
Screen Actors Guild, 193
SDS (Students for a Democratic
Society), 15, 75, 115–16, 139, 188
Sears, Roebuck, 200, 202
Seattle Psychiatric Institute, 176
Seattle Times, 65
Second Civil War, The, 187
Secrest, Charles, 133
Secret Service, 58–60, 107 n
"Secret Six," 58
Security (national), 44, 241; American
Security Council concern with,
200–01, 203, 209–12; government
concern with, 243, 249–50, 252.
See also Surveillance
Segregation, 21, 53, 57 n, 59, 80, 109,
114, 226; schools (desegregation
of), 53, 57 n, 109, 114, 226
Senate. *See* Congress, U.S.
Senate Internal Security Subcommit-
tee, 44, 147, 159, 175, 238
Servants of Apostasy, 125
Sex Education, 21, 47, 127, 128 n,
155
Seymour, William, 105–06
Shadel Hospital, 176
Sharp, Adm. Grant, 32
Shearer, William K., 157
Shelton, Robert M. Jr., 54–55, 61
Shelton College, 125–27
Shifflet, Harold, 164
Shirer, William L., 253–54
SIECUS, 155
Simmons, William J., 52
Sisco, Don "The Hook," 115
Skolnick Report. *See* National Com-
mission on the Causes and Preven-
tion of Violence
Skousen, W. Cleon, 24, 44, 178, 200,
225
Smith, Gerald L. K., 78, 100, 140, 151
Smith, H. Allen, 240
Smith, Ian, 136
Smoot, Dan, 33, 124 n; "Reports"
(radio program), 33, 124 n; *Reports*
(publication), 136

Society for American Military Engi-
neers, 212 n
Society for Rational Individualism,
252 n
Soldiers of the Cross, 78, 88, 154
Sollitto, Robert A., 84
Sommerford, Al, 82
Sons of the American Revolution, 135;
Patriotic Educational Committee
of, of Calif., 43
Sons of Liberty, 113
Sourwine, Julien G., 147, 159, 161–62
Southern California. *See* California,
Southern
Southern California Freedom Councils,
100, 109, 189
Southern California Reformation
College, 130
Southern California School of Anti-
Communism, 178
Spear, Joseph, 145
Spencer-Roberts, 193
Spreen, Johannes F., 233–34
"Square Movement," 186–87; *Aware:
The Square Newspaper*, 187;
"Square Circles," 187–88; "Square
World of Ed Butler," 187; *West-
wood Village Square*, 186–87
Stang, Alan, 24
Stanley, Scott Jr., 30
Statecraft, 93, 113–14; *Statecraft*,
114–15; 164
Steele, Dr. Arthur, 127–28
Steinbacher, John, 165
Stenvig, Charles, 229
Stevenson, Adlai III, 13, 16
Stokes, Carl, 218, 226–27
Stone, Willis E., 31
Stormtrooper, The, 88 n
Stratemeyer, Gen. George E., 153
Strauss, Adm. Lewis L., 207
Strike from Space, 204 n
Students Association Against Totali-
tarianism, 237
Students for a Stable Society, 249 n
Subversive Activities Control Board,
147, 162, 211, 250–51
Support Your Local Police (SYLP), 25,
32, 222 n, 225